BEYOND PRODUCTIVITY

BEYOND PRODUCTIVITY

*Embodied, Situated, and (Un)Balanced
Faculty Writing Processes*

EDITED BY
**KIM HENSLEY OWENS
AND DEREK VAN ITTERSUM**

UTAH STATE UNIVERSITY PRESS
Logan

© 2023 by University Press of Colorado

Published by Utah State University Press
An imprint of University Press of Colorado
1580 North Logan Street, Suite 660
PMB 39883
Denver, Colorado 80203-1942

All rights reserved
Printed in the United States of America

 The University Press of Colorado is a proud member of the Association of University Presses.

The University Press of Colorado is a cooperative publishing enterprise supported, in part, by Adams State University, Colorado State University, Fort Lewis College, Metropolitan State University of Denver, University of Alaska Fairbanks, University of Colorado, University of Denver, University of Northern Colorado, University of Wyoming, Utah State University, and Western Colorado University.

∞ This paper meets the requirements of the ANSI/NISO Z39.48-1992 (Permanence of Paper).

ISBN: 978-1-64642-485-6 (hardcover)
ISBN: 978-1-64642-486-3 (paperback)
ISBN: 978-1-64642-487-0 (ebook)
https://doi.org/10.7330/9781646424870

Library of Congress Cataloging-in-Publication Data

Names: Owens, Kim Hensley, 1974– editor. | Ittersum, Derek Van, editor.
Title: Beyond productivity : embodied, situated, and (un)balanced faculty writing processes / edited by Kim Hensley Owens and Derek Van Ittersum.
Description: Logan : Utah State University Press, [2023] | Includes bibliographical references and index.
Identifiers: LCCN 2023021787 (print) | LCCN 2023021788 (ebook) | ISBN 9781646424856 (hardcover) | ISBN 9781646424863 (paperback) | ISBN 9781646424870 (ebook)
Subjects: LCSH: Academic writing—Psychological aspects. | Report writing—Psychological aspects. | Scholarly publishing—Psychological aspects. | Authorship—Psychological aspects. | Manuscript preparation (Authorship) | College teachers as authors.
Classification: LCC P301.5.A27 B49 2023 (print) | LCC P301.5.A27 (ebook) | DDC 808.02—dc23/eng/20230721
LC record available at https://lccn.loc.gov/2023021787
LC ebook record available at https://lccn.loc.gov/2023021788

Support from the University Research Council at Kent State University.

Cover illustration from *Un Autre Monde* by Grandville (Jean Ignace Isidore Gérard). Public domain image from Wikimedia Commons.

For all of our professors at the University of Illinois at Urbana-Champaign, 2001–2007/8, who let us into grad school all those years ago and who modeled stellar teaching, scholarship, and collegiality.

CONTENTS

List of Figures   ix

Acknowledgments   xi

1. Situating Scholarly Writing Processes across Life Contexts
    Kim Hensley Owens and Derek Van Ittersum   3

2. Sand Creeks and Productivity: A Writer's Reckoning of Personal
    and Academic Selves
    Ann N. Amicucci   24
    Tags: embodiment, critique, identity

3. Relearning to Write in Crip Time (on the Tenure Clock)
    Melanie Kill   41
    Tags: embodiment, technology, adaptability, productivity

4. Process Not Progress (or, *Not-Progress* is Process): A Narrative
    Meditation
    Hannah J. Rule   56
    Tags: productivity, critique, adaptability

5. When Writing Makes You Sick
    Tim Laquintano   72
    Tags: embodiment, adaptability, technology, productivity

6. Speak in the Tongue of Your Father: Disentangling "American"
    Work Ethic and Professional Curiosity
    Kate L. Pantelides   89
    Tags: critique, embodiment, identity, productivity

7. "Embodied Action" as Precarious Process: Writing Productivity at
    the Intersection of Crip Self-Care and Academic Contingency
    Andrew Harnish   105
    Tags: critique, adaptability, embodiment, productivity

viii   CONTENTS

8. Showing Up: Una Manera sobre Writing Process
    Zakery R. Muñoz   124
    Tags: identity, critique, embodiment

9. Writing Queerly: Honoring Fragmented and Embodied Identities in Composition
    Beth Buyserie   142
    Tags: identity, productivity, embodiment

10. Transformative Practices: Black Women Exist Beyond Our Ability to Produce
    Tatiana Benjamin   158
    Tags: identity, productivity, critique, embodiment

11. Undergraduates and Faculty Writing as Partners
    Kellie Keeling, Emily Pridgen, and J. Michael Rifenburg   174
    Tags: collaboration, productivity

12. The School Bus Never Came: How Crisis Shapes Writing Time
    Melissa Dinsman and Heather Robinson   193
    Tags: identity, collaboration, productivity

13. (Intra-)Active Notebooking as Becoming
    Kevin Roozen and Steve Lamos   209
    Tags: collaboration, identity

14. Externalized Process and Writing Tools
    Laura R. Micciche   227
    Tags: productivity, adaptability, technology, embodiment

    Index   245
    About the Authors   249

FIGURES

6.1. Writing Project Dialogic Decision Tree   102
13.1. Photo of Kevin's notebook   214
13.2. Steve's annotations on Kevin's notebook   222

ACKNOWLEDGMENTS

We would like to thank, first, the authors who put so much care and vitality into the chapters in this book. It has been a pleasure to work with each of them. We would also like to thank Rachael Levay, who believed in us and in this book and set us up for success at every stage. We thank our anonymous reviewers, who helped improve everyone's contributions; Ben Brown, who helped us ensure everything was cited properly; and Jennie Swanson, who helped us fix everything we missed. We are grateful for the various technologies that supported this project: Zoom provided a reliable platform for us to meet; Google Docs provided an accessible space in which to draft and collaborate; and our iPhones provided us with the ability to text, plan, and joke across time zones.

Kim would like to thank Ethan and Eleni, for keeping things interesting and musical nearly every minute of every day; Luke, for always listening; Qi'ra, for sleeping through almost the entire process of creating this book and expecting walks when she wasn't; Jupiter (RIP), Butterbeer, Shyla, and Jimmy, for their kittyness that makes the house a home; Kate Scott; Donelle Ruwe, for administrative support that spared her sanity during the constant challenge that was directing a writing program during COVID; Heather Nash, for helping her get over those constant challenges; Arizona, for being beautiful; and specifically Mount Elden, for inspirational hikes close to home.

Derek would like to thank his family, for providing space to write and read; Tim Lockridge, for talking through these and other ideas; and the Internet, for making collaboration across space and time possible and even fun.

Finally, we would like to thank each other for having this idea, for making it fun, and for always meeting our own deadlines. We are excellent to each other.

BEYOND PRODUCTIVITY

1
SITUATING SCHOLARLY WRITING PROCESSES ACROSS LIFE CONTEXTS

Kim Hensley Owens and Derek Van Ittersum

Scholarly writing can be a scattered process, with research and composing time eked out in fits and starts. Teaching, administrative, and family responsibilities can overwhelm even the most dedicated scholars' best intentions for scheduled writing time. Writing and research processes also change over time as circumstances change—as graduate student life morphs into tenure-track or adjunct life; as single life morphs into partnered life, or vice versa; as faculty have children who require different intensities of attention at different stages; as bodies are or become differently dis/abled; and/or as administrative roles replace writing time with back-to-back meetings. The field of writing studies has a long history of looking into the details of how people write, from work that focuses on the cognitive through think-aloud protocols (e.g., Flower and Hayes), to work devoted to freewriting and expressivism (e.g., Elbow), to work theorizing distinctions between different understandings of and approaches to process (e.g., Faigley), to work carefully examining the choices of writers who draft and revise versus those who perfect prose before they set it to paper (e.g., Harris), to more recent work examining how particularly productive faculty members write (Tulley). This collection continues in those traditions, seeing faculty's ways of writing as a form of flexible, evolving knowledge. We seek to examine, explain, and even exult in how writing processes change over time. By exhibiting what is lost and gained through successive rounds of transformation and adaptation over time, we hope to move ourselves and others to a sustainable understanding and practice of process—one that moves us beyond productivity as the primary measure of success.

While we maintain that all writers' scholarly writing practices metamorphize over time as circumstances change, the arrival of the global Coronavirus pandemic resulted in restrictions that challenged even the most flexible scholarly writers, in part by fully eliminating many familiar

---

https://doi.org/10.7330/9781646424870.c001

writing contexts. Schools, libraries, coffee shops, and other spaces were closed, while home working environments now included more people than usual, including, for many, children who needed care and attention and no longer had schools or playdates to attend. In some ways these disruptions were more of the same, as disruptions to scholarly writing plans are nothing new. As various researchers have demonstrated, including Robert Boice with faculty across disciplines and Christine Tulley with faculty in rhetoric and composition, completing scholarly writing when focus and time are fragmented is possible. For some scholars, writing happened somehow, especially when spurred by tenure demands, and for others, making it through the serial crises was sufficient. The challenges of this particular time opened up questions for us about writing processes because we were ourselves wondering how to build more resilient writing habits, how to write with the emotions of the moment rather than in spite of them, how to judge what was enough and when it was acceptable to rest. These questions were in part set in motion by the pandemic but grounded in research and arguments about process that have driven our scholarship for many years.

Trying to write in the midst of the pandemic was particularly incapacitating, as many of us shared with colleagues in private conversations and social media posts. Boice recommends that faculty writers ensure their writing success in part by arranging "external situations to ensure regular writing productivity" (2) (Where was Boice, I [Kim] wonder, when I was trying to write with two kids in separate remote school bands, with clarinet and trombone battling it out simultaneously upstairs?) Boice's advice articulates well with the "environmental-selecting and -structuring practices (ESSPs)" Paul Prior and Jody Shipka describe in their study of scholarly writers' processes. For many writers, the pandemic restrictions eliminated the infrastructure within which we were able to arrange any writing sites outside our homes; we were also unable to arrange "external situations" within those home sites. Tulley details how many of the scholars featured in her book write successfully within small chunks of time, yet pandemic restrictions highlighted the important differences between, for example, writing in between loads of laundry or meetings and trying to write in between helping children with remote school activities or while learning how to safely accomplish everyday tasks—like purchasing food—that had suddenly become potentially dangerous.

While pandemic restrictions are easing as we write this introduction in the early summer of 2021 (and continuing to be perplexing and ever-changing as we revise again in fall of 2022), it seems unlikely that previous contexts will return exactly as they were. We have learned, collectively and individually, about the vulnerabilities of our infrastructures. Even eradicating the Coronavirus wouldn't repair those weaknesses. And so, we are (all) faced with writing within unstable contexts and precarious structures, as in fact many writers had been doing prior to the pandemic or all along. As writers, how can we negotiate these instabilities in ways that are generative and meaningful as well as sustainable and reasonable? In some cases, this negotiation requires learning strategies for working in differently fragmented ways, finding ways to push along a project in less than ideal or even far from ideal conditions. In others, it may mean changing goals or projects altogether.

As we consider how to keep going when it's (beyond) hard, though, we also want to ask if and when we should. We want to interrogate how we can resist the tendencies that push us to meet neoliberal demands of limitlessly increasing personal productivity. When can/should we relax the pressure to write, to constantly *produce*? The neoliberal expectation that we each take total responsibility for our personal efficiency as individuals became even more clear and more starkly absurd in 2020, an absurdity that shows no signs of diminishing in 2022. As writing researchers and as writers, we are called to grapple with these expectations and pressures and consider together what alternatives we might work toward—what might exist beyond productivity.

Our book is situated in what Laura Micciche describes in *Acknowledging Writing Partners* as "cultural time" (74). The specific context of the pandemic and its aftermath is omnipresent and oppressive, but also occasionally generative. It leaves us with some new answers to old questions about how scholars write, and it leaves us with new questions, too, about why they write and when they maybe shouldn't. The disruptions to our infrastructures made visible what we took for granted in terms of time and space (both physical and mental) to write, but also forced us to pause and (re)consider what we had normalized in terms of productivity and pressure. This collection offers personal and scholarly investigations into process and productivity: We want to be sure that the questions the pandemic threw into sharp relief are not forgotten, not allowed to retreat into the background once this moment in cultural time finally passes, but instead faced and answered.

Drawing inspiration from Jessica Restaino's pledge to "determine anew [her] use value" (137) as a scholar after a devastating personal loss, this collection seeks to determine anew the use value of scholarly writing and the processes that produce it, both within and beyond the context of losses, constraints, and adaptations associated with COVID-19. This collection explores how scholars have navigated various workflow changes

6   KIM HENSLEY OWENS AND DEREK VAN ITTERSUM

throughout various phases of their lives and careers. The pandemic context has provided an opportunity to examine how writing processes can be adapted and to examine whether and how writing might be made more precious when it is slowed and fragmented by circumstances wildly beyond our individual control.

In what follows, we first share snapshots of our own recent process disruptions and discoveries, linking our personal experiences with one another's and with the overarching themes of this collection. Then we examine how extant scholarship speaks to issues of process and productivity before previewing the thirteen chapters of the book and its seven intertwining themes—adaptability, collaboration, critique, embodiment, identity, productivity, and technology—reveal about how scholarly writers meet new demands, respond to unstable conditions, and draw on various resources to function in ever-shifting scholarly writing contexts.

A GLIMPSE INTO KIM'S PROCESS

I produce acres of text before I find the square inch of valuable real estate I want to build on. I generally think my writing process is too scattered, too fragmented, too messy—and did long before COVID-19 shrunk my workworld, my husband's workworld, and my son's and daughter's schoolworlds into one shared homeworld for a solid year. I tend to assume as a writer that I'm doing it wrong—that if I could just be more linear, more planful, and have the perfect setup, guarantee X minutes with zero interruptions, I could write quickly, write painlessly, write more that's worth keeping, and no longer "waste" time reorganizing and reframing and rewording. In short, I assume that everything I know about writing—that it evolves over time, that it is thinking, that it is recursive and not linear, that it includes and evolves through activities that are "not writing" (Prior and Shipka), that it almost always benefits from other readers and from revision—does not, or at least should not, in this imagined ideal situation, apply to mine.

As a writing studies scholar, I really know better, but somehow I still don't. And that awareness of what I know but don't know, or know but don't always apply to myself, informs some of the questions that animate this collection. Derek and I and the authors of these chapters are curious about how we and other scholars inquire into their own processes, how we and others in and beyond our field internalize and apply scholarly knowledge about writing processes, how we and they adapt to different constraints of and across time, as careers and complications ebb and flow. It is through individual stories and investigations that we come

Situating Scholarly Writing Processes across Life Contexts   7

to better understand how scholarly writing actually works—not just for those who are at the pinnacle of prolific academic publishing success, as Tulley has illustrated, but for all of us who research and write across different institutional types and in different academic roles and paths.

While my writing process was never evenly sustainable, the pandemic definitely broke the process I had come to rely upon over the previous several years. In a very busy administrative role requiring me to spend my workweek in an office, which, as Michael Faris aptly notes, is for "*office* things" (22), I was not even able to write in the small snatches that had previously worked for me. I had settled into scheduling a single meeting-free morning most weeks, during which I would write at a coffee shop, where (presumably) no one could find me and where I wasn't, as I am in my office, six feet from the copy machine shared by the sixty teachers I supervise. While that schedule was never perfect, never what I would have preferred, it had been (sort of) working.

The pandemic broke that process in every way: location, time, schedule, caffeinated beverage options, people—every aspect was upended—and at first that break(ing) meant a total cessation of writing. And to be clear, as a tenured, promoted professor, I had the privilege to just stop for a while, although that isn't to say stopping felt good or even okay. I was wracked with writer's guilt. And it wasn't just that I didn't have time to write, or couldn't focus when I tried, although both statements would be accurate—I didn't try. I didn't want to. I could not see the point.

Slowly, though, the break(ing) shifted into a remaking. Writing itself always involves transformation—a shift from a whole to parts to a different whole. The process is similar to what Robin Kimmerer describes in the context of a woven basket as a marvel of "transformation, its journey [taking it] from wholeness as a living plant to fragmented strands and back to wholeness again as a basket" (311). The disruptions, time shifts, spatial challenges, and other constraints the pandemic brought also resulted in opportunities for an evolved writing process. While I had many more scheduled (Zoom) meetings, logistical problems, and staffing emergencies to deal with during the pandemic, and while I also had two children remote-schooling from home who needed regular help with everything from math to Zoom to setting up counseling sessions, other constraints all but disappeared. I went from having an almost constant flow of office-related questions, student issues, and coworker drop-ins a day to a trickle of unscheduled calls. While I could no longer slip away to write alone for a full morning with coffee shop treats, I eventually had more small pockets of available time each day than I'd had in years. It took time to relearn how to use such pockets for writing (and to even want to), but I did.

Write first, goes the mantra, *and it's easier to come back to.* While I have never been and will never be the kind of writer who starts at 5:00 a.m. or writes before the family is up for the day, I settled into a routine of writing as soon as the kids were settled into their Zoom classrooms. On the two to three days a week when I managed to do that for part of an hour first instead of immediately falling into the email sinkhole or answering a probably not critical phone call, I wrote then and often again the same day. This new schedule resulted, eventually, and quite unexpectedly, in a bit more writing time each week than I'd had before.

Among the (re)discoveries of writing at home again, or seeing "how writing emerges through the cracks of living" (Rule 5), was: while at the coffee shop, I would of course need to unpack my materials to begin and repack them to end, and I similarly set up and closed up shop at home. To start writing I would first clear and prepare my physical space. I'd get the right drink, open the right tabs, stack the right resources—rituals like these can impede writing if taken to extremes, but for me they prepare the path. As I write, even if it's for a short time, Post-it Notes accumulate, notebooks pile up, pens proliferate. At home, instead of tuning in and out on ambient coffee shop sounds like strangers clinking dishes and snippets of conversations, I had interruptions requiring my full attention—pets throwing up or children asking if they could watch a show, having been released from online school ten minutes into a supposedly ninety-minute class. At the end of a writing session, I clear the space—recycle and move Post-its, put away pens, close notebooks, restack books, close tabs, minimize documents. I also clean up the document, tying up loose ends as best I can; ensuring I've cited sources, changing the color or writing a note-to-self where I'm leaving off, etc. My stopping process, then, is something of a ritualized literal and metaphorical cleaning—although it is not typically as peaceful as that sounds.

Two books I encountered during this time affected how I thought about my changing writing process: a memoir called *Wintering*, by Katherine May, and Robin Kimmerer's wonderful *Braiding Sweetgrass*. May describes a Japanese ritual called *Hari Kuyo*, the Festival of Broken Needles, in which seamstresses and artisans solemnly thank sewing accessories that have outlived their use by placing items like broken needles in tofu. While to a Western ear that ceremonial process may sound odd, anyone familiar with Marie Kondo's bestselling *The Life-Changing Magic of Tidying Up* will recall her recommendation to thank items such as old clothes for their service before neatly folding and discarding or donating them. May quotes her friend saying, "The needle breaks the fabric in order to repair it. You can't have one without the other." This image of breaking to remake is one that lingers for me in terms of writing and writing process. Additions sometimes destroy, and removals sometimes repair. I ruin the pristine whiteness of the page or screen to make my mark(s) on it; I deplete resources of energy, lead, and ink to create sentences; I unmake sentences to remake them—to make them prettier or smarter.

Thinking of writing tools as valuable elements of creative processes highlights the value of both the tools and the processes. Reading about Kimmerer's theory of reciprocity alongside May's book, while considering my writing tools in this new way, led me to think about how I interact with those tools. Kimmerer describes the reciprocal relationship Native peoples have with land, with nature, as one in which people give to and receive from nature *and vice versa.* She writes that "nature asks us to give back, in reciprocity, for what we have been given . . . through gratitude, through ceremony, through land stewardship, science, art, and *in everyday acts of practical reverence*" (190; my emphasis). I started to think about how I could add "everyday acts of practical reverence" to my writing life by including a gratitude practice toward my writing tools and spaces into my wrapping-up stage.

Instead of hurriedly gathering up the Post-its and pitching them into the recycling bin, I started to build a moment of gratitude into my process. Instead of allowing negative self-talk about the quality or progress of my writing to simmer while I clear my space, and instead of cursing various technologies—a habit I can too easily fall into—I started to spend just a few seconds focusing on the value of each physical or technological tool. Giving each notebook, each pen (today it's a blue Uni-Ball Jetstream, medium point; yesterday it was a pink Pilot Razor Point, extra fine point), each Word document, Google Doc, or Zotero file its due for the work it supported and enabled that session proved calming, and perhaps that sense of calm helps me return to write another day.

One of the questions we asked in our call for papers was whether the constraints of writing—shoved into the forefront for many due to pandemic-related restrictions and life changes, but which persist across all contexts in various shapes and sizes—could, counterintuitively, make us more curious about writing, help us deepen our understandings of our writing processes, and make our writing activity more precious. It did for me. In addition to finding ways to use the time and space available to us, thanking writing tools might be one way toward that latter outcome. Below, Derek's process snapshot also focuses on tools, although in somewhat different ways—his is a tinkering-with-tools process. While our methods of meander differ, we share the underlying notes of self-judgment, of discomfort with or embarrassment about what our processes actually look like. We both seem to keep trying to "perfect" our processes, trying to unlock the secret to whatever holds us back or propels us forward.

A GLIMPSE INTO DEREK'S PROCESS

While I have never found myself in conditions that have seemed ideal for writing, I often project out to a future when such conditions will exist and imagine how the words will flow easily and how much I will enjoy it. When I can focus on one project at a time, when I have time for multiple writing sessions in a day, when my wrists and hands don't hurt, when I won't have to spend prime morning writing hours doing childcare. These conditions are unlikely to change for years, if ever, and so I turn my attention to perfecting my "environment-selecting and -structuring practices [ESSPs]" (Prior and Shipka) so that at least I can craft some small container in which the ideal conditions for writing might exist for forty-five minutes or so.

I tend to need time to warm up to writing; that is, it's common for me to sit and stare at the screen for a while, to write and delete a few words for a half hour or so before I can start to generate sentences and paragraphs. It feels a bit like needing to load up all the trains of thought for the project back into my working memory. Because my writing sessions rarely last longer than an hour, I have tried various ways to reduce this warm-up time. Using a Mac app called Tinderbox, I created a visual map of notes (sort of like a mind map but not hierarchically arranged) with common ideas grouped together and other notes linked together with arcing lines showing the connections across the map. Looking at this map, which I had built over months and continued to add to here and there while working on a book project, seemed to help me keep the ideas in mind and reduce the warm-up time somewhat. Crafting this digital environment was an ESSP that has been effective.

And yet it's also kind of embarrassing. Like Kim, I imagine that this process is wrong, that I am wrong somehow for needing it. I spent many hours developing the map with all of the notes, and I wish I could just graduate to writing without needing such a lengthy planning activity. If I didn't need these other tools and what feel like roundabout processes, I could just write.

As useful as these planning tools can be, I also use them as distractions. Tinderbox affords much more than just visually laying out notes (it is almost like a rich programming environment) and I find myself crafting elaborate project-management solutions or time-tracking dashboards

Situating Scholarly Writing Processes across Life Contexts 11

with it. This experience with the application pays off in some respects, as I can use it for qualitative data analysis, for example, but there's a fuzzy zone separating valuable tinkering from avoiding work. It's easy for me to be seduced into playing with the tools, getting the system organized just right. I find it satisfying because when it works, the results are obvious. The project-management notes in Tinderbox can be displayed in the timeline view according to their date data but also can be manipulated in the map view for more free-form arrangement—it works! With writing, it's never clear to me if it works or not until I get feedback, and wrestling with that uncertainty can be unsatisfying, especially when my attention is scattered across different demands during the day.

I feel guilty about tinkering with these systems and like I'm not productive enough, but they do benefit my work and my ability to work. The note mind map I made in Tinderbox was a space I returned to again and again while drafting and revising my book—it helped me draw connections, it helped me build a comprehensive description of the theoretical apparatus. And earlier in the process it helped me organize my thinking and it gave me a place to write when work on the book was stalled, frustrating, or too overwhelming. As research on ESSPs shows, valuable mind states can be generated and/or recalled through these kinds of writing process arrangements.

As Tim Lockridge and I have argued, affect matters for writers' workflows. Writers may write more or less depending on their affective relationship with their tools, their practices, their physical embodiment. While no notebook or pen will "make" anyone write that novel they've been dreaming about or get started on their scholarly article earlier, tuning in to the enjoyment of the materials may create a virtuous circle that builds positive associations with writing. Tinkering with Tinderbox is enjoyable for me, and spending time in the app increases my comfort and expertise with it, which seems to have a positive impact on my use of it for writing projects. With my own case, and as Kim describes her packing and unpacking rituals and her affective relationships with pens, Post-its, and word-processor documents, I wonder how we can take these affective elements into account as writers, writing teachers, and writing researchers. I find myself too easily spinning between extremes: wanting first to show how optimizing for positive affect really will increase productivity and then recoiling and wanting next to say that orienting toward affect, toward ways of writing that are meaningful and pleasurable, is its own end, regardless of how much useful text is produced.

There are no final answers here, no perfect ways of resolving tensions between different orientations toward writing, toward work, toward our fickle or fragmented selves. Personal stories, like those animating the chapters in this book, offer a way to share local, situated knowledge about how writers are negotiating these tensions and how they have solved them "for now" or are living with the tensions or how they have used the (often painful) energy of the tensions to transform. These stories can prompt writers to reflect on their own practices and consider what changes (personal, collective, infrastructural) might lead toward the affective experiences they desire. Furthermore, research with experimental designs investigating the ways tools and practices shape writers' experiences can help writers grapple with the possibility that their affective sense may limit their view of what's possible and effective. While such research could present a risk if the results were interpreted as prescriptive determinations about which tools or practices are universally best for all writers or all contexts, we hope to show through the chapters of this book the many varieties of tools and practices different writers adopt to meet the needs of their different embodied, situated contexts.

STUDYING HOW SCHOLARS WRITE

Christine Tulley's compelling arguments in the first few pages of *How Writing Faculty Write* offer clear reasons why we should be studying how writing faculty write. She suggests that readers can learn from productive writing faculty's writing processes, that anyone in the field can extrapolate lessons from those successful writers to incorporate useful pieces into their own processes. Tulley explains that these scholars know writing research and that when they make known precisely how they follow the paths laid out by the field's scholarship, others can, too. But while Tulley's book provides important information about writing processes, there is much more to examine in this area. She acknowledges that the book is focused on famous people in the field, as were the *Paris Review* interviews with famous fiction writers that inspired her work. Such studies focused on exemplars have value, but we want to hear and learn more from those with very different lives and processes. We need more accounts from more writers in our field, with differing career paths across different types of institutions, and we need to learn not just how they achieve their writing goals but how they think about and negotiate what productivity means for them and what tradeoffs are required.

This book works to create a fuller picture of scholarly writing processes in the field by collecting a broad range of stories focused on process. Like many in the field (Takayoshi; Rule; Prior and Shipka;

Shipka; Prior), we see writing as an activity that greatly exceeds any particular moment of inscription. The accounts in this book continue to expand our pictures of what ways of being in the world (Prior and Shipka) writing can take on, what kinds of differences might be behind our colleagues' and our students' most recent writings, and what we can theorize about how writing works from these nuanced accounts.

Writing "is a matter always of its *conditions*—its places, tools, technologies, movements; how it is inhabited by bodies, by others present and by others who aren't yet there (those future readers in future contexts often unknown)" (Rule 5). Our field still has relatively few accounts from writing practitioners that consider these conditions or focus on helping other scholarly writers understand them. We are working here to continue expanding our field's understanding of these conditions. Laura Micciche argues that "the conditions of academic writing surface through isolated examples rather than overarching narrative" (*Acknowledging* 30), a point our book seeks to underline by providing thirteen detailed examinations of various scholars' academic writing processes, relying on a wide variety of methodologies and scholarly or personal emphases. By gaining further insight into how writers at various career stages have adjusted their processes, their workflows, their arrangements of time and tools, the field stands to learn more about scholarly writing, about ourselves as writers, and about how to best help others—from students to junior colleagues to co-authors—shape and refine their processes. The contributors to this collection explicitly voice the subtle feeling so many academic writers have: We're each doing it wrong somehow. By bringing such self-recriminations into the light and openly acknowledging these fears, we hope to help writers move beyond them.

Our interest in and emphasis on individual processes may seem to ignore, rather than respond to, the broader pandemic and institutional contexts we all find ourselves in and may, in that sense, seem to be subject to individualist criticisms like those levied against institutions that focus on individuals' responsibilities to steward their own "self-care" instead of acknowledging or adjusting damaging work contexts or expectations (Kar Tang and Andriamanalina). But we want to keep the focus simultaneously on individual processes and the contexts they are rooted in to look at the micro as a window into the macro. Rule argues that writing's "situatedness is a continuum, not a choice" between the micro and the macro, between a writer's individual process and the "larger forces" always at play (53). The COVID-19 pandemic is one such larger force, but only one—various broader contexts and systemic and intersectional issues are always in the mix as well.

The accounts in this book help us understand that there is no "normal," so we can learn to appreciate and work with our idiosyncrasies rather than feel embarrassed by them. As Rule has argued, when we see processes as fixed, as a set of steps that can be prearranged or are idealized in some fashion, we frame writing as somehow able to be controlled or existing outside the local specific conditions in which we find ourselves. Drawing on "crip time"[1] and postprocess theories, Rule suggests that "(process) time cannot and should not be systematized or codified in advance" (81). Further, Micciche reminds readers "that writing takes time and is propelled by not knowing, dead ends, and wrong turns" (*Acknowledging* 68). She explains that these detours and screw-ups are "arguably part of the deep structure of academic writing permitted in acknowledgments and other marginal texts but rarely foregrounded in current scholarship on writing pedagogy and theory" (68). This collection seeks, in part, to bring those hiccups and challenges into the light beyond the acknowledgments sections.

This collection provides accounts of writers "taking an inquiry posture" (Rule 109) toward their writing, toward the disrupted situations in which they find themselves, toward the constraints that seem to make writing unlikely or impossible, toward processes that frequently feel off kilter, out of sync, incorrect. Sometimes we can get fixated on attempting to control external conditions to provide the structure we are used to or think we "should" have, but this inquiry posture provides another way, a way of revealing the act of being curious about how our writing is going or what we are experiencing. Further, an inquiry posture can be a productive defense against a tendency to become mired in comparisons, feeling like one's process doesn't meet some idealized standard(s). As we get curious about what conditions we find ourselves in, what happens when we write, we can find ourselves appreciating the fragmented evolutions and start to see our writing as being precious without being perfect.

One element that emerges from this curiosity about our writing is emotions. Alice G. Brand has described an "inexorable intertwining of writing and emotion" (290) in her research on student writers, professional writers, and prospective English teachers. While the field has examined the emotional dimensions of students writing (e.g., Brand and Powell); of teaching (e.g., Micciche, *Doing*; Worsham); and of working as a writing program administrator (e.g., Davies; Wooten, et al.), there has been little focus on emotional components of writing among faculty writers. Zachary C. Beare and Shari J. Stenberg, noting this gap, find in their *College English* study of emotions related to writing toward publication (among faculty at research-intensive institutions) that across career stages, emotions matter. Beare and Stenberg identify four categories of focus for where writers fall in terms of their "emotional habitus related to publishing": "faculty career stage, area of scholarly focus . . . ; preparation in graduate school for publication . . . ; and negative experiences with failure" (107). Their study offers significant insight into emotions about the process of writing for publication among faculty at research-intensive institutions. While their study, like Tulley's, is delimited by a focus on high-achieving writers at institutions where such achievement is demanded, some of the emotions they identify track across institution types and with many writers in our collection. One of Beare and Stenberg's study participants, for example, describes her writing anxiety in terms of a " 'cult of productivity' and 'accountability' " (109), which aligns with what some writers in this collection describe.

Wrestling with emotions while writing may feel like proof that we're dysfunctional in some way, yet scholarship in this area suggests that emotion is an unavoidable aspect of writing; emotion is not something one matures beyond or something that needs to be eradicated. A key emotion that faculty writers especially grapple with is guilt—primarily productivity guilt, a sense that one should be working all the time and should always be perfectly able to balance all the spinning plates of research, mentoring, teaching, administration, family life, and self-care and constantly produce publications. To some extent, such guilt results from norms of idealized bodies and idealized schedules that can dramatically differ from individual writers' bodies, needs, and schedules—challenges contributors in this volume openly address.

Dana Lynn Driscoll, S. Rebecca Leigh, and Nadia Zamin surveyed faculty and doctoral students and found that over half regularly felt academic guilt. They suggest one way to overcome that guilt is to "fram[e] self-care as professionalism," which they argue "gives us the opportunity to deepen our own work and create better work lives. It creates space for us to stop normalizing burnout and academic guilt and to start building a culture where we cultivate spaces to do the best labor that we are capable of doing" (476). Their emphasis on reshaping practices to alleviate impossible tensions and work demands that lead to omnipresent guilt, and explicitly working to reclaim the self as something beyond a producer-of-academic-work, resonates with our goals for this collection. We see these arguments as aligned, if not in total agreement, with those who argue against self-care as a solution to systemic problems. Jasmine Kar Tang and Noro Andriamanalina, for example, present an analysis of cross-disciplinary BIPOC/international dissertation writers that discusses the challenges of institutions focusing on encouraging individual wellbeing (self-care) rather than promoting structural changes that will specifically benefit BIPOC/international students/scholars. We agree that self-care is a problem when it is offered as a solution in a tone-deaf or even disingenuous manner to suggest that individuals must work harder to avoid letting institutions crush them. Yet we also see self-care as a necessary element of any person's life, professional or not, and hope to work to normalize the many ways life events and cycles will shape how writing happens, instead of letting life result in lifelong academic guilt.

Kar Tang and Andriamanalina also describe guilt's sister emotion, shame, with a specific focus on feedback dissertation advisors give to BIPOC/international student-scholars. They describe shame emanating from feedback about their language choices and about their attempts to "bring in the personal." They decry, too, the opposite: praise that overly focuses on sections where such students did bring in the personal or write in a nonstandard dialect. Micciche also brings up shame. She reveals that some writers, such as C. H. Knoblauch and Elspech Probyn, find shame and the anxiety of producing inadequate or inaccurate prose generative, while others, like Mike Rose, find shame a source of writer's block (*Acknowledging*, 48–49). Shame can keep writers from sharing their work, from completing work that didn't get the proverbial gold star on a first draft, from continuing to try to write in less-than-ideal circumstances. One value of the personal stories in this collection is that they reveal how authors feel and sit with senses of shame associated with writing—this exposure helps those authors name, face, and overcome such shame, and helps readers recognize how they might as well.

Beyond guilt and shame, what other emotions do faculty writers wrestle with? The field has little data on this. Kristine Johnson's study of faculty writing advice manuals suggests that most prominent discourse on faculty writing—which is written by people outside our field but promoted within the field on our listservs, our social media spaces where work and social connections blur, and in other professional spaces—takes a behaviorist approach, suggesting that doing the writing for fifteen minutes a day (or whatever set time) is what matters, regardless of whatever emotions one may be feeling or other difficulties one may be experiencing. Johnson describes this advice as "epistemologically current-traditional" (read: outdated) and argues for rhet-comp professionals to add our expertise to this conversation (62). While our discipline may still be grappling with the implications of process, post-process, and more recent approaches to writing, disciplinarity, and invention, the field has acknowledged the serious limits of current-traditional approaches.

This collection shares accounts from writers in the field from a variety of career stages and institutions about their writing processes to continue peeling back the onion. The stories in this collection examine and push back against emotions like guilt and shame; the stories in this collection demonstrate various embodied, emplaced, and seemingly impossible conditions for writing; the stories in this collection pull on the threads of extant scholarship on writing, seeking to weave new tapestries of understanding. We mean understanding here in all senses—foremost, in terms of understanding how scholars write, but also in terms of understanding one another as human beings so we can better advocate for understanding across our collective systems. Ultimately, we see the value of this book not only in its call for the field to (continue to) pay attention to process, but in its call to change what's harmful in the status quo and find a sustainable path forward.

STORIES ABOUT SCHOLARLY WRITING PROCESSES

In our call for proposals, we sought both personal and scholarly contributions to examine the advantages and possibilities as well as the frustrations concomitant with evolving scholarly writing processes. We invited proposals for chapters that would take up, challenge, or augment questions such as:

- How have you reinvented your writing process(es) at one or more stages of your scholarly career or for different types of projects?
- What resources or tools have you adopted for that reinvention? What was your affective experience before, during, and after?
- How does your personal engagement with writing processes shape your engagement with process scholarship or writing studies writ large, or vice versa?
- How does your teaching of writing shape your own writing processes?
- How does your scholarly writing occur within your home, work, and community context?
- How is your scholarly writing process affected by gendered, raced, and/or classed work-life expectations?
- What are the possibilities and challenges associated with your scholarly writing process?
- How could past examples of ideal and/or problematic scholarly writing processes speak to the present? How do you relate to your past processes?
- What do you see as the challenges of creating or sticking to a productive process, and/or how do you push back against a culture that over-values speed and "productivity"?

18   KIM HENSLEY OWENS AND DEREK VAN ITTERSUM

The proposals we received and the chapters authors produced show a diverse set of scholars thinking deeply and very differently about their processes and those of others, and across those differences seven themes emerged: adaptability, collaboration, critique, embodiment, identity, productivity, and technology. Each author addresses multiple themes, so rather than organizing our collection by single themes, which would inevitably emphasize one element over other important elements of each chapter, we've chosen an intersectional approach, through which these overlapping themes reverberate as they recur throughout the book.

Our collection opens with Ann N. Amicucci's contribution, "Sand Creeks and Productivity: A Writer's Reckoning of Personal and Academic Selves." Amicucci describes the processes of reanimating her writing with a sense of her true self, giving herself permission not only to "feel [her]self in [her] body" as she is writing but to write about that self as well. She details how specifically **embodied**, emplaced writing disallows the otherwise easy assumption/perception that a writer is an able-bodied, white male. Inviting readers to join her on walks with soundtracks of podcasters, Amicucci **critiques** perceptions that writing in the field must be disembodied and solely data-based. She shares her struggles with choosing to write either as her "creative writing self" or as her "academic self" and uses this essay to both argue against those distinctions and allow her disparate **identities** to blend.

Continuing with a focus on what it means to write as a person with a body, Melanie Kill describes how "**embodied** interactions with writing technologies affect first how and what we write and then, by extension, who can write." Intertwining her experiences with disabilities and her experiences with various writing **technologies** and temporalities, Kill confronts her own internalized sense of ableism. Her essay, "Relearning to Write in Crip Time (on the Tenure Clock)," lays bare the particular and innumerable challenges of repeated **adapting** in order to write with one disability, and in doing so she demonstrates the unjustness of one-size-fits-all publication **productivity** standards.

Revealing that historically her "writing processes have ridden mostly on fear- and anxiety-driven autopilot," Hannah Rule examines what it means to question the value of continuing apace, or continuing at all, after earning tenure during the pandemic. Her chapter, "In Process Not Progress (or, *Not-Progress* is Process): A Narrative Meditation," questions her own expectations for **productivity** and **critiques** the structures that lead writers to the default position of not writing. She asks how we might account not only for published pieces but also for those that never got written in the first place, for whatever reason(s). Exploring how to **adapt** to these new times and her own shifting perspective, Rule finds that writing processes "are just what happens, where, with what, and how. What it takes to make writing happen changes."

For Tim Laquintano, what it took to make writing happen on a tight tenure deadline was an unhealthy mix of meatball subs, months of long writing days, and pharmaceuticals. In "When Writing Makes You Sick," Laquintano calls for a shift in how scholars in the field acknowledge and relate to the psychophysical demands of writing and the negative **embodied** consequences that result. He shares his own story of **adapting** toward healthier ways of living and writing and his explorations of the complicated array of **technologies**, research, and beliefs available in wellness spheres. Rather than calling for more research, Laquintano asks readers to prioritize health over **productivity** in everyday conversations, rolling our eyes at stories of the hours of sleep lost in service of drafting another article instead of straining to stay up later ourselves.

Kate L. Pantelides **critiques** her inherited, learned, problematic work ethic, passed down from her father, a Greek immigrant to the United States. "Speak in the Tongue of Your Father: Disentangling 'American' Work Ethic and Professional Curiosity" explores how her father's love language—a deeply driven work ethic—connects to advice in academia "about how to write effectively," which she finds "similarly, and problematically, tangled up with American notions of morality, worth, and **productivity**." Pantelides works in this chapter to distinguish the components of her writing process, work ethic, and **identity** that are "beautiful" from those that are "racist and troublesome," teasing out a way to **adapt** to a "healthier, more sustainable writing balance" she can **embody** and model for others.

Andrew Harnish **critiques** academic **productivity** expectations at the expense of **embodied** realities connected to disability in his chapter, " 'Embodied Action' as Precarious Process: Writing Productivity at the Intersection of Crip Self-Care and Academic Contingency." Describing himself as "nourished by the antinormative praxes of queer culture," Harnish seeks to balance his commitment to opposing neoliberalism with his continued search for stable employment within the academy. After a detailed accounting of the various ways he has **adapted** his life and writing process to manage iatrogenic nerve damage that permanently affects his body's ability to regulate heat, Harnish explores and connects two approaches to writing, analyzing each for its particular application to embodied realities their audiences experience.

Taking up the mantles of **critique** of the academy, his **identity** as a Burqueño, and of writing as an **embodied** practice he'd like to literally see in action in seminar, Zakery R. Muñoz offers his story in "Showing Up: Una Manera sobre Writing Process." Muñoz focuses on his *manera* of writing, blending his past experiences as a student with a history of struggle in Albuquerque with his current experiences as a PhD student in Syracuse. Muñoz makes a pointed and fascinating call for the writers in the field to put their physical writing processes on display. He specifically asks those who teach graduate students to demystify their writing processes by working on their writing-in-progress in real time, with students in seminar watching and working on their own writing simultaneously.

Beth Buyserie's contribution, "Writing Queerly: Honoring Fragmented and Embodied Writing in Composition," explores her complicated relationship with writing and the "longstanding and deep-seated anxiety and depression around writing" for publication that causes her to hate it. Buyserie questions how someone who loves to teach writing, and loves to teach writing teachers, can have such an imperiled, negatively **embodied** experience with it. Sharing the stories of her path to a tenure-track position alongside her path to a queer **identity** and the lifestyle shifts each necessitated, Buyserie describes her typical writing process as involving "deep sacrifice and many hours of self-doubt, punctuated by fragments and snippets of frantic writing." Buyserie weaves lessons from counseling with her writing process story to demonstrate how one can help with the other. Counseling helped her change her prevailing internal narrative from a paralyzing fear of academic death to working toward associating writing with joy.

Continuing the theme of **identity** as well as **critique**, Tatiana Benjamin's chapter, "Transformative Practices: Black Women Exist Beyond Our Ability to Produce," illuminates her experience as a Black, female scholar to highlight that the personal is (still) political and to link that concept to inflexible productivity expectations in the academy. Benjamin narrates her personal experiences and writing process adaptations within the context of systems of power she views as designed to fail her. The chapter interrogates how interlocking systems of power normalize hyperproductivity; she explores how her labor, given her **embodied identity** as a Black cisgender woman living with chronic illnesses, is deemed disposable. Benjamin examines the various physical, emotional, and mental health disruptions that affect her writing processes and offers specific strategies for resisting "grind culture."

Kellie Keeling, Emily Pridgen, and J. Michael Rifenburg's "Undergraduates and Faculty Writing as Partners" also focuses on the roles of professors and students. They describe the trio's process of writing across roles, with two undergraduate students and one faculty member working together not only to perform an assessment and course design for their campus but also to follow those activities with **collaboratively** written publications about the outcomes of the partnerships. They liken themselves to a tree, "growing and learning and trying to thrive." The three examine how they resist neoliberal imperatives of competition and increasing **productivity** in part by "accepting coordination over competition," as they describe how they worked together, separately, to write this piece. They further detail how their partnership protected students from labor exploitation.

In "The School Bus Never Came: How Crisis Shapes Writing Time," Melissa Dinsman and Heather Robinson describe how they held onto their **identities** as scholarly writers during the pandemic, when "everyone was home all the time and so work was always around us." They connect their ways of continuing to write with those of other women writers confronted with crises and disruptions. Yet they also notice a difference, sharing how **collaboration** among women academic writers during the pandemic allowed for continued **productivity** and thus the ability to hang on to the writerly identity when so many challenges threatened to disrupt it.

Steve Lamos and Kevin Roozen, in "(Intra-)Active Notebooking as Textual Assemblage," share elements of their own long-term **collaboration**: an autoethnographic study of each of their daily writing habits—what they call their "mundane notebooking practices"—to demonstrate the relevance and value of such practices across decades of writing experience. The authors rely on an "intra-view" methodology and connect to Jennifer Sinor's diary analysis as they work toward a better understanding of both Kevin's notebooking practices and the broader conditions under and through which people make meaning as writers. They focus, in part, on how writers use mundane practices to both display and forge **identity** through writing.

Finally, drawing on her experiences leading writing workshops for faculty and graduate students, Laura R. Micciche, in "Externalized Process and Writing Tools," examines the ways writers respond to the high-stakes **productivity** demands of the dissertation and tenure clock and how their processes differ across genres. She details how writers **adapt** specific software **technologies**, typically those designed for other industries, to externalize and shape their writing processes. Micciche also explores how technologies and tools become more visible when they are required for tasks a body can no longer undertake, examining what happens when issues of **embodiment** interrupt what seems "normal."

NOTE

1. Alison Kafer defines "crip time as being not only an accommodation to those who need 'more' time but also, and perhaps especially, a challenge to normative and normalizing expectations of pace and scheduling. Rather than bend disabled bodies and minds to meet the clock, crip time bends the clock to meet disabled bodies and minds" (27).

WORKS CITED

Beare, Zachary C., and Shari J. Stenberg. "'Everyone Thinks It's Just Me': Exploring the Emotional Dimensions of Seeking Publication." *College English*, vol. 83, no. 2, 2020, pp. 103–30.

Boice, Robert. *Professors as Writers: A Self-Help Guide to Productive Writing.* New Forums Press, 1990.

Brand, Alice G. "Writing and Feelings: Checking Our Vital Signs." *Rhetoric Review*, vol. 8, no. 2, 1990, pp. 290–308.

Brand, Alice G., and Jack L. Powell. "Emotions and the Writing Process: A Description of Apprentice Writers." *The Journal of Educational Research*, vol. 79, no. 5, 1986, pp. 280–85.

Davies, Laura J. "Grief and the New." *WPA: Writing Program Administration*, vol. 40, no. 2, 2017, pp. 40–51.

Driscoll, Dana Lynn, et al. "Self-Care as Professionalization: A Case for Ethical Doctoral Education in Composition Studies." *College Composition and Communication*, vol. 71, no. 3, 2020, pp. 453–80.

Elbow, Peter. *Writing With Power: Techniques for Mastering the Writing Process.* Oxford UP, 1998.

Faigley, Lester. "Competing Theories of Process: A Critique and a Proposal." *College English*, vol. 48, no. 6, Oct. 1986, p. 527. https://doi.org/10.2307/376707.

Faris, Michael J. "Coffee Shop Writing in a Networked Age." *College Composition and Communication*, vol. 66, no. 1, 2014, pp. 21–24.

Flower, Linda, and John R. Hayes. "A Cognitive Process Theory of Writing." *College Composition and Communication*, vol. 32, no. 4, Dec. 1981, p. 365. https://doi.org/10.2307/356600.

Harris, Muriel. "Composing Behaviors of One- and Multi-Draft Writers." *College English*, vol. 51, no. 2, 1989, pp. 174–91. *JSTOR*, https://doi.org/10.2307/377433.

Johnson, Kristine. "Writing by the Book, Writing beyond the Book." *Composition Studies*, vol. 45, no. 2, 2017, pp. 55–271.

Kafer, Alison. *Feminist, Queer, Crip.* Indiana UP, 2013.

Kar Tang, Jasmine, and Noro Andriamanalina. "'I Cut Off My Hand and Gave It to You, and You Gave It Back to Me with Three Fingers': The Disembodiment of Indigenous Writers and Writers of Color in U.S. Doctoral Programs." *Learning from the Lived Experiences of Graduate Student Writers*, edited by Shannon Madden et al., Utah State UP, 2020, pp. 139–55. *Project Muse*, https://muse.jhu.edu/book/76862.

Kimmerer, Robin Wall. *Braiding Sweetgrass: Indigenous Wisdom, Scientific Knowledge and the Teachings of Plants.* Milkweed Editions, 2015.

Kondo, Marie. *The Life-Changing Magic of Tidying Up: The Japanese Art of Decluttering and Organizing.* Ten Speed Press, 2014.

Lockridge, Tim, and Derek Van Ittersum. *Writing Workflows: Beyond Word Processing.* U of Michigan P, 2020.

May, Katherine. *Wintering: The Power of Rest and Retreat in Difficult Times.* Narrated by Rebecca Lee, audiobook ed., Riverhead Books, 2020.

Micciche, Laura. *Acknowledging Writing Partners.* The WAC Clearinghouse; UP of Colorado, 2017.

Micciche, Laura. *Doing Emotion: Rhetoric, Writing, Teaching.* Heinemann, 2007.

Prior, Paul. *Writing/Disciplinarity: A Sociohistoric Account of Literate Activity in the Academy.* Lawrence Erlbaum Associates, 1998.

Prior, Paul, and Jody Shipka. "Chronotopic Lamination: Tracing the Contours of Literate Activity." *Writing Selves/Writing Societies: Research from Activity Perspectives,* edited by Charles Bazerman and David R. Russell, The WAC Clearinghouse; Mind, Culture, and Activity, 2003, pp. 181–239. https://doi.org/10.37514/PER-B.2003.2317.2.06.

Restaino, Jessica. *Surrender: Feminist Rhetoric and Ethics in Love and Illness.* 1st ed., Southern Illinois UP, 2019.

Rule, Hannah. *Situating Writing Processes.* UP of Colorado, 2019. https://wac.colostate.edu /docs/books/situating/processes.pdf.

Shipka, Jody. *Toward a Composition Made Whole.* U of Pittsburgh P, 2011.

Takayoshi, Pamela. "Writing in Social Worlds: An Argument for Researching Composing Processes." *College Composition and Communication,* vol. 69, no. 4, 2018, pp. 550–80.

Tulley, Christine E. *How Writing Faculty Write: Strategies for Process, Product, and Productivity.* Utah State UP, 2018.

Wooten, Courtney Adams, et al., editors. *The Things We Carry: Strategies for Recognizing and Negotiating Emotional Labor in Writing Program Administration.* Utah State UP, 2020.

Worsham, Lynn. "Going Postal: Pedagogic Violence and the Schooling of Emotion." *JAC,* vol. 18, no. 2, 1998, pp. 213–45.

2

SAND CREEKS AND PRODUCTIVITY
A Writer's Reckoning of Personal and Academic Selves

Ann N. Amicucci

Tags: embodiment, critique, identity

My townhome faces the back of a shopping plaza, and between my home and the liquor store and the dentist's office is a sand creek, a fifty-foot-wide expanse of sand whose banks are covered in basketball-sized red rocks. In March 2020 when the COVID-19 pandemic began, snow coated the sand. In April, dandelions appeared, and prickly pear cacti showed their green. By June, the prickly pears sprouted flowers, and large papery white poppies bloomed at the sand creek's edges. There's a delicate flower I took a picture of that summer, butter yellow and both spiked and gentle. It's called a bractless blazingstar, and maybe this flower with its thick and thin petals competing for attention is a metaphor for how our identities, our selves, intersect. In July, black-eyed Susans bloomed. By September, the sand creek was brown again, the Susans gone, the poppies trampled.

A RESEARCH AGENDA CHANGES

Before the pandemic, I was a researcher who studied students' writing practices with digital technologies. The central value of this research agenda is gathering student perspectives to inform how we use digital tools in first-year college writing courses. I had spent the months leading up to March 2020 designing a study to learn about intersections students perceive and teachers foster between students' social media writing and their learning of rhetorical concepts in first-year writing.

But as COVID-19 spread and campuses moved to remote learning, this line of inquiry no longer seemed important. I couldn't ask teachers and students to spend time participating in a study when the world was navigating the early weeks of a pandemic. And so, having only just begun collecting data, I paused the study and said I'd come back to it in a few

https://doi.org/10.7330/9781646424870.c002

months, when things would be back to normal. We all remember saying "when we're back to normal" for some time before accepting that there would be no more normal to go back to.

We found out on a Friday that we'd start teaching remotely on Monday, and I walked with my colleagues Michelle and Heather from a committee meeting back to our offices. Heather and I couldn't stop giggling at the absurdity of the quick transition to come. We were boisterous and disruptive, and I fell to the carpet laughing, a more public display of emotion than any I'd ever risked at work. Michelle, one of my closest friends, didn't join. She said she'd been in that space of bleary disbelief a few days before but was now just afraid. I can't tell you this story without telling you that Friday was the last time I would sit in a conference room with colleagues, or any room with any group of people, for more than a year. And I can't tell you this story without telling you that Michelle would take her own life later that year, a death from depression exacerbated by pandemic isolation. I share this story for two reasons. First, because we each have a story of our early time in the pandemic, the cognitive dissonance, the fast changes to our work. And second, because this is what it looks like to bring who we are as writers to the page: to tell each other what our bodies do in our stories (crumple to the carpet with laughter) and to share how our writing is shaped by the lives we live (by surprise, change, loss).

The first week after the quick pivot to remote learning was a fast barrage of emails and explanations of how to teach online, then spring break came, and suddenly I was alone with a laptop on my knees and no qualitative data for the foreseeable future. I would prepare my tenure dossier that summer, and I wanted to demonstrate that in the face of needing to pause data collection, I could maintain an active research agenda.

Though I'd been for twelve years the type of researcher that collects data and writes IMRAD[1] articles, I had once been a student of literature and existing texts, mining what I read for meaning and exploring that meaning through literary analysis. There's a dichotomy in English studies: some of us study existing data in what I'll call professionally published texts, whether novels or poems or public tracts or websites, and apply a theoretical lens to words that exist largely in final, polished form in the world. Some of us collect our own data, whether through surveys or interviews or the examination of less-polished writing artifacts like student work or social media interactions. When I joined a department where nearly all the other researchers work with existing professional documents, I discovered just how little we talk about the differences between these two camps—because I had to learn to explain how my research processes worked to scholars whose processes differed greatly, despite our being in the same field. But during the pandemic, I recognized that I could cross this chasm. Since I had to pause being one kind of writer, perhaps I could dip my toe into being the other kind.

I spent spring break exploring my interests outside of students' digital writing practices and brainstormed a range of topics but discarded them when it felt like I was just trying to come up with a project to fill time. I began asking, What's my "essayistic impulse" (Hesse et al.)? I kept coming to my curiosity about ethos and self-construction in writing, and I kept thinking about the concept of "embodied rhetoric"—an area I knew nothing about. And so, I began to read.

I can't stress enough how thrilling it was, global pandemic notwithstanding, to spend a spring break reading down a rabbit hole of scholarship. That week was a time when, conscripted to stay home for safety and entered into an unspoken agreement with my colleagues that we would largely leave each other alone for spring break while we adapted to our new reality, I suddenly had whole days to discover what I cared about as a writer.[2]

What I read about embodiment resonated. Christy Wenger writes that we can "reconceiv[e] our ethos as materially connected to our bodies so that we see our rhetorical authority as stemming from the body. For writers, presence is a conscious inhabiting of the body so the felt experience of writing is one in which the body's role in composing is acknowledged and the body itself is understood to leave traces, embodied markers, on our writing" (79). With Wenger's guidance, I came to feel myself in my body that spring, in a nine-by-eleven-foot home office with bookshelves and a desk that a friend had given my father in the 1960s that I rarely sat at. I had participated in a felt sense activity led by Sondra Perl a few years before and remembered how powerful it had been to ground my body in physical space before writing ("Composing"). Perl writes that "once we realize that we have access to this knowing in our bodies, we can learn to cultivate it. We can practice directing our attention to it" (*Felt* 4). I recalled fledgling attempts to bring my students into their own bodies by replicating Perl's activity in my classroom yet realized I did nothing to acknowledge my own physical self in my writing process. Wenger made me question how long I was willing to sit with that laptop on my knees and tune out everything I was feeling—hunger, muscle strain, longing to watch reruns of *Superstore*—when I got lost in writing.

PANDEMIC BODY AT REST

In the COVID-19 pandemic, my face ached, all of it, and the sides of my neck and my jaw and my shoulders, from sleeping in a firm comma and grinding my teeth. My jaw and my neck hurt from straining. So much time was spent in video conferences and, despite trying to do otherwise, I held my face in a strained upward shape, trying to smile, to show the people on the other side of the screen that I was managing.

I want you to know what the pandemic felt like in my body: sore spots on the calves from crossing one leg over the other and then the other over the first, back and forth and back and forth, trying to be comfortable. Eyes sore from the constant blinking against television screen, computer screen, window screen. Eyes sore from the constant blinking against tears.

My seven-year-old niece sent me a life-size drawing of herself complete with paper arms to wrap around my body because I mentioned on the phone that I hadn't hugged anyone in months.

BODYLESS WRITING PERFORMANCES

Twinned forces in my doctoral program had led me to remove more and more of myself from my writing. First, a professor, to my great benefit as a teacher and scholar, had me read Stephanie Vandrick's *Interrogating Privilege: Reflections of a Second Language Educator* to prompt reflection on my own white privilege—and this and other texts gave me the sense that maybe I shouldn't be speaking or that maybe, if I didn't have an oppressed or marginalized perspective, I didn't have a valuable perspective to share at all.

Second, my dissertation advisor, despite trusting my teaching expertise in the classroom, drilled out of me any trust in my teaching expertise in my writing. When I began the doctoral program, I had taught college writing for five years across three institutions, and I often wrote what I knew to be true from my experiences in the classroom. It interested me to describe how I could feel a frisson of energy when a discussion went smoothly or how I'd frame an activity in a particular way so students would take directions coming from a young woman seriously. But my advisor was adamant that I only make claims based on data I had systematically gathered and analyzed. I internalized the idea that what mattered to the profession was not my lived experience but what I observed and described through research.

I became a defensive writer in graduate school—anticipating and addressing any possible critique a reader could have—and in the process became less present in my writing. Even now, years later, my early drafts of manuscripts are conversational. My natural orientation as a writer is to describe how I understand a concept from a vantage point shaped by my particular years of teaching, shaped by my aged and gendered body. But as I refine and revise, my manuscripts become blanker prose with little flash and no sense of who the writer is behind the page. Academic writing socializes us into leaving the personal off the page and, more specifically, keeping the writer's multiple identities and embodied experience out of our prose.

There's a problem in being absent from our writing. We all write from somewhere, from some body. Embodied writing—purposefully writing from the body and its identities (Knoblauch 57–58)—shows how the stories we tell and the arguments we make come through the lens of our embodied selves. As A. Abby Knoblauch explains, embodied writing allows us to understand that "the way my body moves through this world is often different than the way that your body moves through this world" (59). Or in Victor Villanueva's terms, embodied writing is "someone saying something to someone from a particular view of reality that seeks to make that reality known" (52). Yet the disembodied writing that emerged in composition studies' social turn in the late twentieth century as we moved away from expressivism and toward purportedly deeper or objective engagements with discourse has meant we are often no body in composition scholarship (Banks 22; Hindman, "Making" 88; Hindman, "Writing" 98; Welsh 106; Yoo, "My Child" 259). When we write from no body, we risk writing the every*body*, a hegemonic everyperson who elides oppression, marginalization, and lived experience (Banks 33; Knoblauch 58–59; Lim 84). When we enact an everyperson on the page we inadvertently suggest that we are all white and male because readers will assume we are all white and male unless they know otherwise. Or, if readers can see in our bylines that we are not all white and male, readers will inadvertently assume we are all able-bodied and cisgender because we have been socialized to assume voices of authority come from such bodies.

We have many forces working against us: training in academic writing tells us to be objective rather than bring ourselves to the page, much of the academic writing produced serves as a model for performing an everyperson identity, and it is tempting to think we'll benefit if reviewers see us as a blank slate rather than a complicated human with multiple identities such as that of a graduate student or an early career researcher or a person from a background different from reviewers' own. Despite all this, I join the chorus of composition and rhetoric scholars calling for bodies to be present on the page: for us to explore our views and experiences from and through the body, despite the risks this choice presents. Kristie S. Fleckenstein writes, "In sacrificing bodies to some illusion of either transcendent truth or culturally constituted textuality, we cut ourselves adrift from any organic anchoring in the material reality of flesh" (281). When we write of/from/through the body, we recognize "the cultural, historical, and ecological systems that penetrate and reconstitute these material places," places Fleckenstein calls the "concrete spatio-temporal contexts" each writer occupies (281). We bring our identities, our lived perspectives, our specific—if fractured, still-forming, never-formed—identities to our readers.

In the face of a bodyless professional writing tradition, we can listen to those who bring their embodied experiences to the page, who seek to break from easy categories in writing. Min-Zhan Lu calls for us to "struggle for a different kind of nervous system when reading the writings produced through alternative routes" and to "pay more specific attention" to ways writers break free of binary thinking (54). Villanueva says it is "risky business" to write as he has, to explore critically one's racialized and classed lived experiences (50). Yet any temptation to hide this personal experience and "stay private and make public a display of the dispassionate, the intellectually known" conflicts with Villanueva's central argument as a public intellectual, that our epistemologies are always shaped by our individual identities and contexts (51). I imagine any reader of this chapter could provide a short list of writers who, like Villanueva, bring their lived experience to the page. Yet I am troubled by how short and canonical that list likely is. Bringing our embodied selves to the page as a collective would mean this practice is so valued and so welcomed that we could no longer list only the few writers who do so.

Teija Löytönen et al. demonstrate such a practice in resisting traditional academic knowledge-making in the development of a professional workshop. The authors question a disconnect in dance education where, in teaching students about the physical body, faculty do not always draw on embodied knowledge. Co-author Eeva Anttila writes, "We tend to lose our innate bodily wisdom when we become more trained and skilled in dance" (Löytönen et al. 241). In a workshop the group leads, co-author Anita Valkeemäki initiates "a 'moro-reflex,' a startle. Her arms and legs swing wide open, her head and spine arch backward." The startle movement Is repeated by co-presenter Anttila, then repeated by Löytönen and co-author Hanna Guttom in the audience, and "from here, a wave of startles and breaths emerges" (255). The authors disrupt boundaries of typical workshops by involving attendees in movement

ANN N. AMICUCCI

and of typical scholarship by presenting their article as side-by-side conversations on the page that weave together the authors' personal and professional lives. Such boundary-disrupting scholarship demonstrates possibilities for new meaning we can access by embodying writing.

PANDEMIC BODY IN MOTION

I set out walking daily with the podcast *Write-minded* in my ears. I've come to think of its co-hosts, Brooke Warner and Grant Faulkner, as friends or confidantes because they have been on all my walks through the pandemic, with me when I say hello to a neighbor or nod at the teenagers who hesitate at the edge of the ducts beneath Constitution Avenue, waiting for me to pass so maybe they can add their own words to the graffiti.

Brooke starts one episode with the greeting, "Hello persisters, survivors, secret-keepers, and anyone who's sick of playing it small" ("Writing"), and I have hit the path early in the morning before the sun strengthens because I don't want the burden of carrying an umbrella along with my keys and my phone because my summer clothes have no pockets.

Grant begins an episode, "Welcome, hard-working writers, strenuous procrastinators, multi-brained multi-taskers, jumping jugglers, and every kind of do-it-aller" ("Productive"), and my feet cut again through dry grass to the path where my shoes sink into tire marks and sandy footprints left by frisbee golfers and dog walkers and bikes.

Grant says, "Welcome poets, lyricists, transformationalists, and recreators" ("Creating"), and I find I can walk and listen to the podcast or think of nothing at all or think of other things, like how long it's been since I've seen my family and whether my father will live until our next visit or how uncertain I am, now that the pandemic has separated us, that moving across the country was a good idea.

Brooke intones, "Hello choosers, visualizers, and achievers" ("Getting"), and the podcast has become a chant, my ritual, my sacred space where other writers recognize how uncertain things are this year and always. I had for years thought of my academic and creative writing selves as separate identities, but because I don't have a degree in this area, don't teach in this area, and haven't published much in this area, my creative writing self always lurked in the shadows while my academic self, whose strictures I resist but whose work my CV legitimizes, is on display. Heather Fester shares a story of one of her own insights-while-walking moments as a scholar:

> I went for a walk earlier to clear my head so I could write the current leg of this draft. As I was walking, I was studying the sidewalk and thinking about belief. For a long stretch of sidewalk, I had to watch my step closely. The concrete ground was broken into jagged pieces beneath my feet. . . . The roots pushing up through the broken surface made me think of the subconscious or latent content and assumptions or values that protrude through our belief structures. But every so often, I also saw a landscaped yard where "contraction joints" had been planned into whole swaths of concrete . . . there was a "give" to the surface that allowed for the natural shifts underneath. (144)

Fester's contrast between traditional concrete where disruptive values have no choice but to leave the surface in jagged pieces as they push toward the air and joints that anticipate a shifting foundation provides a metaphor for the reckoning I faced as a writer in the pandemic: I could continue to maintain rigid adherence to an academic writing self that ignores another, contradictory, creative writing identity informed by embodied experience beneath it, but only if I ignored the possibility that one would eventually break through and dismantle the other. In those months of working from home, of my work coming to incorporate walks that took me beyond the boundaries of the sidewalk and into the sand creeks, of those walks having a soundtrack of craft theory that inevitably seeped into how I thought about academic writing, I began to recognize and see the potential for disrupting the boundaries of my academic writing practice.

WRITING SELVES IN CONFLICT

What makes me feel alive as a writer: When my sneakers stumble on the unsteady sand, when I climb the rocks to traverse the boundary between one sand creek and a perpendicular other, when I take photos of individual flowers in portrait mode. When I notice their petals' yellows. When I think of my own: propping a yellow cast on my broken foot up on a lawn chair in the backyard at ten years old with a coloring book in my lap; the jokes boys made about the too-tight fluorescent yellow t-shirt I wore at fifteen after a trip to the Toronto underground mall; a friend slipping ice cubes into the bottom of my yellow two-piece swimsuit at sixteen. I am alive as a writer when I recognize the "essayistic impulse" of common threads through lived experiences (Hesse et al.). When I recognize the "glimmers" of objects or moments in the physical world that call out, "Hey, writer, this is for you. Pay attention to this" (Houston). When I worry less about publication status and citation politics and feel instead the music and rhythm of words and phrases on my lips, on readers' ears.

32   ANN N. AMICUCCI

What academia teaches us about how to win the career game of publishing or perishing: First, write every day, in the morning, before doing other tasks, preferably for hours at a time. David Brooks' new wife thought that as like-minded intellectuals they would have leisurely conversations over coffee every morning, but he says this isn't the case. "I don't talk until I've written a thousand words," he quips, telling an audience, many of whom are college students with complex schedules and jobs and family responsibilities and many of whom are working professionals whose jobs consist largely of nonwriting tasks, that he writes from seven in the morning until noon each day.

Second, if you cannot block out hours at a time to write, write in tiny chunks, because successful scholars claim writing time in whatever bits they can find it. Christine E. Tulley's interviews with writing studies superstars reveal Jacqueline Jones Royster's concept of "quick focus" as a label for what many of these scholars do to stay productive by taking what time they can find and narrowing in on a writing task, even if only for a few minutes. Tulley explains, "Dànielle DeVoss, Cindy Selfe, and Chris Anson argue for keeping writing projects on screen and returning to them often during the day even just to tweak a sentence, add a reference, or reread a difficult section to let it percolate before a meeting" (*How* 24).

Third, if you think you can't block out time to write, you're wrong. Paul J. Silvia takes issue with claims that academics can't block out such time, calling the lament "I can't find time to write," one of many "specious barriers" to establishing a productive writing schedule (*How* 11–12). Silvia writes two hours each morning, five days a week, and he occasionally enters "cave mode" when he declines most requests for reviews and doesn't answer email quickly (*How* 14; "Cave").

And fourth, make sure to have multiple projects in your research pipeline at all times. Erin Marie Furtak writes, "A common bit of wisdom I've heard shared among academics is the 2-2-2 rule: Always have two manuscripts in preparation, two under review, and two in press." The version I learned in graduate school was ABCD: always be collecting data, so that when you write up one study and send it out, you'll have new data ready to work with.

I've benefited greatly from all this advice—in fact, I devour it and let it nourish my productivity. I choose multiple journals with similar readership and manuscript parameters at the start of a study so I can submit my work to one journal and then go down the list if a manuscript is rejected (Silvia, *Write* 29–30). I end writing sessions by putting an "up next" note in large font on a manuscript so I can dip back into it without having to reorient myself to what I should be writing next (Tulley, "Avoiding"). I maintain a Trello board with categories for Reading, Study Design, Data Analysis, and so on (Furtak) so I can know what project is in what stage and then continually berate myself for not having enough projects moving along this conveyor belt.

And what type of writer have I become in the process? My research can be boiled down to the following missive: Students do amazing things as digital composers, and I want to tell you, teacher readers, about what they do and what this can mean for your teaching. But I can't just say, "Here's this student from my class and I'm going to tell you about the amazing work they've done." I can't just say, "Here are some neat teaching ideas that I know will work because I've been teaching for years." I quite love the research process. But I wish *I* were valued more within it, that my lived experience mattered more. And I wish I could move more slowly in the world as a writer: notice more, read more, think more.

We hear similar calls in the "slow scholarship" movement, which compels academics toward collective action in opposition of productivity metrics and ever-increasing demands (see Berg and Seeber; Mountz et al.). Alison Mountz et al. remind us, "Given the chance to marinate, ideas ripen, often resulting in some of our most thoughtful, provocative, and important work" (1237). Ruth Ray Karpen writes that slow scholarship "serves as a counterpoint to the fast-production mentality of contemporary academic life" and calls for "forms of inquiry that are more time- and labor-intensive" (398), and Louise Wetherbee Phelps calls this long game of scholarly work "more difficult but richer than episodic composing . . . intermittent, distributed across temporal discontinuities, while unrelated activities and commitments—on different timescales—interrupt and distract" (307). I'm unaccustomed to this type of slowing down. I spent years feeling I was trying to hack the game of scholarly productivity, and now that I have, I've forgotten whether it's a game worth playing.

I lead a group of twenty-six full-time faculty who are largely (not always, but largely) fulfilled by their work and our collaborations, who feel they can say something when something is wrong, who feel they can be creative in their teaching, and I consider this a great success, but it has meant I don't have a daily writing practice. I ask, Do I know anyone who has a regular, sustained, lifelong writing practice and is also a successful administrator? I suppose I do; I can see them in Tulley's book, writing in five-minute intervals and leaving Post-it Notes on their computers for what to write next when a minute presents itself.

I've done this. I've written sentences in the minute and forty seconds it takes my tea to heat in the microwave. I've taken notes toward article

34   ANN N. AMICUCCI

manuscripts on my phone while walking across campus between committee meetings. I'm writing this paragraph knowing that in eight minutes I have a meeting to discuss a faculty member's annual performance evaluation. But do I know anyone for whom this is all sustainable? Who actually likes this pace?

I don't see how it will be possible for me to keep subscribing to academia's productivity mantras and also have a sustainable lifelong writing practice. Or I don't see how it will be possible for me to continue being the productive writer that academia wants me to be and also exist as a writer who pauses, notices the world, revels in the craft, and delights in the process.

The verb for the writing that sustains me is "ponder." The verb for academic writing is "churn."

EXPANDING OUR ATTENTION TO INCLUDE EMBODIED WRITING

What would it look like for us to break down the siloes around our writing selves and invite embodied experiences into our academic writing? As a first step, we can expand how we teach our students to write. I can present IMRAD-style articles to my undergraduates as only one of many possible forms to imitate in composing academic scholarship. Faculty who teach graduate students can assign students to read scholarship that disrupts traditional scholarly writing forms. For example, in the exploration of ideological transparency in teaching where Fester employs the metaphor of jagged versus "jointed" concrete, she chooses not to analyze students' reflections as a traditional qualitative study might but to "include their voices alongside my own to comment on and interrupt my narrative of our shared classroom experience." Carrying her metaphor forward, Fester writes, "I will let the voices of these students push up through the text without comment, and I'll let the reader decide if the concrete beneath our feet shifts naturally with the many voices moving through it or if it, too, becomes broken ground" (145). There are many voices we might invite to move through our own and our students' writing: lines of text from our journals, insights from letters we've received, moments from music or movies or other popular culture artifacts we encounter in daily life. Expanding our attention could mean validating more personal voices and personal artifacts as worthy of joining the conversation in a scholarly text.

Just as Fester invites her students' voices to disrupt her writing, Gloria Park welcomes multiple versions of her own story into her work. Park begins her autobiographical study of how her hybrid Korean-American identity has shaped her experiences teaching in the United States and Korea with a poem she authored in high school, then structures her manuscript around "autobiographic poetic waves" that share and analyze personal stories (11–15). The methods of Park's study disrupt the bodyless tradition that renders scholars hegemonic in writing. She explains that "by encouraging genres of writing such as autobiography, autoethnography, poetry, narrative inquiry, and other personal narratives in academia, there is a collective push toward revealing how gendered, racial, linguistic, and classed identities have further (dis)enfranchised individuals" (9). Fester's and Park's publications stand as examples of how important scholarly arguments can be made—and hegemonic practices disrupted—through nontraditional writing forms.

THE SHADOW CV

As a second step in inviting embodied experiences into our academic writing, we can talk openly about what our writing and research processes look like in lived experience, beyond the sterilized record of those experiences on a CV. In 2021, I received news from a journal that an article I wrote would finally be published, following a pandemic delay. It had been six years since I'd collected data and four years since I'd sent a manuscript to this journal after having earlier versions rejected by two others. My notes for that publication are a litany of frustrations: unreturned emails, documents never seen by the journal during an editor transition, and months upon months of waiting. Yet when the piece was published, readers would never know the path that led to it.

Each of us has an official document listing things we've actually published, presentations we've actually given. And we each have a shadow CV, the work behind that work (Looser). If I were to write a shadow CV for 2020, it would list a proposal written and accepted to a conference that was cancelled, a rejected grant proposal, an application to a research mentoring program that was put on hold, a rejected proposal to a special issue of a journal, all the time designing and field testing surveys for the study I paused and eventually put on hold indefinitely, a conference panel proposal I was asked to spearhead on a topic I was unfamiliar with and so did extensive reading in order to shepherd a group into writing a proposal that was rejected, and the forty-some hours that go into composing a tenure dossier.

Among creative writers, it's a badge of pride to amass rejections (Liao; King 28–29). But most academics don't talk openly about shadow work. Joli Jensen argues that "even the most prolific and successful of

36   ANN N. AMICUCCI

us feel that we need to keep our writing struggles under wraps" (3, 8). I only talk about my rejected manuscripts with close friends, afraid that mentioning them to colleagues will raise questions about the quality of my work.

What would it look like for faculty to tell students stories of rejection and persistence? We can teach students what revision and messy, recursive writing processes look like for professionals as a way of making our lived experiences as writers visible. Doug Downs writes:

> Primary and secondary education routinely wind up teaching students "the" writing process: prewriting, drafting, revision, editing. In schools, though, this process is rarely able to be truly implemented as professional writers experience it: genuinely iterative, recursive, developmental, and chaotic. Rather, it is usually presented as stepwise and linear: we do not draft until we have pre-written; we do not revise until we have drafted. Many college writing courses begin to chip away at such stepwise linearity conceptually, yet assignments designed to promote or require truly non-linear processes (not merely multiple revision loops) are rarely described in our literature. (34)

In response to Downs's call for us to teach students about the messy writing processes professionals engage in, we could talk openly about the shadow CV. Lu writes that we need to "become as interested in the act of writing as in its content: that is, to be as attentive to what the writer is trying to do—how does the writer go about approaching certain lived experiences and why—as in what the writer finds to say about those experiences" (54). Our professional communities—visible in the books, journals, and conferences that showcase the products of our research—demonstrate that we largely aren't interested in scholars' and other professional writers' processes outside of collections such as this one and select others (see Elliot and Horning; Lockridge and Van Ittersum; Tulley, *How*). Perhaps each piece of scholarship we publish could be accompanied by a footnote or brief video to tell the story of how it came to be: the circuitous reading, the rambling drafts, the attempts to connect with different readers, the rejections.

INSISTENCE ON THE PERSONAL

Just as we can expand our attention to the types of writing we teach and make our writing processes visible by writing about the messy work behind our CVs, we can insist on the value of bringing ourselves into our writing, to embody writing through our lived experience and identities. Renee Gladman recounts a scene in *Calamities*, a collection of flash

Sand Creeks and Productivity   37

nonfiction essays, that may be an actual event—perhaps a lecture or workshop she is leading—or may be an imagined sequence or metaphor for what she hopes to accomplish as a writer. She shares:

> I began the day trying to say the word *body* as many times as I could, for myself and for everyone in this room. . . . I wanted to exchange the word with all my correspondents. I wanted to say "body" to them: how is your body or writing through the body or how the body activates objects in the room. . . . I hoped to reach a point in speaking where when it was time to say "body" I could go silent instead. I'd pause and everyone in the room would sound the word within themselves. I'd go, "Every time you put a hold in the _____," and demure. (89)

Gladman incants the body again and again until, she hopes, the group recognizes that the body is an ever-present, ever-important layer to our knowing the world and comes to fill in "the body" or "my body" or "bodies" in her sentences. Gladman's message here is twofold: that the body is important enough for us to be reminded of again and again and that the way we become collectively conscious of the body and its importance is through repetition, through insistence.

Joanne Yoo's scholarship is a story of what such insistence on presence on the page can look like. Yoo first published an exploration of her own hesitation as an academic writer and her struggle to find an authentic voice. Her writer's perspective reflects, "*This new-found desire to communicate creatively has disturbed my writing path. I rebel against the institutional discourses that silence my own voice*" (Yoo, "Writing Out" 446). She then published a series of articles that test out these new possibilities as a writer. These manuscripts describe experiments with "writing dangerously" by exploring the personal within academic prose ("A Year" 354), ways academics can access new planes of meaning by writing creatively ("Writing Creatively"), connections between breathing and writing ("Learning"; "Tracing"), and stories of her son coming to terms with his racialized body ("My Child"). Taken collectively, Yoo's scholarship is insistent, like Gladman repeating *body*, in showing us what a wealth of riches we can access when we invite and celebrate stories of lived experience.

I call for us to expand how we think of ourselves as writers and readers, to expand the networks within which we have scholarly conversation. Let's stop teaching graduate students they should cite their professors for posterity and teach them instead to consider whose stories and whose identities they are amplifying through citations. Let's start teaching students to read smaller, independent journals that disrupt the boundaries of what scholarship looks like and whose lived experiences we are called to witness. Let's give ourselves permission to allow all our thinking and reading to inform our writing. We stand to gain more readers this way: Yoo argues that composing in ways that resemble creative more than academic prose means more readers can access and understand a writer's ideas ("Writing Out" 447). And perhaps even more importantly, we stand to gain a holistic understanding of our whole selves as writers, to gain a writerly voice that allows all of who we are to come to the page.

NOTES

1. The acronym IMRAD refers to articles with sections titled Introduction, Methods, Results, and Discussion.

2. For readers who question why I haven't recounted overwhelm at having to move my teaching online, I'll share that I'm comfortable with technology and, as an administrator who was only teaching one course that semester, found it fairly easy to transition my course to synchronous online meetings. But I'd be remiss not to mention that the year challenged me deeply as an administrator in the extensive support I provided to other faculty making these transitions.

    And also, my defensive reflex as a writer insists that I answer a question I imagine you're asking: no, I don't have children or a partner.

WORKS CITED

Banks, William P. "Written through the Body: Disruptions and 'Personal' Writing." *College English*, vol. 66, no. 1, 2003, pp. 21–40.

Berg, Maggie, and Barbara K. Seeber. *The Slow Professor: Challenging the Culture of Speed in the Academy.* University of Toronto Press, 2016.

Brooks, David. "Leadership: Centering Relationships and Building Trust." Leo Hill Leadership Speaker Series, 23 Feb. 2021, University of Colorado Boulder, via Zoom.

"Creating in Uncertainty, featuring Devi S. Laskar." *Write-Minded*, podcast, hosted by Brooke Warner and Grant Faulkner, 28 Dec. 2020. https://podcast.shewrites.com/creating-in-uncertainty/.

Downs, Doug. "Double Standards and Sunshine: Exploring Expectations for Professional and Student Writing in FYC." *Stories from First-Year Composition: Pedagogies that Foster Student Agency and Writing Identity*, edited by Jo-Anne Kerr and Ann Amicucci, The WAC Clearinghouse and UP of Colorado, 2020, pp. 23–42.

Elliot, Norbert, and Alice S. Horning, editors. *Talking Back: Senior Scholars and Their Colleagues Deliberate the Past, Present, and Future of Writing Studies.* Utah State UP, 2020.

Fester, Heather. "Transparency as a Defense-less Act: Shining Light on Emerging Ideologies in an Activist Writing and Research Course." *On Teacher Neutrality: Politics, Praxis, and Performativity*, edited by Daniel P. Richards, Utah State UP, 2020, pp. 143–61.

Fleckenstein, Kristie S. "Writing Bodies: Somatic Mind in Composition Studies." *College English*, vol. 61, no. 3, 1999, pp. 281–306.

Furtak, Erin Marie. "My Writing Productivity Pipeline." *The Chronicle of Higher Education*, 6 June 2016. https://www.chronicle.com/article/my-writing-productivity-pipeline/.

"Getting Intentional with Your Writing, featuring Deesha Philyaw." *Write-Minded*, podcast, hosted by Brooke Warner and Grant Faulkner, 22 Feb. 2021. https://podcast.shewrites.com/getting-intentional-with-your-writing/.

Gladman, Renee. *Calamities.* Wave Books, 2016.

Hesse, Doug, et al. "What Should be the Nature of First-Year Writing and Its Relationship to Larger Curricula?" Writing the Range conference, 14 Nov. 2014, University of Denver, Denver, CO.

Hindman, Jane E. "Making Writing Matter: Using 'The Personal' to Recover[y] an Essential[ist] Tension in Academic Discourse." *College English*, vol. 64, no. 1, 2001, pp. 88–108.

Hindman, Jane E. "Writing an Important Body of Scholarship: A Proposal for an Embodied Rhetoric of Professional Practice." *JAC*, vol. 22, no. 1, 2002, pp. 93–118.

Houston, Pam. "Craft talk." Visiting Author Series, 10 Mar. 2021, University of Colorado Colorado Springs, via Microsoft Teams.

Jensen, Joli. *Write No Matter What: Advice for Academics.* U of Chicago P, 2017.

Karpen, Ruth Ray. "Afterword: Toward an Even Longer View." *Talking Back: Senior Scholars and Their Colleagues Deliberate the Past, Present, and Future of Writing Studies*, edited by Norbert Elliot and Alice S. Horning, Utah State UP, 2020, pp. 392–403.

King, Stephen. *On Writing: A Memoir of the Craft.* Pocket Books, 2002.

Knoblauch, A. Abby. "Bodies of Knowledge: Definitions, Delineations, and Implications of Embodied Writing in the Academy." *Composition Studies*, vol. 40, no. 2, 2012, pp. 50–65.

Liao, Kim. "Why You Should Aim for 100 Rejections a Year." *LitHub*, 28 June 2016. https://lithub.com/why-you-should-aim-for-100-rejections-a-year/.

Lim, Shirley Geok-lin. "Lore, Practice, and Social Identity in Creative Writing Pedagogy: Speaking with a Yellow Voice?" *Pedagogy: Critical Approaches to Teaching Literature, Language, Composition, and Culture*, vol. 10, no. 1, 2010, pp. 79–93.

Lockridge, Tim, and Derek Van Ittersum. *Writing Workflows: Beyond Word Processing.* University of Michigan Press, 2020.

Looser, Devoney. "Me and My Shadow CV." *Chronicle of Higher Education*, 6 Nov. 2015. https://www.chronicle.com/article/me-and-my-shadow-cv/.

Löytönen, Teija, et al. "Playing with Patterns: Fumbling Towards Collaborative and Embodied Writing." *International Review of Qualitative Research*, vol. 7, no. 2, 2014, pp. 236–57.

Lu, Min-Zhan. "Reading the Personal: Critical Trajectories" in Brandt, Deborah, et al. "The Politics of the Personal: Storying Our Lives against the Grain. Symposium Collective." *College English*, vol. 64, no. 1, 2001, pp. 41–62.

Mountz, Alison, et al. "For Slow Scholarship: A Feminist Politics of Resistance through Collective Action in the Neoliberal University." *ACME: An International E-Journal for Critical Geographies*, vol. 14, no. 4, 2015, pp. 1235–59.

Park, Gloria. "My Autobiographical-Poetic Rendition: An Inquiry into Humanizing our Teacher Scholarship." *L2 Journal*, vol. 5, no. 1, 2013, pp. 6–18.

Perl, Sondra. "Composing in the Here and Now." Conference on College Composition and Communication, 19 Mar. 2015, Tampa Marriott Waterside & Tampa Convention Center, Tampa, FL.

Perl, Sondra. *Felt Sense: Writing with the Body.* Heinemann, 2004.

Phelps, Louise Wetherbee. "Identity Work: Continuities and Transformations in the Senior Years." *Talking Back: Senior Scholars and Their Colleagues Deliberate the Past, Present, and Future of Writing Studies*, edited by Norbert Elliot and Alice S. Horning, Utah State UP, 2020, pp. 294–307.

"Productive Procrastination, featuring Bridget Quinn." *Write-Minded*, podcast, hosted by Brooke Warner and Grand Faulkner, 3 Aug. 2020. https://podcast.shewrites.com/productive-procrastination/.

Silvia, Paul J. "Cave Mode = Out of the Cave." *Paul J. Silvia*, https://sites.google.com/a/uncg.edu/paulsilvia/cave-mode.

Silvia, Paul J. *How to Write a Lot: A Practical Guide to Productive Academic Writing.* 2nd ed., American Psychological Association, 2019.

40   ANN N. AMICUCCI

Silvia, Paul J. *Write It Up: Practical Strategies for Writing and Publishing Journal Articles.* American Psychological Association, 2015.

Tulley, Christine. "Avoiding the Stalled Academic Writing Project: Advice for Increasing Faculty Writing Momentum from Rhetoric and Composition Superstars." Conference on College Composition and Communication, 7 Apr. 2016, George R. Brown Convention Center and Hilton Americas, Houston, TX.

Tulley, Christine. *How Writing Faculty Write: Strategies for Process, Product, and Productivity.* Utah State UP, 2018.

Vandrick, Stephanie. *Interrogating Privilege: Reflections of a Second Language Educator.* U of Michigan P, 2009.

Villanueva, Victor. "The Personal" in Brandt, Deborah, et al. "The Politics of the Personal: Storying Our Lives against the Grain. Symposium Collective." *College English,* vol. 64, no. 1, 2001, pp. 41–62.

Welsh, Susan. "Writing: In and With the World." *College Composition and Communication,* vol. 46, no. 1, 1995, pp. 103–07.

Wenger, Christy I. "Embodied Ethos and a Pedagogy of Presence: Reflections from a Writing-Yogi." *The Journal of the Assembly for Expanded Perspectives on Learning,* vol. 23, 2017–2018, pp. 76–91.

"Writing with Urgency, featuring Marcelo Hernandez Castillo." *Write-Minded,* podcast, hosted by Brooke Warner and Grant Faulkner, 13 July 2020, https://podcast.shewrites .com/writing-with-urgency/.

Yoo, Joanne. "Learning to Write Through an Awareness of Breath." *Qualitative Inquiry,* vol. 26, no. 3–4, 2020, pp. 400–06.

Yoo, Joanne. "My Child and His Beautiful Body." *Qualitative Inquiry,* vol. 26, no. 3–4, 2020, pp. 257–61.

Yoo, Joanne. "Tracing the Immaterial Spaces of *You.*" *Qualitative Inquiry,* vol. 27, no. 1, 2021, pp. 64–69.

Yoo, Joanne. "Writing Creatively to Catch Flickers of 'Truth' and Beauty." *New Writing,* vol. 18, no. 1, 2021 pp. 74–83.

Yoo, Joanne. "Writing out on a Limb: Integrating the Creative and Academic Writing Identity." *New Writing,* vol. 14, no. 3, 2017, pp. 444–54.

Yoo, Joanne. "A Year of Writing 'Dangerously': A Narrative of Hope." *New Writing,* vol. 16, no. 3, 2019, pp. 353–62.

3

RELEARNING TO WRITE IN CRIP TIME (ON THE TENURE CLOCK)

Melanie Kill

Tags: embodiment, technology, adaptability, productivity

In the fall of 2010, the episodic migraines I have experienced since childhood "transitioned" into chronic migraine, no longer a part of my life to get through once or twice a month but a chronic daily neurological condition that required attention, management, and a complete transformation of the ways I live and work. At the center of much of this change was the fact that my computer screen became a barrier rather than a portal. The light that screens emit—flashing imperceptibly and always moving in obvious and subtle ways—is both a trigger and exacerbating factor in my variable everyday experience of pain, nausea, dizziness, and fatigue. Over the past decade, I have had to reimagine my relationship with both time and technologies of writing as I've learned to live, think, and work within both the physical constraints and discriminatory systems that act on my now disabled being. I've done this in the context of a rapidly expanding range of available tools for writing. And I've done this in the context of the tenure clock: taking a tenure-track position at a research-intensive university four months after being diagnosed with chronic illness, doing my work while also navigating disability disclosure and a faculty accommodations process being developed as I showed up to ask about it. Within my disabled, misfit (Garland-Thomson) status, and through my unexpected encounter with what it means to incohere, I've found possibilities for depth of thought and ethical understanding of writing technologies and writing processes that I could not have imagined outside them.

As a scholar of digital rhetorics, a disability that disrupted my interactions with computers initially seemed like some absurd joke. Over time, I've come to see my previous exposure to such a narrow range of digital devices and software as the limited and limiting framework. Life with chronic illness has vastly expanded both the variety and complexity

---

https://doi.org/10.7330/9781646424870.c003

of my interactions with technologies for writing. I have found that, as disability studies scholars have been arguing for decades, "disability enables insight—critical, experiential, cognitive, sensory, and pedagogical insight" (Brueggemann 795). Disability has enabled me to crip (Sandahl) the technologies I study and the ways they configure particular relationships not only between thought, writing, and action but also between individuals and institutions.

In this chapter, I consider the lessons of a decade of personal experiments with writing technologies and workflows from the critical perspective of disability rhetoric, which "situates disability itself as positively meaningful and meaning-making" and offers "imperfect, extraordinary, nonnormative bodies as the origin and epistemological homes of all meaning making" (Dolmage 4, 19). I examine the ways embodied interactions with writing technologies affect first how and what we write and then, by extension, who can write within institutions of higher education. Taking up the concept of crip time (Kafer, *Feminist, Queer, Crip*; Kafer, "After Crip, Crip Afters"; Samuels; Price, "Time Harms") to think about crip temporalities as productive even though noncompliant within capitalist ideologies (Russell), this chapter offers a critical exploration of lived experience to argue against an exclusive, and exclusionary, focus on fast writing as the measure of success for intellectual labor. In response to these exclusions and in recognition of the need for attention to equity in institutional structures, I explore the value of disabled habits of writing and knowledge-making that incorporate "rest and coasting amidst the labor of making" and recognize "the mind's need for incoherence, to rest, coast, spread out, incohere" (Berlant and Lasky).

WRITING TOOLS AND WORKFLOWS

Over the past decade, I've experimented more and less successfully with a range of writing technologies and workflows. This process of figuring out how disabled writing works for me has happened alongside the other practical and social labor involved in acquiring a disability. I have come to think of learning to write while disabled as a kind of experiential design brief. Disability—as a dynamic configuration of embodied, material, and social conditions—presents me with a set of questions that can be both framed and addressed in myriad ways (Hendren 7). I have moved roughly through three stages of framing—apparent only in retrospect—and through too many different tools, strategies, combinations, and permutations to count or document. When I first encountered chronic illness, I did not understand it at all. I acted on my own deeply internalized ableism, approaching my body as a problem that could be fixed by medical or technological intervention and would just have to be ignored in the meantime. I worked more and slept less than ever with the goal of passing and pushing through. When I became too ill to function, I took a year of leave without pay, began seeking formal disability accommodations, and moved myself into a second stage. With passing no longer an option, I found a new layer of work in repeated disclosure and explanation, but I was also freed up to experiment more openly. I started wearing my tinted migraine glasses out in public. I began to pay attention and untangle some of the intricate webs of cause and effect between my writing tools and practices and my health. I discovered that relearning to write in the context of disability was going to require me first to understand what I knew and believed about writing before disability. I reshaped my habits, environments, and the paths I moved through with the aim not of pushing through a rough period but of learning to live a life I still very much wanted even with chronic illness. In short, I stepped out of crisis mode and began openly to figure out what adaptations and accommodations would help and could be made. In a third stage, where I find myself now, I am working to let go of the shame and guilt I've carried in my disabled being. I am working on asking for what I need without apologizing for who I am. I am working to accept my bodymind as it is now and explore its reconfigured constellations of possibility.

Carolyn Miller proposes that "if rhetoric is the art that adjusts ideas to people and people to ideas, we might characterize technology as the art that accommodates the material world to people and people to the material world" (Miller x). Technology, then, is fundamentally about accommodation(s); it is a form of material rhetoric that is both world building and world defining. It presents us with configurations of tools and procedures that offer more affordances to some and more barriers to others, that normalize access for some and deny it to others. Rosemarie Garland-Thomson offers the terms "fits" and "misfits" to "theorize disability as a way of being in an environment, as a material arrangement," which is to say that disability is not so much in a body, or bodymind (Price, "The Bodymind Problem"), as in the relation between a body, its tools and contexts, and the socially determined meanings of that relation (Garland-Thomson 594). For example, the idea that some technologies are "assistive" or "adaptive" technologies, while others are categorically not, is grounded in normative ideological frames that place some accommodations—along with the bodies that rely on them—as within the normal range and others outside it (Hendren 25–26). "The

44 MELANIE KILL

dynamism between body and world that produces fits or misfits," Garland-Thomson explains, "comes at the spatial and temporal points of encounter between dynamic but relatively stable bodies and environments" (Garland-Thomson 594). In this view, disability is relational and dynamic, which is to say that a writing technology (i.e., an accommodation) that works well for some bodies will not work for all bodies in all times and spaces.

It is almost certainly the case that my issues with screens would not have impacted me professionally before computer screens became ubiquitous writing tools. The expectations about what scholarly outputs should look like are based on normative ideas about what people should be able to do using common writing technologies like the laptop. In this section I consider my own experiences with the onset of chronic illness and my adaptation to the many misfits it introduced to explore the possibilities of the dynamism between body and writing technology that have transformed my writing practices.

Before it made me sick to do so, I spent a ridiculous amount of time on my computer. Having grown up using word processing software, my writing practices involve a process of laying out and weaving together ideas and arguments that does not start at the upper left and continue across and down from start to finish. I have never planned out my writing before beginning. I have always written to discover what I want to write, working through an iterative process of reading, writing, and revising. Before I became disabled, writing basically meant sitting down at a computer repeatedly until I had a polished text. I did not need to think through the various stages or tasks involved in my writing, so I gave no thought to the process: reading until I had something to say, drafting a lot of text, honing an abstract, sorting and structuring text, and then moving through many rounds of revision and editing in which I would print and mark up each version by hand, before entering the changes and printing again. Word processing software got me used to both seeing the whole and being able to manipulate it fluidly; which is to say that my writing practices had developed around the affordances of my writing tools. We learn to write, and to write with technologies, over decades—in living rooms, bedrooms, and classrooms, in collaboration with others, and in different home, community, institutional, and professional settings. Part of the work of becoming disabled has involved the need both to train myself into new ways of working and to find tools to replicate my familiar ways of working while minimizing my reliance on the computer (screen) itself. Changing writing habits and technologies is a messy and experimental process, and there I was, on the tenure clock, studying myself undergoing profound change as a writer as much as I was experimenting with writing technologies.

I have no tidy chronological narrative to capture my experiments with writing technologies because this was not a tidy process. It was and is a complex, ongoing, and iterative project of integrating, emphasizing, upgrading, deprecating, and using many tools in concert and continuously adapting my workflow to my capabilities in a given day or hour. Not being able to use a computer screen for extended periods of time has required using more writing tools (e.g., draft printout, mechanical pencil, notecards, and e-ink tablet) and searching out new ways to get text into digital form (e.g., scanner, voice dictation, handwriting recognition). Among the first things I learned about screens is that there is no holy grail that allows me to use a computer the way I once did. Over time, however, I have discovered that not only light but also motion and high contrast patterns are triggers for me. Understanding this enables me to select, set up, and switch between types of screens and other writing surfaces as needed.

Each of the tools and technologies I use offers different possibilities for how I position, support, and relax my body; how I input text; how I define writing tasks; and how I break up, organize, and manage longer text. These choices in turn impact how I think and organize ideas and how I write and structure that writing. In these ways, they also direct me toward particular kinds of writing. I can write for longer using one tool; I can write more quickly using another. What I can no longer do is write without thinking about writing, for marathon-length stretches, at a fast pace, without interruption.

Because of the friction illness introduces, I've become keenly aware of the various tasks involved in writing and have had to create systems for coming back to tasks I am not able to complete at a particular time. I have sought a range of ways to accomplish each task and move between them, and a flexible procedure for prioritizing tasks and projects that accepts doing what is possible at the time rather than getting hung up on tasks that are objectively more important but not feasible. I select writing tasks based on a combination of which are most urgent and which tools, given my current symptoms, I am able to work with at the time. Some tasks are completely dependent on a particular device. For example, I have no choice but to use my computer if I need to insert footnotes or citations drawn from my citation management software. If I am drafting and planning, I have a lot of flexibility. Other tasks involve a one-way move after which I can work with them only on my computer. Work that I used to experience as organic, even if it was not, has become hyperarticulated, and steps that used to be invisible or previously unnecessary have become manifest and manifold. The technologies that enable my writing also break it up. Like the hiccups, stilted cadences, and mispronunciations of screen readers, they roughen the production of research. Negatively or positively, they add drag.

These tools require expenditures of time and energy even before they are put to use. Perhaps one of the most embarrassing expectations I had when I became disabled was that someone would be able to tell me what assistive technologies I should now use. Finding and figuring out how to use new tools has become part of my writing workflow. It requires significant resources including (1) time and energy to discover and research; (2) time, energy, and money to acquire; and (3) time and energy to set up, troubleshoot, and develop or adapt routines.

Through my loss of ease at the computer, I have gained a few lessons from friction. Take, for example, the delays inserted by the technologies themselves in screen-refresh rates, lag times, and time transferring text between devices. Because of these I have gained the ability to *not* forget my tools and to *never* imagine them as neutral, and the same can be said for composition. Finding my way back to some degree of ease with writing, I discover how hard it must be for many people to get there in the first place. I am also better able to grasp, in a more variegated and knowing way, how different kinds of writing are possible with different devices and software. This was something I had long been aware of because of my specialization, but in a mostly conceptual way. I have additionally gained insights into the panoply of obstacles faced by other writers, professional and nonprofessional, who have disabilities that are functionally cognate with mine. Below, I will say more about the positive possibilities of losing ease at the computer, for writing and more generally for intellectual labor and equitable employment. Now, I turn to examine how work and disability interact in an institutional context. Friction is only a problem under pressure.

BODYMINDS WORKING IN CRIP SPACETIME IN HIGHER ED

Becoming disabled on the tenure clock has left me with a distinctive perspective on the ways writing technologies structure relationships between individuals and institutions. Assumptions and expectations about the writing technologies people do or should use play a significant role in who can write fast, who can pass as abled, and who can secure accommodations. When we fail to attend to the role of writing technologies in academic work, we unthinkingly turn the pre-tenure probationary period—essentially an extended-timed writing exercise—into a test of who has the best tech for their body, the most resources, and the most reliable support systems. All junior faculty bodies, we tend to take for granted, have a given length of time to cohere to the standard set by tenure and promotion benchmarks, but there are vast inequities in the supports they have to do so. "Need" is a way of describing a mismatch, not an objective state.

Margaret Price observes that although the multidisciplinary field of disability studies is flourishing in US universities, "disabled *people* in academic life seem to be struggling" ("Precarity" 192). To put this another way, the intellectual value of disability is increasingly recognized, even as the intellectual worth of disabled people remains largely unimaginable within the ableist systems of academe. "Disability myths" (Dolmage 34–37) play a significant role in this simultaneous valuing of disability as an abstraction and devaluing of disabled people as human beings. But beyond the tropes that guide subconscious ideas about people with disabilities, it is also the case that neoliberal demands for fast work render disabled people temporally inconvenient.

As Susan Wendell explains, "When the pace of life in a society increases, there is a tendency for more people to become disabled, not only because of physically damaging consequences of efforts to go faster, but also because fewer people can meet the expectations of 'normal' performance: the physical (and mental) limitations of those who cannot meet the new pace become conspicuous and disabling, even though the same limitations were inconspicuous and irrelevant to full participation in the slower paced society" (Wendell 59). Everyday technologies play an important role in setting this pace, and as long as we assume them to be neutral tools, supporting ease and productivity equally available to all, we are effectively excluding those who do not have access to or cannot use them with ease.

By representing the perspectives of disabled people, the concepts of crip time (Kafer, *Feminist, Queer, Crip*; Kuppers; Samuels) and crip spacetime (Price, "Time Harms") theorize and validate lived experience around non-normative temporalities. While the collective recognition of crip time can itself be liberatory, it does not change the fact that crip temporalities are a challenge to the normative ideologies supporting capitalism and used to justify discrimination. As Alison Kafer has explored, we live within the unspoken normative consensus that "any future that includes disability can only be a future to avoid" (*Feminist, Queer, Crip* 2). And yet disabled people persist in living "engaging and satisfying" lives (*Feminist, Queer, Crip* 2). While I personally would love to be less sick or even cured, I still value life with disabling chronic illness, and I still want a future. And like Susan Wendell, despite feeling grief and loss for other potential lives, I cannot wish I had never become disabled. As Wendell explains, disability "has made me a different person, a person I am glad to be, would not want to have missed being, and could not imagine relinquishing" (Wendell 83). I do not want pity; I want not to be crushed and discarded. I want to be allowed to do my work in the world without having to justify my right to exist at every turn. The number of people who have asked me why I don't just quit if I am really so sick seem to me to lack any sense of what it would be like to turn away from their own scholarly work, investments, and responsibilities.

For a disabled academic, doing one's work in the world takes extra time and labor, as does acting on an enhanced capacity to help others who are not physically able and/or politically willing to self-optimize in order to meet advanced capitalism's extractive demands. This additional labor extends across research, teaching, and service. While service and mentoring responsibilities are highly visible though undervalued, the affective burden of social justice work, of arguing against one's own subjectivity as a problem, goes uncounted.

Once I began to openly identify as disabled, I sought accommodations. And I encountered the, let us say, varied responses of colleagues and administrators: sympathetic, supportive, knowledgeable, uncomfortable, skeptical, dismissive, suspicious, or simply bewildered. No matter the response, the intellectual and emotional labor involved in seeking disability accommodations is exhausting. This includes the labor of faking well and fitting in, including what Irving Goffman terms masking and others refer to as covering or passing. Disclosure is exhausting, but so is pretending I didn't just run to the bathroom to throw up and then come back to the meeting. The labor burden on individual disabled people also includes "access fatigue" (Konrad), such as the work of compelling medical professionals to write letters and fill out forms on my behalf. This unaccounted-for labor of seeking accommodations is underlaid by continual unpredictability. The most crucial accommodation on the tenure clock is extended time, and (at my institution at least) extensions are considered only one year at a time. Never knowing how much time I had held me in a state of repeated, impending crisis. Within my department and upper administration, many of the people receiving these requests and making these decisions are also tasked with evaluating me for tenure and promotion. To be required to take up the role of supplicant rather than colleague in these interactions is not without consequences.

My experience of accommodation therefore tracks with what Price describes: "Accommodation is by definition a move put in place to address ('accommodate') some problem" that "tends to operate in the neoliberal university more like an attempt at cure or eradication than like an attempt to actually include disability as part of university life" (Price, "Precarity" 195). This begins to explain why time, which would seem one of the least burdensome or expensive accommodations to provide for tenure-line faculty, is so closely guarded an accommodation. Disabled people can and do self-accommodate, for example by working many more hours, but there is a limit to what any person can do, and, particularly for people living with chronic illness, digging too deep into time for basic needs like sleep, food, and symptom management comes with consequences. For instance, it may be possible to take a late night to meet a deadline, but only if you can afford to lose the following days to the incapacity of a major symptom flare. Similarly, if denied the time it takes to be productive and disabled, there is no way to manage the tradeoffs, and your remaining available time shrinks to create unlivable conditions. For disabled faculty, therefore, the tenure clock can be a hard limit. Should they endure market conditions to be hired in the first place, they encounter the direct inverse of crip time—a system set up to eliminate them.

Alternatively, disability could be embraced insofar as it considerably diversifies academia. But demographic data is hard to come by because it is not collected. And chronic illness and other invisible disabilities are overlooked still further, falling outside commonplace mechanisms for locating disabled bodies or making them legible. Migraines, along with other neurological impairments like epilepsy, are considered physical disabilities under the ADA. But, unlike epilepsy, the external signs of a brain's reaction to particular stimuli in a migraine attack are subtle, and often made even more subtle by the migraineur's learned skill of masking pain and other symptoms. When they are observable, signs like sensory sensitivities, vomiting, and difficulty with balance and coordination can even be mistaken for an alcohol or drug use disorder, playing out a version of "disability drift," where less stigmatized forms of disability are equated with more stigmatized forms, or "disability drop," where a more socially acceptable type of disability is faked as a cover story (Dolmage 46), thus making disclosure and accommodations more fraught.

In moments of disability disclosure, I have often been met with the assessment that I have some mysterious and medically unprecedented condition, which is sad for me but not anything that could be addressed systemically. Chronic migraine is well-studied in medicine and disability studies (Kempner; Honeyman; O'Shea). It is a long-duration chronic daily headache disorder that affects approximately 1.29% of women and 0.48% of men in the United States. Rates are highest in women ages forty to fifty in low household income brackets. It is influenced by hormone fluctuations (i.e., menstrual cycles and menopause) and correlated to income and, via income, to race, which means it disproportionately impacts working-age women of color. If one in one hundred women and one in two hundred men in the United States live with chronic migraine, it is not chronic migraine that is unusual, it is me, a chronically ill, disabled person working in a university.

These are not merely personal struggles. They are encounters with systems—ideology expressed in policies—that cannot account for the lived experience or the intellectual potential of disabled faculty members because they have so far functioned so successfully to exclude disabled people from academia. There are time-sensitive elements of a junior faculty member's workload, especially in terms of teaching and service: students need feedback, grades need to be submitted, and programs need to be administered. Time for scholarship is different: it is common for faculty members to produce scholarship in different forms at different rates and even to go through more and less productive periods in their careers. After tenure, time ceases to matter in the same way.

The accommodations process at many universities seems to operate less as a resource and support system and more as a test of who has the resources and determination to navigate bureaucratic barriers. The payoff once disability accommodations are institutionally approved may be low, as it is up to individual professors, supervisors, and administrators—who may neither have the resources to support their implementation nor understand the profound inequity of failing to do so. People cannot demonstrate what they are capable of (with accommodations) unless they receive the accommodations they need. As Margaret Price argues, "Crip spacetime makes it obvious that we cannot rely on some individuals to articulate 'needs' and others to bestow 'accommodations' in order to achieve justice" ("Precarity" 205). Price goes on to observe, "The landmarks of crip spacetime are well known to most disabled faculty members, and in fact to all minoritized faculty members: surveillance, disbelief, minimizing, apparent inability to understand straightforward requests, gaslighting, microaggressions, open cruelty" ("Time Harms" 272).

She asks what, by contrast, collective accountability might look like. To conclude, I take up Price's question and explore another: What do we gain when we genuinely make space for disabled researchers, scholars, writers? Both questions concern knowledge production—its who and its what, its ethics and its forms.

RETHINKING PRODUCTIVITY, WRITING TOWARD EQUITY

We need people in higher education thinking and writing about access and illness and not just for the benefit of institutional critique. Illness is in so many ways such an ordinary state, so universal and fundamental to the human experience. With attention to race and gender, Jacqueline Jones Royster makes the point that

> knowledge is produced by someone and that its producers are not formless and invisible. They are embodied and in effect have passionate attachments by means of their embodiments. They are vested with vision, values, and habits; with ways of being and ways of doing. These ways of being and doing shape the question of what counts as knowledge, what knowing and doing mean, and what the consequences of knowledge and action entail. (Royster 280)

Disabled embodiment is generally associated with disorder, but, in fact, along with other dimensions of diversity, it offers a range of alternative orders. It is disruptive to specific ways of conceptualizing productivity, and it brings others into focus, to the advantage of all. As Leah Lakshmi Piepzna-Samarasinha tells us, "One of the gifts of disability and moving on 'crip time'—slowly—is that we notice things that people moving quickly typically miss" (Bader). Disabled academics bring richness of observation. This can patently benefit a researcher in a field such as urban studies who, for instance, is analyzing inequitable public transit systems. But it also benefits disciplines characterized by close analysis of discourse and textual artifacts. Some of the under-remarked consequences of intensified research expectations across disciplines and divisions include predictability and sameness. Understandably, researchers, especially junior and contingent faculty, are often operating with expedience as their lead. When you have to produce quickly you are more likely to conduct highly targeted research and to commit to paper the most conspicuous relationships or patterns you observe in the materials at hand. Studies conducted under pressure will of necessity privilege a working focus that is less likely to let in less conspicuous connections, as well as less immediately relevant content. And researchers trying to work fast will be less likely (less able) to examine their objects of investigation from several angles. They are not given license (time) to allow the mind to expand around an idea or set it aside. When you stop looking directly, sometimes you catch a glimpse of something unexpected, sometimes you see around your own assumptions. Less time hinders discovery, inattention, surprise, imagination, rest and coasting, and empathy; crip time born of crip embodiment advances them.

Outside the field of disability studies, the intellectual and institutional value of slow inquiry has been well-established and received: "If there is one sector of society that should be cultivating deep thought," it is academia (Berg and Seeber xviii). Collective accountability of the kind Price calls for, on behalf of disabled researchers, would protect against the flattening of knowledge production, through securing for all researchers the time for discovery-led and experimental work, not to mention careful rewriting and deep revision. Genuinely accommodating disabled scholars diversifies tertiary institutions both in terms of their makeup and their knowledge creation. Crip time in the research setting further allows for careful, fair, and involved (ethical and slow) collaboration. Finally, crip time, insofar as it challenges discriminatory productivity standards, makes institutions more organizationally robust. Accommodations and accessibility systems will only become effective if the individuals navigating them feel they can report on what works and what does not work, without risking job security. A parallel can be drawn with the tenure narrative: Tenure was established to protect the intellectual freedom of researchers so that they would not have to censor or abort their research questions out of fear of losing their jobs. Disabled academics who feel secure in their employment can advance their home institutions by helping them better function. They can describe the machinery of accommodations. In their status as vitally included, they can bring difference to a sector that is in danger of becoming an epicenter of high-achieving bodyminds and an avatar of the undesirable descriptor, elite. That takes time.

How small or hidden should scholars be expected to make their lives to make room for intellectual work? Collin Bjork and Frida Buhre call for rhetorical studies to "better account for the multiplicity and asymmetricality of the temporal regimes that structure rhetorical relations and, at the same time, work towards articulating and enacting more just temporal frameworks" (Bjork and Buhre).[1] The answer offered by disability scholarship is that work time and life time are not at odds. While this claim may sound familiar—a rehash of productivity literature and wellness advice—it is different from the neoliberal idea of work/life balance in which our private lives are arranged in service to our work with the aim of maximizing our economic value. In which it is assumed that if your life is difficult, your work will suffer. It is a system that does not provide the resources required to outsource the tasks of daily life so as

Relearning to Write in Crip Time (on the Tenure Clock)   53

to reduce our lives down to a casual side project; however, those who have those resources are richly rewarded. It is suspicious of the vulnerable specifically for their precarity. I claim work and life as inseparable because intellectual activity fills up my life, and it need not overtake it in order for my work to have value.

With respect to the work of writing, both disabled and abled writers are "blocked" in various ways, many of which are not only psychological. Writing advice that frames productivity as a matter of will power and determination participates in a particular kind of blame and shaming that is at odds with diversity and equity. It is part and parcel of a system that relies on privilege to provide the support and resources it does not. It also fails to recognize the difficulty of writing and persisting within institutions that are hostile to your existence as a scholar or student. Doctoral students on the academic job market, for example, are advised to try to conceal from potential employer institutions any life events that may have slowed their time to completion and reduced their research outputs. Having an ill parent or partner or developing a disease or disability are strikes against you. The key is not to be discovered and not to gain a tag. As Dolmage notes in a similar vein, "Disability is often used rhetorically as a flexible form of stigma to be freely applied to any unknown, threatening or devalued group" (Dolmage 4). The tenacity of ableist expectations for academic workers makes plain that advances within institutions organizationally speaking—diversity statements, campus centers, offices, and degree programs—are not addressing root problems.

The work of writing is especially instructive for institutional critique because of its overlooked materiality. It is easy to assume, for instance, that someone who is in a weakened state cannot chair a panel but can still write, because the labor is not physically and performatively demanding. Foregrounding writing as an embodied activity also foregrounds the harm it can produce if the body is neglected in service of a research deliverable. If I work against my body, I am too sick to write. If I work with my body, I can write differently. My workflows are not efficient. They shape and push my work in unexpected ways. One of the keys to my workflow is to break focus regularly so that I remember my body and attend to it. My body is not something to be overcome, it is how I move through the world. It is what makes writing possible. And the friction of my interactions with writing technologies is a live and dynamic thing. Friction is what makes movement possible. Light friction is, after all, associated not only with pleasure but also with heightened awareness.

It is my hope that by acknowledging the material interaction between my particular bodymind, my writing tools, and my writing—both the practices and the product—I might call attention to the considerable influence of bodies on writing and also to push back against ableist ideologies and policies that frame those of us with temporally marked, noticeable, and misfit bodies as unfit for academic work. Perhaps the lessons of my bodymind could be lessons that suggest we might all expand—take up more time and space—to hold ground against constricting neoliberal definitions of productivity. As Moya Bailey writes, "We can make a decision to push back on expectations of overwork through how we design our research and, when we are in positions of power, the kinds of scholarship we value for promotion and tenure" (Bailey 295).

What is precious about scholarly writing is not its mere proliferation but the useful distillation of intelligence, experience, determination, curiosity, adaptability, and deep care for this world and the knowledge more just futures require. I hope we can learn from the COVID-19 pandemic that the support structures many temporarily lost were never available to everyone. We need an ethics of pace that allows us to move together toward our social justice goals and allows us to build trust and engage with the perspectives of our collaborators, whether they are community members or colleagues. We are sometimes impatient with those who have less power, with those who are struggling. I call on us to be impatient instead with systems that dehumanize and with a pace of structural change that is unethical.

NOTE

1. To illustrate some of the ways the writing technologies on which I rely slow my writing processes, the following text is what the voice dictation tool in Microsoft Word generated when I read this quotation: "better And in symmetric ality of the temporal visions that structure that will presentations and. Articulating and acting more just to. I don't listen. Holiday at the temple visions that strike you're that welcome dictation. Working together Justin."

WORKS CITED

Bader, Eleanor J. "Reimagining Disability Justice: An Interview with Leah Lakshmi Piepzna-Samarasinha." *Los Angeles Review of Books*, 27 Nov. 2018, https://blog.lareviewofbooks.org/interviews/reimagining-disability-justice-interview-leah-lakshmi-piepzna-samarasinha/.

Bailey, Moya. "The Ethics of Pace." *South Atlantic Quarterly*, vol. 120, no. 2, Apr. 2021, pp. 285–99. https://doi.org/10.1215/00382876-8915966.

Berg, Maggie, and Barbara K. Seeber. *The Slow Professor: Challenging the Culture of Speed in the Academy.* U of Toronto P, 2016.

Berlant, Lauren, and Dorothea Lasky. "I Don't Understand the God Part: A Conversation Between Lauren Berlant and Dorothea Lasky." *MAKE Literary Magazine*, Feb. 2014. https://www.makemag.com/interview-berlant-lasky_new/.

Bjork, Collin, and Frida Buhre. "Resisting Temporal Regimes, Imagining Just Temporalities." *Rhetoric Society Quarterly*, vol. 51, no. 3, May 2021, pp. 177–81. https://doi.org/10.1080/02773945.2021.1918503.

Brueggemann, Brenda Jo. "An Enabling Pedagogy: Meditations on Writing and Disability." *JAC: A Journal of Composition Theory*, vol. 21, no. 4, 2001, pp. 791–820.

Dolmage, Jay. *Disability Rhetoric.* Syracuse UP, 2014.

Garland-Thomson, Rosemarie. "Misfits: A Feminist Materialist Disability Concept." *Hypatia*, vol. 26, no. 3, 2011, pp. 591–609.

Hendren, Sara. *What Can a Body Do?: How We Meet the Built World.* Riverhead Books, 2020.

Honeyman, Susan. *Child Pain, Migraine, and Invisible Disability.* Routledge, 2016. https://doi.org/10.4324/9781315460932.

Kafer, Alison. "After Crip, Crip Afters." *South Atlantic Quarterly*, vol. 120, no. 2, Apr. 2021, pp. 415–34. https://doi.org/10.1215/00382876-8916158.

Kafer, Alison. *Feminist, Queer, Crip.* Indiana UP, 2013.

Kempner, Joanna Leslie. *Not Tonight: Migraine and the Politics of Gender and Health.* The U of Chicago P, 2014. *WorldCat Discovery Service*, http://chicago.universitypressscholarship.com/view/10.7208/chicago/9780226179292.001.0001/upso-9780226179018.

Konrad, Annika M. "Access Fatigue: The Rhetorical Work of Disability in Everyday Life." *College English*, vol. 83, no. 3, 2021, pp. 179–99.

Kuppers, Petra. "Crip Time." *Tikkun*, vol. 29, no. 4, Oct. 2014, pp. 29–30. https://doi.org/10.1215/08879982-2810062.

Miller, Carolyn. "Rhetoric, Technology, and the Pushmi-Pullyu." *Rhetorics and Technologies: New Directions in Writing and Communication*, edited by Stuart A. Selber, U of South Carolina P, 2010, pp. ix–xii. *WorldCat Discovery Service*, http://site.ebrary.com/id/10635890.

O'Shea, Kathleen. *So Much More Than a Headache Understanding Migraine through Literature.* The Kent State UP, 2020. *WorldCat Discovery Service*, http://public.eblib.com/choice/PublicFullRecord.aspx?p=6244599.

Price, Margaret. "The Bodymind Problem and the Possibilities of Pain." *Hypatia*, vol. 30, no. 1, 2015, pp. 268–84.

Price, Margaret. "The Precarity of Disability/Studies in Academe." *Precarious Rhetorics*, edited by Wendy S. Hesford et al., The Ohio State UP, 2018, pp. 191–211.

Price, Margaret. "Time Harms: Disabled Faculty Navigating the Accommodations Loop." *South Atlantic Quarterly*, vol. 120, no. 2, Apr. 2021, pp. 257–77. https://doi.org/10.1215/00382876-8915966.

Royster, Jacqueline Jones. *Traces of a Stream: Literacy and Social Change among African American Women.* U of Pittsburgh P, 2000.

Russell, Marta. *Capitalism & Disability: Selected Writings by Marta Russell.* Edited by Keith Rosenthal, Haymarket Books, 2019.

Samuels, Ellen. "Six Ways of Looking at Crip Time." *Disability Studies Quarterly*, vol. 37, no. 3, Aug. 2017. https://doi.org/10.18061/dsq.v37i3.5824.

Sandahl, Carrie. "Queering the Crip or Cripping the Queer?: Intersections of Queer and Crip Identities in Solo Autobiographical Performance." *GLQ: A Journal of Lesbian and Gay Studies*, vol. 9, no. 1–2, Apr. 2003, pp. 25–56. *Silverchair*, https://doi.org/10.1215/10642684-9-1-2-25.

Wendell, Susan. *The Rejected Body: Feminist Philosophical Reflections on Disability.* Routledge, 1996.

4

PROCESS NOT PROGRESS
(OR, *NOT-PROGRESS* IS PROCESS)
A Narrative Meditation

Hannah J. Rule

Tags: productivity, critique, adaptability

Recently, daily living has felt more like living history. It seems like every day we're processing current events like pages in a history book—an unrelenting global pandemic, the murder of George Floyd by a Minneapolis police officer, the January 6 attack on the Capitol. The list goes on. This era—"long-2020," as a colleague of mine off-handedly called it—still beats on in calendar year 2021 (and beyond), as the pandemic and public heath disinformation continues to rage, as wildfires burn, as we pessimistically watch efforts wither to reform policing and voting rights, as we negotiate half-returns to campus. We've mostly been at home all the while, often experiencing events up close through unrelenting streams of content and trying to maintain life's mundane responsibilities. While individuals' circumstance and privilege make the experience of these times quite different, I do think long-2020 has us questioning everything. I have felt this strangeness chronically and in various ways, including in the slice of my life in which I am a scholarly writer. I work at a public research university, so in some ways my professional life is to be driven by my writing output. But, long story short, it hasn't been going well, not in my estimation.

Since starting in my current position, my writing processes have ridden mostly on fear- and anxiety-driven autopilot. No time for pausing, just nose to the pavement. I got my tenure and promotion letter in May of 2020, at the height of global surreality (I compiled and submitted my file in the pre-COVID fall of 2019. Others admirably managed to assemble files, wait out the long review process, and get a decision all within the long COVID year [Carney]). The twin events of weighty professional stress relieved amidst cascading global horrors—or the malaise of the post-tenure "slump" intersecting with deep existential angst in

https://doi.org/10.7330/9781646424870.c004

Process Not Progress (or, Not-Progress Is Process)   57

the country and in the world—put me in a strange headspace, to say the least. I am apathetic and unmoored; I am skeptical of everything I have published or might write. I am questioning everything.

At the same time, when I step outside myself, I do see that I've basically been doing fine. I've pushed writing projects along and benefited tremendously from collaboration. But I've *felt* strange and disengaged as a scholarly reader, researcher, and writer. How can my small stuff matter at all when worlds out there burn? This question makes me linger in worry and apathy.

There have been signals over this long year, inside and outside academia, that others too are questioning business as usual, with many calling for different orientations to work. There has been encouragement to shorten the work week—though, not surprisingly, arguments for it tend to focus on the economic, not the humanistic, sense it would make (McKeever). There has been some much overdue attention paid to the mental health and wellbeing of faculty (Cliburn) and to the disproportionate effects the pandemic has had on women and caregivers who are also academics, especially those of color (Farinde-Wu; Skinner et al.). There has been some institutional grace for, and needed questioning of, tenure clocks and conventional models of faculty research output (Butler). Even still amidst this reconsideration, I've equally felt a strong undertow of *overcoming* (a thoroughly ableist trope, as Allison Harper Hitt reminds). We take in messages of coping, of innovating, of "using" all our "extra" time, of learning real fast how to expertly deliver online education to your students (and while you're at it, your children), of getting into sourdough, of finally finishing that article you didn't have time for before. Of nevertheless being "productive."

Likely these latter messages are coming mostly from "inside the house," a dynamic that I think may be relatable. By this I mean that likely it is mainly me who is the one continuously judging my disinterest in scholarly writing. I am the one feeling like I've been doing something wrong; I am the one feeling like an imposter as I try to summon any bit of energy to write anything at all or as I procrastinate in painful ways I never have before. I know that periods of being fallow in scholarly writing is normal, even in "normal times." But that's not how it *feels* to me.

As such, I've been thinking about how to conceptualize *not* being productive as a scholarly writer—or how to understand periods of *not-progress*—as legitimate, okay, a norm, an inevitability. Acceptable to me but also to the academic cultures and communities in which we work. How do we center an ethic of mindful not-progress on scholarly writing rather than giving it this one-time, halfway, long-2020 exception?

58   HANNAH J. RULE

How can *not making progress* be experienced and understood as a meaningful part of all scholarly composing processes? These questions are certainly exigent now, and they continue to be so if we want to create more humane and equitable conditions in academia. In what follows, I turn to work in writing studies and adjacent fields to find ways of seeing scholarly writing processes *not* as an orderly march toward publishing nor a mechanized devotion to "being productive." I instead want scholarly writing processes as wayward experience and exigence, as effortful writing and *not-writing*. What follows is a first-person effort,[1] one of contradiction and questioning, that I hope connects.

2. For some evidence of my attempts at pandemic-era, post-tenure productivity, see this very chapter. Working on it has mostly consisted of repetitiously writing in my calendar that I need to start it. Thereafter, my process has been totally different from my standard. Typically, I start a project with a huge chunk of before-writing time devoted to gathering and organizing all my sources, reading everything, and writing extensive notes to reference. Typically, I never read while drafting. I rarely even quickly reference a book (I prefer the books I've read to just be stacked orderly nearby). Everything this time was different. For one, I started writing first, setting up the introduction (initially, basically a series of copy-and-pastes from my proposal) to function, I think I hoped, like a prompt. Then I cobbled together a list of sources I might want to read or return to. I'd start each drafting session by reading what I had written, looking for a thread or momentum to propel me into the next section. I'd placehold the section with a few topic words and then read whomever I thought could help (I always read in a particular armchair in my living room, one that leans back and has short arms. The ergonomics of this chair make it basically impossible to handwrite anything. That is, it was not an advantageous physical choice, but one I nevertheless repeated, marking unsteady straight lines in the margins of texts I read to indicate lines and moments that stuck out). I always drafted with books or pdfs open. I did have my separate note file, the one that started as that list, but I found myself starting to write in there too, right alongside my notes and captured quotes. It was all mixed up. I never had much of a sense of where I was going, at any point.

2, again. I should say too, I needed an extension to get the first draft of this done. If I'm honest, the bulk of this essay I drafted during that extension period. I had to hurry. I hate hurrying.

2, and again. I want to confess, though it probably doesn't communicate right, that this whole thing (that is, writing this essay) feels like a self-indulgent, maybe whiny, enterprise. Everything about scholarly writing has felt this way to me recently.

3. A few months ago, a friend from another institution asked me to present at a virtual writing retreat for faculty across their campus. The set-up for this retreat seemed dreamy; community energy for writing seemed especially crucial during pandemic isolation. With my co-presenter and the hosts, we decided to focus on confronting writing blocks. It should be no surprise that I was far from feeling like I had something to offer—what was *my* writing schedule, *my* ethos for speaking on what this friend defaulted into calling a "faculty writing productivity panel"? To help me pull off the bluff, I centered my comments on a moment in writing scholarship that always sings out to me. It comes from Keith Hjortshoj's *Understanding Writing Blocks*. Hjortshoj challenges the ways blocking becomes a catchall for all manner of writing difficulty by first outlining what a block is not. Blocks for Hjortshoj are not delays or detours (those are routine in writing of all kinds) nor a lack of motivation, inspiration, or ability; they are not chiefly psychological or emotional or rhetorical challenges nor the outcome of certain personality types. Rather, blocks are best seen as behavioral, even physical, matters. To avoid blocking is to counteract inertia by nurturing steady momentum, continuous contact, or unremitting rhythm with writing. It's also about adjusting assumptions.

One big myth Hjortshoj takes down is that successful writers are those that cannot *not* write. As this myth goes, "real" writers simply must write in spite of any odds or resistance or criticism stacked in the way. He pushes the opposite of this view, naming persistence as the defining quality of successful writers—but not in a grit or stick-to-it-ive-ness way. He writes,

> What distinguishes successful writers from everyone else, however, is *not* that writing is or has become easy for them. They are accomplished writers, instead, because they keep writing, in spite of the difficulties they encounter. . . . Whether they have [an] innate drive or do not, successful writers have found the time, methods, resources in themselves to continue writing in spite of continual opportunities to stop: when a word, a sentence, or a draft goes wrong, or when they get criticism, rejection slips, bad advice, bad grades, or bad reviews. Those who are not helpless to stop have found ways, nonetheless, to stop stopping. (45)

Find ways to stop stopping. I'm taken with this. To me, Hjortshoj is telling us that not-writing is the default. Writing is not some inhuman(e)

60   HANNAH J. RULE

ideal of progress or productivity. Rather, the human condition of writing is quitting. Writing is a continual invitation to stop or to never start in the first place. Worlds stand at the ready to block writing from happening at all. That any of us manage to eke out time, space, resources, and energy to nurture a writing fire at all should really be something to behold.

4. On the matter of not-writing or stopping-writing as writing's essential condition, I think of Tillie Olsen's *Silences*, a book that continues to smack me with its premise. Focusing on literary writers, Olsen asks, what of all things unwritten? The infinite works and creative potential never realized because writers found themselves in circumstances that got in the way? Silences, like stopping, pervade writing. Silences far outpace that which manages to be written. Olsen's are not what she calls "natural" silences—the expected pause for renewal or the "natural cycle of creation" (6). She speaks rather of the gaping, inexplicable ones (like Melville's thirty-year silence after *Moby Dick*) or the "hidden" ones (8) where work is abandoned or never appears. She speaks of the silences of cultural or political censorship (9) and of the silences preceding achievement. Most importantly, she evokes the resounding silences of "lives that never came to writing"—of the "mute inglorious Miltons," as she names them, "whose waking hours are all struggle for existence; the barely educated; the illiterate; women" (10). Writing does not avoid entanglement with circumstance, with identity, with the ways that history and social systems mark and position us in terms of "class, color, sex; the times, [the] climate into which one is born" (Olsen n.p.). Such entanglement works to precipitate silence.

I wonder about academics' silences. Circumstances can capriciously change and sometimes can be changed by us, but more they are thrust upon us, often as enforcers of systemic bias and exclusion. I know too there are systems and roles that get in the way. Many are in professional positions that by design inhibit writing by not sanctioning time or resources for it. I've known several exceptional book projects left unrealized in these circumstances and writers who nevertheless take on some sense of personal failure for that silence. How to make legible these and other silences? How can we log the unwritten, the abandoned, the not-allowed, the potential of scholarly insight and innovation left to silence?

5. Just one way might be that we multiply the forms we recognize and embody for becoming written. This makes me think of Wendy Sharer's recent observation that the limiting strictures of dominant scholarly

genres "work against the participation of many colleagues in the field because of the time demands that accompany those genres" (194). She argues for spaces—for the publishing of "venues" instead of or alongside articles, for example—in which "smaller chunks" (192) of research endeavors, or the insights and innovations discovered in situated practice, could be shared in conditional form. Such a broadening of genre could retain rather than erase the dynamic "research *process* rather than present a research product" (184). It would also stimulate inclusivity, a wider range of contributing voices of those who, from different kinds of institutional and identity positions, happily steer their scholarly energies more toward social activism, teaching and mentoring, community work, and/or program administration; those who long for time to write and research but are saddled with interfering labor demands (administrative, contingent, familial, and so on); those who may feel "discomfort (or, perhaps, disgust)" (194) with conventional scholarly forms and "the cultural lineages from which they have descended" (194).

This makes me think also of Jacqueline Jones Royster's observation that we tend to make academic discourse into "an *it*" (25). We speak as though academic discourse is one thing, some pre-formed unity or force of nature enduring out there somehow separated from us (25). It's/They're not. Discourse is always discourses that are multiple, intersecting, moving, historical, Royster tells us. Academic discourses are always "embodied" and "endowed" and, thus, can't be anything but a "*people-centered* enterprise" (25). Discourses, or "acceptable" genres of scholarship, are never a preformed system of conformity or immovable rules.

I'm thinking that, to this point in my career, I have similarly been making scholarly writing—that stuff sanctioned by my institution, laced as it feels with the counting of publications, the ranking of their "kind," and the unstated but strong edict to publish or perish—into too much of an "it." I have been making scholarly writing into one kind of thing with one right way of doing it; I've been making it something only imposed on me and conducted to satisfy the institution first. Publish or perish. (Systems have a way of pressing on us, don't they.) But scholarly writing, too, is only ever people-driven.

5, again. On the matter of possibility and options, I'm thinking of a colleague who is writing beautifully about choosing not to write while in a tenured position at a research university. I was thinking, "You're allowed to do that?" I literally did not know that choice was possible. But now I do.

6. A headline yelled out to me recently as I mindlessly scrolled a news aggregator app: "Lockdown was not a Sabbatical." The article subtitle reads, "Don't worry if you haven't grown as a person during the pandemic." I took this as a direct address (and I suppose it is this sense that drives the whole idea of "news" aggregators. Can the machine somehow see me doing my daily monologue of fretting about not writing?). The title was inspired by a tweet that said: "I don't want to alarm anyone, but I've just been asked in a job interview if I used lockdown 'to pursue any passion projects or personal development.' The market really does want us all to think we've just had a generous sabbatical" (Buñelo). Both this Twitter user and the author of this *Vox* article, Anna North, are warning us of the slick forces suggesting long-2020 was some kind of extended break from life, a fount of extra time and space, and the opportunity to be *more* "productive." At the same time, I'm thinking about the work "sabbatical" is doing here, with its logic that time and space away from other responsibilities of an institution will reliably produce work, and passion to boot. First, time (and time away) is necessary, but not sufficient stimulus in itself. Second, I am suspicious that anyone fully gets away. Can scholars ever really cloister themselves? Should they even?

7. Time, of course, is also relevant here. I've started calling my recent pace at academic work slow (rather than disinterested, pained, or other pejoratives). Or maybe not slow exactly, as I recognize that word betrays an allegiance to normative time—that clock-ticking, scheduled, calendar time; epitomized by the tenure clock among other imposing mechanisms. Disability scholars have long been cracking these regimes of "normate" time, a term coined by disabilities scholar Rosemarie Garland-Thomson for an imagined everyperson, "cripping" them to bend "the clock to meet disabled bodies and minds" (Kafer qtd. in Samuels) rather than bend persons to meet clocks. I must continue to recognize that whatever this pace is, it's fitting and fine. Don't submit to bending. I'm in a position to resist it now, for myself, for others.

Slowness has become an appealing salve for the sped-up, corporatized, managerial university. Maggie Berg and Barbara Seeber, forwarding the tenets of the slow food movement, make a case for the "slow professor." Slow profs resist the hyper-speed machinations of contemporary higher ed through habits like purposeful deliberation, patient reflection, collaboration and dialogue, resiliency, and open-ended inquiry. Slow profs shun frenetic busyness and the impossibilities (and, we should add, normativity) of sliced-up, packed schedules that valorize behaviors like rising at 4:00 a.m. to write before the family wakes up.

Somewhat in the same vein, my mentor Laura Micciche has argued for the virtues of "slow agency" in WPA work. Extending the analogy of hypermiling—vigilant driving that conserves fuel using methods like cruise control, removing cargo, or just keeping under the speed limit (74)—slow agency in institutional work for Micciche amounts to strategic waiting. Slow agency opens space to assess complex problems, call in stakeholders as collaborators, and use careful documentation of process to diffuse snap, top-down decisions and ensure instead wise, fitting, and sustainable change. This kind of holding off is counterintuitively a powerful enaction of our agency, Micciche says, "not necessarily a sign of powerlessness, inactivity, or dereliction of duty. On the contrary, [being slow] creates much-needed space for becoming still and getting places, allowing for regenerative returns" (74).

I think I'm pro-slow in the ways these writers differently describe it. At the same time, I'm skeptical of the currency of slow in matters of scholarly (rather than administrative) production. Micciche emphasizes the value of documenting expended labor in administrative projects as a way to reassure stakeholders and to get credit for process. But, for scholarly writing, I can't help but picture the annual report genre and its built-in expectation that works listed as "in-progress" move quickly to the "published" list. Moreover, as Christine Tulley emphasizes, entities of higher ed tend to erase writing entirely from the work faculty do, focusing instead on "'research' and in turn implying that academic writing is a task to be hurried through or just a small and easily navigated stage where findings are 'written up'" (148). Until it's somehow a slow university, the slow scholarly *writer* seems like they always must gird against the hurried tide.

I'm pro-slow, even when it's not achievable. And I am pro-whatever time it takes. And I'm also remembering that I've advocated publicly for slow's opposite. In an interview in *Pank Magazine* (Reddy), I talked about some benefits of hurrying up in writing processes, a view I cheekily identified as antithetical to the very foundations of the process paradigm and its clarion call for more time for (student) writers to deliberate, invent, develop, and draft. I described how I was using different timed invention exercises across my writing courses and, similarly, how I found my own practice that getting writing started straight away (often in emails addressed to myself) could help me sidestep toiling anticipation or mounting dread and make writing "feel much less Herculean." When I read this now, I do see the influence of the ticking tenure clock I was standing under. "Don't think about it, just hurry up and do it" was a kind of survival strategy for writing I didn't even know I was using.

64   HANNAH J. RULE

Micciche too differently voices the allure of hurrying, why it can nevertheless appeal to us or seem obvious. How can it be bad to prioritize getting where we're going as fast as possible? And anyway, how can the WPA (or scholarly writer) possibly slow down the pace of crises small and large begging for expedient attention? Couldn't acting slow sometimes be unwise or even unethical? Or isn't slowness a luxury or privilege that can't be afforded? Indeed, we often (think we) don't have the *time* to slow down, a sentiment echoed by Berg and Seeber (11).

In all this, I remember that slowness or hurrying or conserving of these sorts isn't so much measured by a stopwatch marking how long something takes. Slowness for its advocates is more an orientation—care and attention for just how we expend our energy (a limited resource), at what modulations, and to what ends. Paying this attention can help us realize that there may not be much difference in how we arrive or what our totaled outcomes are. Maybe it's one fewer line on the CV, a fine exchange for sustainability, for steadiness rather than shallow freneticism, for possibly even some joy. Hurrying too isn't about time to complete a draft; it is equally an orientation, a move to fend off the internal saboteur that shows up straight away to make those first sentences or ideas or brainstorms feel too enormous, weighty, impossible. Hurrying is a habit of mind (not a habit of time, really), like slowness, that is sometimes fitting.

Any gear—slow, hurried, hypermiled—itself isn't the final key. Any pace or orientation isn't consistently possible nor enduringly advisable because our work and lives are always contingent on conditions. Hypermiling, after all, is a practice that has to account for its environment in order to achieve its conservation goals. Some optimal hypermiling practices, like coasting or using tailwinds (see Micciche 75), just aren't possible if conditions aren't right. Another, driving barefoot, is against the law (I love lingering to extend this part of Micciche's metaphor—sometimes you must break the rules in the name of sustainability, wellbeing, and other worthy causes. This is a good lesson for me). In other words, a savvy hypermiler does not concern themselves with the operation of the car alone but with the car and its interface with the ever-changing terrain, road conditions, traffic. So, I'm pro-slow and, at the same time, I'd still defend hurrying. But only sometimes. It's not about humming at one pitch-perfect speed but in practicing oscillation, discerning when it's fit to hurry up a bit, slow down, take a full break, downshift, or kick it into high gear. It's about letting people, and their writing, take the time they take.

8. Speaking of time, when I started my job, I spent a lot of it looking for faculty writing advice. I needed a guide; I needed sources I could learn from in secret. As many do, I found Robert Boice. Based on his extensive research on faculty writers (e.g., "Procrastination"; *Professors as Writers*), Boice undermines assumptions about the time faculty think they need to write. He always lands on this familiar advice: write in short chunks, every day, because the larger swaths of time we think we need are never coming. Faculty who write a little bit every day are actually the most prolific and successful, Boice tells us. He's seen it work over and over.

I was in. I knew that I squandered large chunks of time in most parts of my life and that I'd easily get stuck in a doom loop if I thought too much about how I "have to" write today. I knew that regimes requiring set word count goals were a complete nonstarter for me. And Boice's time prescription seemed to work. Like maintaining an exercise regime (which, admittedly, I'm very much only okay at), just do X number of minutes, then you can stop (but probably you'll do a little more than that). And suddenly you have a habit.

Boice's work also made visible to me how pervasive writing difficulties are with faculty, normalizing that no one is finding this endeavor entirely rhapsodic. Our literature sometimes confirms this, too. I often think of "scratch an academic and you'll find a problem with writing," a sentence I think is Peter Elbow's. There's also this one from Maxine Hairston, which sounds similar, making me doubt that I've correctly attributed the previous: "Almost any publishing academic with whom I have talked about their writing admits to having trouble" (qtd. in Tulley 6). I feel similarly buoyed reading Christine Tulley's recent book, *How Writing Faculty Write*, to hear prolific scholars I admire forefront difficulty. Tulley quotes Howard Tinberg saying writing has never come easy for him "so it can be a bit of struggle to get the meaning out and onto the screen" (15). Further, she reports that Jessica Enoch sees herself as a "slow writer"; Cindy Selfe feels scholarly writing is a "slog" (15). Tulley confirms too that these comp/rhet scholars tend to embody Boicean practices of working in short bursts or enacting habits of "quick focus," to use Jacqueline Royster's term (24). Chris Anson, for example, describes leaving an in-progress project open on the computer so it's always there "staring at you" (qtd. in Tulley 24), unable to be ignored.

In long-2020, the magic of Boice has expired for me. His advice for a daily session or Anson's put-it-right-in-front-of-you strategy only works when you are *willing* to pay the writing any attention, when you think it's worth something. And I haven't wanted to pay attention to much of any scholarly thing recently. Work on my own writing has felt like an exercise, not an exigence. In this headspace, I tripped on the pages of Tulley's interviews in which scholars conveyed the view of the "overall academic writing process as joyful" (19). In their words (qtd. in Tulley 18–19), scholarly writing can be "extremely satisfying" (Yergeau) and "really fun," even "the best feeling in the world" (DeVoss). Apparently some also "love working on it" (Enoch) and "think writing is in [their] DNA" (Yancey). I have not felt anything close to this in some time.

So I guess there is some rhapsody out there for some. And though I am now judging anew my own lack of desire to write, I also must remember the times. I can't assume the satisfaction these scholars describe is necessarily their enduring feeling. Indeed, it's easy to fall into thinking we remain eternally one way as writers. But it's so important to acknowledge that our feelings about writing change. And it's true at the same time that while we can't expect to always feel them, positive feelings—not consistent ones, but little doses of positivity on one morning, or for five minutes, or even for one sustained week sometime when it's sunny—do drive scholarly writing that brings us satisfaction. The bottom line is that feelings, those about writing projects and the world, will not be cajoled by regimes of minutes or where I store the draft I'm uneager to write. There has to be some allowing for conditions.

I think I'll try to follow more after Helen Sword, who takes aim at Boice's all-purpose, near-religious mantra to write little chunks every day. Through a study of around thirteen hundred international research faculty, Sword found that the most productive scholarly writers do not write every day, and that "the correlation between daily writing and high productivity is a tenuous one at best" (313). Instead, Sword highlights terrific range in how faculty writers write, including opposing strategies and even shunned ones like Boice's much maligned "bingeing." Sword's point is not that we should never do Boice's short writing sessions but that sustaining academic writing isn't about consistency with one particular method or approach. What she wants is less puritanical, guilt-driven, and stringent discussions about sustaining scholarly writing and suggests "explicitly linking productivity with craftsmanship, people, and pleasure" (320). I'm in.

9. I'm realizing that I was actually a little Sword-like in that writing retreat panel. To help all of us with the cause of stop stopping, I offered a handout of material and environmental process practices we might experiment with—ideas like setting up your workspace at the end of a session so it is ready for the next, using a voice recorder or typing in an

Process Not Progress (or, Not-Progress Is Process)   67

email window to start a draft, or writing alongside a friend for an hour over instant messaging. I shared my sense that we can hold tight to what we perceive as *our* writing process—our unique, possibly quirky habits perceived as requirements for writing. Such commitment to consistency though can become limiting, more ritual than process. Writing processes, I think, are better seen as not solely ours to control nor enduring across time and place. Processes are just what happens, where, with what, and how. What it takes to make writing happen changes. What worked last time may not right now. Attending to the options in your day, schedule, feelings, deadlines, places, tools, time, and so on are what reveals the best—or much more often, the *make-do*—ways we write today.

9, again. I think that's generally right, but I also failed to convey in that panel session what I really wanted to emphasize: No matter how we arrange things or the "productivity" tips we try, the fact is that it's just plain hard to write during a global pandemic and its many other catastrophes. The world, not our writing, has been calling our focus. I just ended up saying something like, "Look, I have to say, it's hard out there, everything's scary. I'm not one of those over here baking bread. I'm not doing much of anything. Not at all." A person wrote me afterward to say thanks for saying that.

9, and again. I have to say too: Long-2020 is a shared experience of disruption and challenge. We can all see the things that have been getting in the way, and we have mostly given one another grace on deadlines, expectations, attention to coursework, or even just responding to an email, "given these challenging times" (a refrain we've had to say for so long, it kind of enrages us now). But there have always been and will continue to be catastrophes and circumstances everywhere, on smaller scales, in individual lives, too. That is, "The System" is always messing with people's ability and space to do their work and thrive.

10. Writing processes are susceptible (this is something I write a lot [e.g., Rule 146–51]). What I think I mean by this is that writers don't get, and shouldn't wait for, some illusory opportunity to hermetically seal ourselves and our writing, always behind the proverbial closed door of the scholar's study. Writing processes are not separable from life. But in spite of its practical impossibility, cloistering is often an expectation we foist upon ourselves as working writers, even in the face of evidence to the contrary (for some of this evidence, just look back to Tulley's interviews, which show scholarly writers finding minutes for process *in-the-*

68   HANNAH J. RULE

midst of things, in little bursts rather than rarefied time and space away).

I picture Kristie Fleckenstein's notion of somatic mind on this point. Somatic mind highlights the ineluctability of being *placed*. The (writing) self is always a "view from somewhere," a roiling, constantly reconstituting, interconnection among bodymind and material place as "concrete socio-temporal contexts" and the "cultural, historical, and ecological systems that penetrate and reconstitute" (281) them. In other words, we can't help but be where we are as writers. We can't escape our milieu, as it reconstitutes perpetually at levels of scale. Let me here replace Fleckenstein's term "organism" with "scholarly writer"—I think it works:

> Both [scholarly writer] and place can only be identified by their immanence within each other; [a scholarly writer] in this place (body, clothing, cultural scene, geographical point) is not the same [scholarly writer] in that place. Who and where (thus, what) are coextensive. Survival—ecological, psychological, political—does not depend on the fate of a discrete, atomistic reproducing [scholarly writer] (or subjectivity) because such [a scholarly writer] does not exist. Instead, what exists (and what survives or expires) is the locatedness of [scholarly] somatic mind: being-in-a-material-place. (286)

The scholarly writer is not one consistent actor; the scholarly writer changes, depending on conditions. The survival (and thrive-al) of the scholarly writer doesn't depend on its ability to "atomistically" and separately (re)produce scholarship because, well, such a separated entity just doesn't exist. The scholarly writer is always constructed by place, systems, positioning; how they move and adapt is always some response to local conditions. To assume otherwise—to assume they can act independently of their ecologies—is to assure their expiration.

11. Maybe what I'm trying to get at is some kind of in-between, a place from which we as scholarly writers can recognize that sometimes "the world" is just too much with us. I read a few months ago a compelling essay that described how, in our modern life generally and acutely during the pandemic, we could use a cultural return to recognizing a case of the "nerves." In his *Atlantic* essay, "Bring Back the Nervous Breakdown," Jerry Useem recounts how once it was acceptable—at least for the very privileged some—to retreat from life for a time. It was routine (again, for some) to declare "a sort of temporary emotional bankruptcy in the face of modern life's stresses," and devote oneself to physical and mental recuperation. In other words, a case of nerves was not an enduring medical condition, but a rational, socially shared response to "the way people are encountering the moment" (Sterns qtd. in Useem). The everyday

wear-and-tear of the modern world alone was enough to precipitate this sanctioned retreat.

The thrust of modern psychology, however, has instead over time "turned us inward to our personal moods and thoughts—and away from the shared economic and social circumstances that produced them" (Useem), making people's challenges in dealing with what's going on their own problem, literally. In appealing to a time when we saw nerves as a routine condition, I don't mean to minimize clinical depression or generalized anxiety or any other state of mental health. I do think though that collectively we could use socially sanctioned retreats to nurture ourselves through the shared case of nerves that is long-2020. Fear, malaise, anger, worry, sleeplessness, and disinterest are more than justified for what we are all enduring. Dedicating ourselves to recuperation or even just feeling how we feel is not something to question or see as unusual. Having a case of nerves is nothing other than a part of (scholarly) living now, a response to the times.

12. What most of this comes down to I think is also exigence. As I've struggled with my scholarly writing over long-2020, I found myself asking, "What does any of this really *matter*?" This is a drumbeat question we should be asking all the time. For a good long while, asking this question made me fret. Frankly, I've felt nothing matters much this year.

12, again. I have said aloud to myself a number of times while writing this that all I'm actually talking about is writing with clinical anxiety and panic, a long-standing condition and part of me amplified intensely by the conditions of long-2020. I have repeatedly imagined writing an email to the editors saying I would not write this essay, because I couldn't find anything to say.

13. I'm thinking now of a work on process that I love: Jack Selzer's "Exploring Options in Composing," published in the process heyday of the 1980s. Selzer cautions the compositionists keen to leap from nuanced empirical study of writers-in-process to generalized prescriptions for writers in the classroom. Selzer wants instead a pedagogy of process options, not a regime. Writers need different approaches to prewriting or revision because it is the details of situation that dictates, or should dictate, what processes look like. Selzer asks, "Do writers always 'need to seek the dissonance of discovery' through revising, even when they write a routine news story or an essay answer on an economics test?" (278). His answer is no. It's detrimental to imply that processes are each time

one way. And writing teachers must remember something easily forgotten: Import is everything. Let me here sub the term "school writing" with "scholarly writing": Writers, Selzer says, "who truncate their writing processes for [scholarly writing], who plan and revise [scholarship] only superficially, may well be doing so not out of ignorance or intransigence but because they regard [scholarship] as relatively unimportant" (281).

Okay, granted, academics should find their writing important sometimes. But I'm realizing that it's okay, and inevitable, that my scholarly writing *doesn't* matter right now. And it is always small. Often writing projects may not be widely kairotic, and do not beg to be written now. That's okay. For where I am and my surrounding conditions, it's just not important that I write right now. And that's more than okay; it just makes sense. What matters is Black lives; what matters is the safety and protection of ourselves, our families, and our communities from COVID-19; what matters is being a vigilant and engaged citizen; what matters is showing up for our students (and sharing with them that you didn't sleep either). It just doesn't matter that I didn't write.

13, again. But, also, I did write. I wrote this. It did not need to be written. So many things encouraged, even begged, me to stop writing it. But I did manage somehow to stop stopping. And it doesn't matter, but I do feel kind of different now.

NOTE

1. By first-person effort, I emphasize positionality—the intersections of my identity that show and those that mostly don't. Many of the former, like that I'm a cisgender white person, gain me privilege and shielding of various kinds. The latter are mostly invisible and sometimes erupt and interfere with the writing I'm to perform in my institutional role. They feel risky or confessional to disclose. As I work to position myself in this essay, I know I'll fail to some extent. I nonetheless aim to write this from the wheres I am in the hopes it connects with you, in your different wheres.

WORKS CITED

Berg, Maggie, and Barbara K. Seeber. *The Slow Professor: Challenging the Culture of Speed in the Academy*. U of Toronto P, 2016.

Boice, Robert. "Procrastination Busyness and Bingeing." *Behaviour Research and Therapy*, vol. 27, no. 6, 1989, pp. 605–11.

Boice, Robert. *Professors as Writers: A Self-Help Guide to Productive Writing*. New Forums Press, 1990.

Buñelo, Elvis [@Mr_Considerate]. "I don't want to alarm anyone, but I've just been asked in a job interview if I used lockdown 'to pursue any passion projects or personal development.'" *Twitter*, 8 June 2021, https://twitter.com/Mr_Considerate/status/140224512007 0664193.

Butler, Todd. "Beyond Tenure Clock Management." *Inside Higher Ed*, 19 Jan. 2021. https:// www.insidehighered.com/advice/2021/01/19/tenure-clock-extensions-arent-enough -help-support-researchers-and-their-work.

Carney, Megan A. "Nothing Normal about Getting Tenure this Year." *Inside Higher Ed*, 2 July 2021. https://www.insidehighered.com/advice/2021/07/02/significant-challenges -newly-tenured-scholars-confront-today-opinion.

Cliburn, Erik. "Faculty at Risk: Colleges Can Support Faculty Mental Health During Stressful Times." *Insight into Diversity*, 17 Nov. 2020. https://www.insightintodiversity.com /faculty-at-risk-colleges-can-support-faculty-mental-health-during-stressful-times/.

Farinde-Wu, Abiola. "Pregnant Mother Scholar in a Pandemic." *Inside Higher Ed*, 8 May 2020. https://www.insidehighered.com/advice/2020/05/08/added-challenges-dealing-race -and-gender-issues-during-pandemic-opinion.

Fleckenstein, Kristie S. "Writing Bodies: Somatic Mind in Composition Studies." *College English*, vol. 61, no. 3, 1999, pp. 281–306.

Garland-Thomson, Rosemarie. *Extraordinary Bodies: Figuring Physical Disability in American Culture and Literature*, 20th anniv. ed. Columbia UP, 2017.

Hitt, Allison Harper. *Rhetorics of Overcoming: Rewriting Narratives of Disability and Accessibility in Writing Studies*. NCTE, 2021.

Hjortshoj, Keith. *Understanding Writing Blocks*. Oxford UP, 2001.

McKeever, Vicky. "A 4-Day Work Week Might be Edging Closer: Here's Why." *CNBC*, 5 Feb. 2021, https://www.cnbc.com/2021/02/05/covid-may-have-pushed-us-closer-to-a-four -day-working-week.html.

Micciche, Laura R. "For Slow Agency." *WPA*, vol. 35, no. 1, fall/winter 2011, pp. 73–90.

North, Anna. "Lockdown was not a Sabbatical." *Vox*, 19 June 2021, https://www.vox.com /22536756/covid-pandemic-quarantine-lockdown-productivity-hobbies-work.

Olsen, Tillie. *Silences*. Delacorte Press/Seymour Lawrence, 1978.

Reddy, Nancy. "The Speed of Writing: An Interview with Hannah Rule." *PANK Magazine*, 19 Feb. 2020, https://pankmagazine.com/2020/02/19/the-speed-of-writing-an -interview-with-hannah-rule/.

Royster, Jacqueline Jones. "Academic Discourses, or Small Boats on a Big Sea." *Alt/Dis: Alternative Discourses in the Academy*, edited by Christopher Schroder, et al., Boynton/ Cook, 2002, pp. 23–30.

Rule, Hannah J. *Situating Writing Processes*. WAC Clearinghouse/UP Colorado, 2019.

Samuels, Ellen. "Six Ways of Looking at Crip Time." *Disability Studies Quarterly*, vol. 37, no. 3, 2017. http://dsq-sds.org/article/view/5824/4684.

Selzer, Jack. "Exploring Options in Composing." *CCC*, vol. 35, no. 3, 1984, pp. 276–84.

Skinner, Makala, et al. "The Disproportionate Impact of the Pandemic on Women and Caregivers in Academia." *Ithaka S+R*, 31 Mar. 2021. Accessed 28 June 2021. https://doi .org/10.18665/sr.315147.

Sharer, Wendy B. "Opening the Scholarly Conversation." *Retellings: Opportunities for Feminist Research in Rhetoric and Composition Studies*, edited by Jessica Enoch and Jordynn Jack. Parlor Press, 2019, 183–201.

Sword, Helen. "Write Everyday!: a Mantra Dismantled." *International Journal for Academic Development*, vol. 21, no. 4, pp. 312–22. https://doi.org/10.1080/1360144X.2016.1210153.

Tulley, Christine E. *How Writing Faculty Write: Strategies for Process, Product, and Productivity*. Utah State UP, 2018.

Useem, Jerry. "Bring Back the Nervous Break Down." *The Atlantic*, 8 Feb. 2021, https://www .theatlantic.com/magazine/archive/2021/03/bring-back-the-nervous-breakdown/617 788/.

5
WHEN WRITING MAKES YOU SICK

Tim Laquintano

Tags: embodiment, adaptability, technology, productivity

In 2013, Kim Hensley Owens and Derek Van Ittersum, the editors of this volume, wrote about the growing prevalence of computing injuries among students. They noted that despite extensive engagement with themes of embodiment over the years, writing and rhetoric studies has typically used embodiment as an epistemologically generative site with less attention paid to the physical body composing. As they trained their focus on writing injuries and the role of pain in composing, they argued that "students' health cannot benefit from the practice of literacy if the practice of literacy is itself damaging to their health" (88). And practicing literacy with a computer could mean repetitive interactions that can lead to a variety of injuries.

The implications of their claims have not, I would argue, been met with the attention they warrant. Theirs is one attempt to pull us out of entrenched currents in the humanities that have suppressed concerns about how writing may harm physical health. These currents are pervasive and powerful, and a cursory and incomplete list would include: (1) a "life of the mind"/body split that many theories of embodiment have attempted to dissolve in the last decades but that still persists quite durably; (2) a cold war legacy that created distance among the humanities and the life/physical sciences; (3) multiple forms of literacy myths that led many of us to tacitly if not openly believe that more literacy is always better for us—at both an individual and community level; (4) a body of literature that mostly comes from psychology that shows personal narrative is capable of particular kinds of physical and emotional healing, which makes it difficult to recognize other kinds of damage writing can do; (5) and, perhaps most important, lingering legacies from the Romantic model of authorship that went some way to create a tolerance if not glorification for unhealthy lifestyles associated with the writing life (more on this below).

https://doi.org/10.7330/9781646424870.c005

Although there are some subfields that have trained sustained attention on the physical body writing (e.g., disability studies), the currents above are at least partially responsible for what seems to be the questionable health status of many academic writers. In their crucial 2020 article on self-care as professionalization, Dana Lynn Driscoll, S. Rebecca Leigh, and Nadia Zamin present a survey of the woeful state of self-care practices among doctoral faculty and students, citing a 2014 report from the University of California, Berkeley, that found "64% of doctoral students in the arts and humanities were clinically depressed" (454). But what stood out to me in that article, which documented the health sacrifices we feel we need to make as graduate students and faculty, was that the authors began the project with a "hushed" conversation at an National Council for Teachers of English (NCTE) conference (459). Let's meditate for a moment on how sick that is. In the last twenty years, in the United States, we've seen an explosion in rates of obesity, autoimmune disorders, and chronic diseases. These are what Michael Pollan, among many others, calls "diseases of civilization," diseases that many attribute to unhealthy lifestyles brought on by the "Western diet," lack of physical activity, poor sleep habits, and chronic stress. And here we are, writing for much of our day (if not for publication then for institutional requirements), in a professional constellation where talking about our physical and mental health must happen in "hushed tones."

It is thus unsurprising that claims about writing injuries haven't resonated as they should across our discipline. This is incredibly problematic given the possibility that we can push Hensley Owens and Van Ittersum's claims even further beyond the realm of computing injuries. Rather than say "students' health cannot benefit from the practice of literacy if the practice of literacy is itself damaging to their health" (88), we might go further to say that, unless there are rigorous wellness protocols in place, information-lifestyle careers dominated by writing and literacy are likely inherently damaging to our health. Writing can be really bad for you. As the biomechanist and science communicator Katy Bowman notes, what we teach students in school—more than math, reading, and writing—is to sit. And as academics, most of us have learned these lessons, and many of us practice what we preach. We need to move from hushed tones to a professional atmosphere where we talk candidly about how to solve what is likely a disastrous model of health the academic writing life can impose on us: sleep disruptions, sedentary behavior, stress, excessive screen time exposure, and the expectation that we sever local personal and family relationships multiple times across the course of our career to move institutions.

74   TIM LAQUINTANO

A number of subfields have tried to undo the hushing legacies that have led to considerable silences in our conversations about writing and the body. Disability studies, activity theory-oriented studies of writing, and studies of identity have attended closely to embodiment and the material and nonhuman world we interact with when composing. The rapidly growing fields of the rhetoric of health and medicine and the medical humanities have also forged new paths among the humanities and health sciences. But, when it comes to the physiological consequences of writing, we still have much to discuss. Coffee shops are a writing space to us, a culture, but we speak little of that fact that coffee is a performance-enhancing writing drug (as are ADHD pharmaceuticals, nicotine, and, if you believe the lore, microdosing with psychedelics and sativa-dominant strains of cannabis that allegedly boost creativity). Self-help books about writing rarely go beyond the cursory advice to eat well, sleep well, and exercise (and research is conflicted on whether exercise can negate the dramatic health costs of sitting for long periods). In his book *Why We Sleep: Unlocking the Power of Sleep and Dreams*, the sleep scientist Matthew Walker notes that Quintilian recognized the importance of sleep to memory and learning, but I had to read outside of rhetoric and composition before I was exposed to Quintilian's thoughts on sleep. One conclusion we may draw from Walker's work about the importance of sleep to physical and mental health is that getting good sleep might be the single most important thing our students can do in the short-term to improve their writing. However, I have yet to see this advice in an undergraduate student handbook, and most people writing self-help books for graduate students spend just a few sentences on it. If Walker is correct about the importance of sleep to mental performance, most of those writing self-help guides should have an entire chapter on sleep, and it should be the first chapter.

Even though we have a variety of subfields centering issues of embodiment that will allow us to speak openly about health and not in "hushed" tones, and even if the pandemic has, potentially, forced a reckoning with work/life balances, we still have some thick ideologies to wash away. Of the currents of thought listed above, which militate against a reassessment of the relationship of writing and physical health, the Romantic legacy of authorship deserves special mention. Rebecca Moore Howard listed four characteristics of the traditional author: autonomy, originality, proprietorship, and morality (58). We might add a disregard for health to that list. As George Becker notes in his overview of the relationship between creativity and mental health, "the Romantics produced not only a logical connection between creativity and madness but also one in which madness was simultaneously a piteous and exalted condition that stood in sharp contrast to what they regarded as dreaded normality" (4). This new ideology provided Romantic writers with a "clearer" sense of their identity, but that identity "precluded the possibility of total health and sanity on the part of creative individuals" (4). To the extent that this legacy persists centuries later, it helps explain why it is not taboo to venerate authorship practices that lead to poor health outcomes (like sleep-deprivation pride); sacrificing one's health for one's writing in this paradigm seems to be evidence we're on the right track.

In what follows, I am going to narrate the poor health decisions I made to complete a scholarly monograph in time for a tenure decision, a physical history of a book. I hope to show the health sacrifices I made for the book, some of which I knew I was making at the time, and some of which I didn't. This will lead to a discussion about the health dangers of the writing life in general and the steps I made to attempt to reverse the damage, which was complicated by the horrifyingly contradictory advice of the wellness industry and the dubious nature of nutrition science. I ultimately hope to produce not calls for more research but calls for a more robust culture of writing fitness—hallway and social media conversations—where, as writing academics, we don't just talk about, think about, and prioritize our physical and mental health but also recognize that writing is a physically grueling activity capable of inducing poor health outcomes. There are now physical therapists and personal trainers that specialize in helping professional video gamers stay fit. What would the equivalent look like from a writing trainer?

Before I begin narrating a brief physical history of my writing life, I'd like to make two notes. The first is the difficulty of talking about the relationship between writing and physical health. At least from my perspective in the United States, writing and its attendant activities are nested in more expansive cultures of unwellness. Writing for professional publication is nested in our lives as academic information workers, a culture that comes with its own health risks (e.g., being forced to cut local relationship ties multiple times over the life span as we move to different institutions). Likewise, academic work is nested in a larger information economy saturated with cutthroat competition and physically and mentally invasive networked technologies, a culture that is further nested in a society often built around cars, processed food, and artificial light. Teasing out which culture is responsible for the poor health we might experience as academics is, unfortunately, incredibly difficult, a point I will return to below.

The second note addresses comments from an external reviewer who helped make this chapter better. The two most poignant comments from the reviewer called the tone of my chapter "condescending" and that it reads like "advice" the reviewer "didn't ask for." I'm not sure these are unfair remarks. My general academic tone is that of deadpan humor combined with whimsical self-contempt. That translates better in my public speaking than in my writing, but I mean no condescension. Second, I am in no way qualified to dispense health advice of any sort. I can say that I trashed my health for tenure, and I can document the research and steps I took to improve it. It is up to the reader to decide whether or not to seek more information if my narrative resonates with them. By the end of this chapter, however, I hope the readers understand that I am adamant that the glorification of unhealthy practices (e.g., sleep-deprivation pride) that I have witnessed in academia needs to stop. We may be on that track, as the pandemic may have forced a broader conversation about health and wellness.

A BRIEF PHYSICAL HISTORY OF A COMP-RHET MONOGRAPH

From dissertation to printed work, my book took about eight years, with two years in graduate school and about six as an assistant professor. My project was too expansive. In addition to eighty interviews and follow-up interviews across four different groups of writers, I had hundreds if not thousands of pages of online discussion I was analyzing. I am not sure I had a day during those years when I wasn't looking at data, thinking about data, or writing in my head or in front of a screen. My children used to ask me why my lips were moving as I drove them to the zoo. I told them I was writing.

I exercised steadily in graduate school and through the first couple years of my time as an assistant professor—I biked to school, walked, and strength trained. That fell away as I became busier. As a new assistant professor, I designed new classes, worked on the writing program, performed college service, and attended conferences. I worked on my post-PhD education in the summer at the Dartmouth summer program on research methods, a seminar on the history of the book, and the Rhetoric Society of America institute. I wrote through most of the summers, and in late July and early August, I spent unhealthy time in academic third space. That is the nebulous space where I exhausted my energy to be productive, but guilt and anxiety told me that I should be working. It was neither a healthy break nor was it a time when I was getting much done. I mostly stared at the screen in a stupor and checked social media too often.

Much has been said about the perversity inherent in the tenure clock, especially its gender bias, as it tends to coincide with periods of prime child-rearing, the work of which often falls disproportionately on women. In my case, I had young children and a looming divorce in the mix as an assistant professor, along with the knowledge that as a humanist I might only ever get one shot at a tenure-track position. That represented a sharp set of blades I used to shred my health. In the fifth year of work, I received feedback from university press peer reviewers confirming that my project was too capacious (the reviewer wrote that I had "at least three books" in the manuscript). I reverse engineered the time it would take the book to go through the publishing process in time for my tenure review. I decided I needed to complete all of the revisions in the course of a single summer. With chaos in my personal life, I was not in a position to be able to tie my shoes, let alone concentrate my scattered attention on the most challenging portion of my writing project, which at that time held about as much attraction to me as molding goat cheese heavily dotted with yellow crusties. I could have invoked a clause in the faculty handbook and delayed tenure for a year, but with the angst of a pre-tenure faculty member and the suspicion that the longer my book took to complete the less likely it would be completed, I did not entertain the idea.

Totally unable to write, I talked to a colleague who recommended a cheery doctor with, let's call it, a generous disposition toward the academic condition and its challenges. After explaining all of the symptoms that were flattening my writing tires, the doctor declared that I had depression. He agreed that the most appropriate treatment would be a "motivator" that would help me write. After filling the prescription, I called a relative in the healthcare industry to ask about potential side effects of the pharmaceuticals, and she responded: "What is it with you academics and your damn motivators?" It was reassuring knowing I was beginning my summer writing sprint in the apparent company of many other academics willing to negotiate the side effects of modern science for the purpose of publishing.

Motivators were only one part of my productivity stack. Wawa was another. Wawa might be the only convenience store in America with a cult following. It has colonized the heavily trafficked intersections of Philadelphia and southern New Jersey. Its iconography and cheap coffee are as Philadelphia as the Eagles. Who knows what's in their meatballs? When Phillymag.com ranked Wawa sandwiches, the meatball hoagie got little respect, coming in at number five. It's likely an environmentally unethical sandwich, and I would guess the meat is sourced from dirty industrial farms, the animals stuffed on a diet of grain. The meatballs are spongy with only the vaguest hints of being rubbery. But when you douse them with a sugary tomato sauce and parmesan, then combine that with a twelve-inch white roll with extra provolone, all the chemical ingredients are there to make it hyperpalatable. It's a processed monstrosity, and I don't know what brain chemicals it releases, but it is all of the good ones.

I survived on a meatball sub each day that summer, as the pills mostly killed my appetite. I told myself that I didn't have time to spend minutes shopping, preparing food, or doing the dishes. There was, of course, a family-owned Italian deli several blocks down from Wawa that produced far better fare, but I judged the ten minutes of walking time too long of an interruption to my writing, and Wawa had cheaper coffee. And I wrote. I used the *Don't Break the Chain* app to measure it. I wrote for eighty-seven days in a row, for between twelve and sixteen hours each day. The pills worked. I couldn't keep my eyes off the screen, and for three months I could not do anything but be a productive writer. I had quit smoking many years earlier, but with the stress, I relapsed to nicotine gum, which is itself a potent stimulant (and some believe a nootropic that is helpful to concentration). It might not have been the healthiest stack, but combining coffee, nicotine gum, motivators, and meatball subs crushed my writer's block: it created something of a prolonged writer's high, although I don't know what my resting heart rate was. I'd venture it was not healthy.

I've always been able to fall asleep after about five minutes in bed. But with the pills, I didn't really sleep. I spent six hours or so with vivid dreams before my eyes snapped open at five in the morning just before I leapt out of bed. I drove the half mile to my office instead of walking in the sunshine down green streets and across a flowered campus. I didn't want to waste time. I skipped any sort of vacation and rest, and I finished the manuscript on the eighty-seventh day of work.

CONSEQUENCES

Although the article on writing injuries by Hensley Owens and Van Ittersum speaks of repetitive disorders from writing on computers, the repetitive movements of hands and wrists often take place in an embodied constellation of sedentary behavior and—for me—sacrifices of diet, sleep, and movement. By the time the book was published, my life as a graduate student and writing professor had produced about four years' worth of lower-back spasms that would flare up quarterly. They usually required an excruciating day or two in bed and then they lingered as lower-back pain for several weeks. I treated my back issues with expensive sessions of physical therapy and muscle relaxers as needed on the advice of a physician. I had raging heartburn that I treated with omeprazole on the advice of a physician. I had seasonal allergies that I treated with loratadine on the advice of a physician. Before the publication of my book, I also had a terrible full-body auto-immune rash for three weeks that made me want to take a dip in a tub full of calamine lotion. I treated it with topical steroids on the advice of a physician. That rash settled on my wrist and lingered there for more than two years. The physician told me to live with it.

After submitting my tenure portfolio, I downloaded some podcasts from the health and fitness industry. The health and fitness podcasting industry is a terrible and wonderful place. It's a blend of Western nutrition and sports science, functional and alternative medicine, and "bro" science and locker room lore. It's populated by athletes, trainers, scientists, physicians, techno libertarians, "bio-hackers" seeking to extend the longevity of their lives, credible entrepreneurs hawking supplements, snake oil salespeople hawking supplements (some of which may help and some of which may hurt), and people who have been failed by Western medicine. It's a place where you can listen to a two-hour interview with a world-class metabolic researcher, and a two-hour interview with so-called experts who, metaphorically speaking, sell exquisitely crafted tin foil helmets. During the pandemic, the sphere was used to sow vaccine hesitancy and even political discord. When I found it, I almost turned off the first podcast. The guest was talking about the dangers of wheat. That was crazy talk. On the advice of the government and my doctor, I ate *whole wheat*, and it had fiber! However, it did help that I had just spent eight years studying vernacular knowledge production in online spaces, and I continued listening and tried to rely on the critical mass of information literacy skills I had acquired. After listening to a rotation of about four different podcasts, I began yoga and I cut wheat, corn, and soy from my diet. I began avoiding meat from industrialized farms, and I cut out vegetable, canola, and sunflower seed oil. My grocery bill tripled, and my pharmaceutical bill dried up. My back pain went away. My allergies went away. My heartburn went away. And the rash on my wrist cleared.

Here's where it becomes incredibly difficult to tease out a causal relationship between the activity of writing, being a professor, and living in an unhealthy culture. Typing on a keyboard may cause repetitive stress disorders, but was it the stress of pre-tenure life that gave me a rash? Or the wheat? Was it the writing and sitting that was killing my back? Or the lack of core strength from avoiding exercise? Inflammation was

80   TIM LAQUINTANO

likely the common denominator among many of my health ailments, but so too were the values I had acquired as a graduate student and a pre-tenure professor: work above all else; publish or perish.

MOVING BEYOND THE HUSH

In 2018, I began reading two books about writing: John McPhee had published *Draft No. 4: On the Writing Process*, and Joanna Penn had published *The Healthy Writer*, a book she co-authored with Euan Lawson, a British medical doctor. On the one hand, McPhee's book comes from a legendary nonfiction writer and an illustrious publisher. It's a relatively disembodied treatise on the writing process. On the other hand, Joanna Penn is something of a self-publishing guru whose name I learned while doing research for my first book. She is an adventure/thriller writer with a dozen "how to" books to her name about writing and self-publishing. In the early days of self-publishing, the joke was that the only way to make money from it was to write books about how to do it. I don't know if that still holds true (or ever held true). But even though one book has silky prose and a pedigree from a legendary writer, I'd like to argue here that of McPhee's book and Penn's book, published right around the same time, the latter book, whose prose pales in comparison, is by far the more important. I am not sure I would even call it a "good book," but to my mind, the table of contents, which includes sections on pain, sedentary behavior, caffeine, alcohol, and loneliness, is so alien to most discussions about writing I've ever encountered, I would call it groundbreaking. I've never seen a frank discussion of irritable bowel disease among high writing society. It's the kind of table of contents that might only emerge when writers see each other complaining on Twitter daily about the physical tolls of the job, which of course are also inseparable from living in environmentally toxic societies.

Penn leveraged her considerable social media following to conduct a survey about the health of writers. Over one thousand respondents complained of "sedentary behaviors/sitting too much, stress, back pain, weight gain, anxiety and sleep problems" (3). Others reported "headaches, eye strain, loneliness and depression, digestive issues, and repetitive strain injury" (3). Penn doesn't do much reporting on the survey methodology, and so we certainly can't attribute any sort of causal relationship to writing and these issues; moreover, we can't tell from her reporting whether or not writers suffer these maladies at rates greater than the general population. But what we can do is look at the physical maladies reported by these writers and see our own issues reverberate with them, as I did.

OPENING SPACES FOR REFORM

There are some currents of belief in academic fields that are notoriously difficult to surface. I have long believed that reading peer-reviewed scholarship is an inadequate way of locating the deep beliefs and values of a field. Articles have been washed and sanitized by multiple peer reviewers and an editor before being published. Rather, I believe it is the conference hallway snipes in between panels, late night jokes with colleagues, social media quips, and classroom asides and editorializing that betray our deepest beliefs. The rolling eyes of mentors I have admired have likely done more to forge my beliefs about my academic field than all of the peer-reviewed scholarship I have read. I didn't leave literary studies because there was snobbery on the pages of *PMLA* or in the headnotes to the *Norton Anthology of American Literature.* I left literary studies because of the hero-worshiping culture I encountered in the hallways of conferences, and the "Marxist" professor who made jokes in class about the "illiterates" at less prestigious institutions. It wasn't literary theory that exasperated me but rather the embodied performances of chin stroking and vigorous head nodding and scoffing that surrounded literary theory at conferences, which pushed me toward composition and rhetoric (where I have found such performances do still exist but, fortunately, not with the same conviction).

That some of our deepest beliefs are so difficult to pin down is a serious problem (as it has been as we try to eliminate racism, misogyny, and ableism from our field). When we publish, we are supposed to find a "problem" in the literature as our exigence, but it is likely the case that some of our most acute problems and collective beliefs are not articulated baldly in bodies of academic literature. And so, on the whole, I make the following claim not based on a rigorous examination of scholarly literature, but on the basis of being in the field of writing and rhetoric studies for fifteen years and spending time with its people: Generally speaking, many of us in writing and rhetoric studies believe writing to be good for us. We encourage writing to learn, we encourage writing for social and economic empowerment, and we encourage writing to heal and cope with trauma. In fact, I sometimes wonder whether or not we have unconsciously generalized the "writing can be physically good for you" research that comes from psychology research to other rhetorical situations and genres when in fact most of that body of research is based almost entirely on a specific kind of writing (expressive personal writing). Writing, as I practiced it in graduate school and early in my career, was certainly not good for my health.

The issue with living in a world saturated with text, reading, writing, and literacy practices is that we can just as easily identify contexts where writing disempowers and disenfranchises. Literacy can be used to regulate bodies, inflict symbolic violence, and as a long tradition of research has shown us, devalue the identities of populations who don't speak dominant discourses. This widespread plurality has been noted in Vieira and colleague's work, "Literacy is a Socio-historic Phenomenon that Can Liberate and Oppress." Likewise, in the same way that writing might have potential for the physical healing of trauma, we can just as easily create a laundry list of how writing habits can be physically bad for you as well. In addition to what we consider mental health issues documented in Driscoll, Leigh, and Zamin's article on self-care in the profession, such as anxiety and impostor syndrome, consider other physical tolls of literacy work: excessive sedentary behavior that can be associated with reading and writing; isolation combined with the fact that we are willing to sever human relationships multiple times across the course of our careers; the financial precariousness and time constraints of graduate school or contingent teaching that can make it extremely difficult to eat a diet of local, seasonal, organic produce and meat (assuming we even live in an area where such food is widely accessible); low vitamin D levels associated with working inside; and the invasive information work we carry with us in our heads (or at least I did) that can disrupt sleep and saturate most of our waking moments. And while most of these stressors have solid scientific research behind them backing their deleterious effects on physical and mental health, there are also a variety of other emerging concerns largely associated with the modern world but that can be especially acute for information workers such as writers and academics. These concerns have been considered woo woo in Western science and medicine but have of late received more serious attention (e.g., blue light from screens as well as other forms of artificial light disrupting our circadian rhythms; our lack of physical connection with the earth, aka "grounding").

In the same way we need to consider literacy's power to both oppress *and* liberate (Vieira et al.), we need to consider in a much more sustained manner literacy's potential to both heal *and* physically harm. But this is incredibly difficult. First, much of the scientific research that has identified the deleterious health effects of information work has of course not isolated writing but rather focuses on an entire spectrum of information work practices that lead to high stress and sedentary environments. But if we do accept Deborah Brandt's premise that writing has become the engine of the information economy, we need to think of how writing and literacy as we practice them are complicit, and how we might talk about the physical components of writing in a way that makes writers aware of the potential consequences of such work.

The other issue is that trying to understand what makes a healthy life in modern America borders on a fool's errand. Many health professionals seem to agree that practicing good sleep hygiene, avoiding processed foods, getting exercise, and limiting stress are baseline components of leading a generally healthy life. But once someone attempts to determine through research how this advice might be operationalized in their writing or academic life, they are going to run into a morass of issues that are embedded in a hot mess of conflicting advice.

Take diet, for example. Let's say we convinced ourselves that our current diet is responsible for health concerns and that it is leading to a complete lack of writing productivity. We might not have been told this by our Western-trained doctor, as nutrition has been a small part of many medical school curricula and generally neglected by Western medicine. We could look to government recommendations and eat many whole grains and avoid saturated fat, but as Nina Teicholz has shown in her investigative science journalism, such recommendations are typically subject to the special interests of the food industry, and quite a few of the recommendations might have been premised on faulty or insufficient data. We then might turn to published scientific literature to see if individual foods are good or bad for our mental well-being, but that literature can suffer from serious methodological issues, and much of it has been funded by the food industry. We could enter the realm of the health and wellness podcasts, in which case we might be intrigued by anecdotal reports of intermittent fasting, ketogenic diets, and mushroom coffee sharpening mental acuity, but then we have to worry about how such advice might be tainted by the supplement industry, shadow sponsorships, and faddish sales of snake oil. We would also need to worry about entering an exclusionary space, as contemporary online health and wellness spheres are not free from ableism, body shaming, and neoliberal ideologies that place on individuals the burden of becoming healthy in a collectively sick society.

But once we spend the incredible amount of time required to familiarize ourselves with potential diet options, we then have to consider how any given diet is going to interact with our personal history, our genetics, and our epigenetic expression. Recall that in Jody Shipka's work on transmodalities, she builds on Laura Micciche's work to argue that a robust understanding of the composing process would account for "partnerships" with extensive arrays of human and nonhuman matter (254). Shipka's list includes keyboards and clothing but also "blood sugar, food, medication, intestinal bacteria, and pets" (254). I thought of Shipka's work after informally studying nutrition for some time, as I wondered whether sharp spikes and crashes in my blood sugar might be responsible for the incredible difficulty I have had when writing in the afternoon, which because of my teaching and childcare schedule has been the only time I have had to write during certain semesters. In 2020, despite being on a four-year streak of maintaining an exercise regimen and eating mostly whole foods, I was concerned that a decade of avoiding self-care had put me on a path to be prediabetic (my A1C was borderline) like 88 million Americans ("Prediabetes"), and I wanted as much information as possible on how different foods and diets affected my blood sugar. I was told I could consult the glycemic index, a system for determining how a particular food might affect blood sugar variability. However, a famous Israeli study attached continuous blood glucose monitors to research subjects and found extraordinary variation in how different research subjects reacted to different foods (Zeevi et al.). This study—and others like it—have begun to suggest that the glycemic index scale has most of its value at the population level, much like the body mass index, which can be helpful in population studies but highly problematic when applied to individuals.

I had been testing my own glucose routinely in the morning for the purposes of being self-informed, but that was a single snapshot of a single point in the day. I wanted a continuous blood sugar monitor. But first I had to find a doctor progressive enough to prescribe one, as many won't unless you are already diabetic. And insurance would likely not cover the cost, because even though they would pay to have me see an endocrinologist once I did have diabetes, they won't cover many things that will help prevent diabetes. The best hope I thought would be to find the youngest doctor I could who might be familiar with emerging trends in nutrition. I found one who prescribed me a monitor after seeming somewhat amused at my self-experimentation.

In addition to a continuous glucose monitor, I have experimented with multiple kinds of self-quantification technologies like sleep trackers, movement trackers, micronutrient calculators, ketone monitors, and heart rate monitors that tracked my heart rate and heart rate variability. I learned something using them all (and as an aside I will also say that personal experience leads me to believe heart rate variability as a measure of stress may have exceptional promise as a predictor of writing productivity on any given day). However, the new-fangled self-quantification technologies and metrics we can use to learn more about our health have serious issues: they're not accessible, especially to the poor; the data can be hard to interpret and finding someone to interpret the data can be prohibitively expensive; and they generate extraordinary privacy issues. It's not hard to imagine a dystopian system where fitness tracker companies partner with health insurance companies to adjust your health insurance rates in real time in response to data flows. Moreover, as the pandemic hit and all of my health metrics took a nosedive, I became too fearful to even quantify my (lack of) movement or heart rate variability during quarantine. They were of little help in times of crisis.

But if we eschew self-quantification technologies, we could take a much simpler route in our quest to optimize our writing health through diet. (And by optimize, I don't mean be more efficient so we can work more; I mean get work done in as short a period as possible to allow for time developing human relationships, pursuing hobbies and crafts, and being well). We could simplify everything and follow Michael Pollan's level-headed advice to "eat food, mostly plants, and not too much" (1). But even within this relatively simple advice there are a host of questions related to health, preparation and time, ethics, and sourcing. If I buy avocado oil to avoid refined oils like canola oil, has it been adulterated? Is it even avocado oil? If I want greater sources of plant protein in my diet, what do I do if legumes spike my blood sugar? What if I don't have the time or the understanding to prepare them in traditional manners like soaking and sprouting and that leads to digestibility issues? What if my leptin and ghrelin hormones, which play a role in whether we feel hungry or satiated, are wonky from a past history of wild weight swings that came as a result of living in South America where I shed and then regained twenty-three percent of my body weight over the course of eighteen months? What if this episode led to metabolic damage and eating plant-based carbohydrates makes it difficult to "not eat too much" because blood sugar variability leads to carbohydrate cravings? If I eat tofu, is it coming from monocropped soybeans that are degrading the soil? If I include animal products, can I locate a source of grass-fed butter or cream that will have an appropriate ratio of omega-3 to omega-6 fatty acids and that also comes from regenerative agriculture? Can I afford it if it does? And, as an expert in local food systems pointed out to me, if the farmer is claiming that they use only grass-fed dairy to produce butter, how do I know they aren't lying? The environmental writer Roy Scranton writes from the perspective that we have already reached a tipping point in global warming and catastrophe is inevitable. Once you start digging into personal questions of diet as they relate to

86   TIM LAQUINTANO

the American and global food system, it is difficult not to reach a similar conclusion.

GOING WHERE?

While it may seem that the diets of cows are far afield from writing, that's just the mind/body split tugging at our sense of disciplinarity. The traditional move here might be to call for more research and greater attention to how writing is complicit in the profoundly unhealthy information environments we work in, but I think the more effective move would be a collective reckoning that we need to create a culture of writing fitness that is passed on through the informal yet powerful channels of collective disciplinary belief formation. In this world, sleep would be sacred. We could unleash microaggressive eye-rolls at conferences against senior colleagues who glorify the priority of one more publication over solid sack time. We could talk about the ways we incorporate movement into our writing protocols, from keeping balls to juggle in our office to hourly stair-climbs in our buildings. We need to get rid of the hushed tones we use to talk about our health. In this model, we would have to be mindful about the ableist norms embedded in much health and fitness, and any new paradigm also needs to avoid normative assumptions about what constitutes good health, too, as this also can be a highly individualized question, which is still very much open to debate. In this model, we would still be free to sacrifice our health for our careers, but the point would be not to venerate such choices but rather discuss them openly in some sort of cost/benefit analysis.

As a card-carrying member of the humanities, I have heard thousands of critiques of neoliberalism throughout my career from my colleagues. But as I think about the first half of my career, I think about what I did and what I was willing to do for this profession: I severed my ties to local communities and my family multiple times in my life for my career; I worked for poor wages for years in graduate school with the dream of a tenure track job; I held a willingness to work contingently for unlivable wages should that job at first be elusive; I prioritized work above everything else, even in times of upheaval when I should have been thinking of self-care. I specialized in a body of knowledge that took so much time to learn and was so narrow I was unaware of the source of my food and what it was doing to me, and what it was doing to the environment. The list goes on. I was not a resistor of neoliberalism as we tend to fancy ourselves in the English department. I was neoliberalism's darling worker. And thus, I am thinking of writing fitness as something slightly different from self-care. I've thought of self-care as a retreat from the toxic and cutthroat information environments we work in (this is most definitely impressionistic on my part; it is a capacious term). I think of writing fitness as a ground-level rebuild of our writing and work environments and attitudes that takes a holistic view of mental and physical health, a space where we prioritize health over productivity, or at least recognize what writing productivity can do to our health. This most definitely can be critiqued as the highly privileged (and highly ironic) stance of someone who has already earned tenure through unsustainable writing practices, but of course that putting well-being over productivity seems privileged is the essence of the problem to begin with.

As I think about the materials I have used to become healthier as I try to rebuild my writing practices around sustainability and longevity, I want to conclude with a particular barrier we might face to becoming fitter writers (and critiques my own position might face). In the last few years, I consulted many materials that might be considered "self-help," and I quantified many things about my health, fitness, and writing process. Years ago, when I wrote a chapter on self-published memoirs in my book, I had to research the memoir trend in the publishing industry. I came across dozens of humanist critiques of both memoirs and self-help literature that suggested that self-help operates within neoliberal ideologies and should therefore be dismissed because it locates the source of a variety of problems (health, loneliness, alienation) in individual pathology instead of corrupt and unjust social structures. I would tend to agree. But none of those critiques spent much time considering whether or not self-help actually works to solve certain problems that come from living in unhealthy cultures, or, more importantly, whether or not we could slice out some tips from that body of literature and appropriate them to serve our own goals while ignoring the genre's neoliberal tendencies (or in some cases sardonic libertarian tendencies). Moreover, I would say, among certain experts and podcasters in the wellness industry, there is an awareness in much new self-help that social structures and corporations have collectively conspired to destroy our health.

I am something of a pessimistic pragmatist. Take movement, for example. I don't believe the zoning and building practices that have made it impossible for me to walk to school without traffic endangering my life will see some sort of radical reversal in the next twenty years (unless the cost of operating a car hits astronomical heights). Without being able to walk to school, I need to plan movement into my day in other ways. I will continue to support politicians and activists who fight for pedestrian- and bike-friendly planning, and when I'm done with the practical restrictions I face that force me to live in my current area to co-parent, I hope to move somewhere more pedestrian friendly. But in the meantime, I've used the suggestions of a variety of self-help books to force movement into my daily work routine. These texts clearly put the burden of movement on me when my inability to walk as a matter of course is the general fault of lobbyists and urban planners who have planned a country around cars. Is it legitimate for us to critique the books I have read because they suggest I need to respond individually to conditions collectively orchestrated by unhealthy urban planning? Maybe. But those books are also helping me ward off a heart attack while waiting for a more perambulatorily just society to arrive.

WORKS CITED

Becker, George. "A Socio-Historical Overview of the Creativity-Pathology Connection: From Antiquity to the Contemporary Times." *Creativity and Mental Illness*, edited by James C. Kaufman, Cambridge UP, 2014, pp. 3–23.

Bowman, Katy. *Grow Wild: The Whole-Child, Whole-Family, Nature-Rich Guide to Moving More.* Propriometrics Press: 2021.

Brandt, Deborah. *The Rise of Writing: Redefining Mass Literacy.* Cambridge UP, 2014.

Driscoll, Dana Lynn, et al. "Self-Care as Professionalization: A Case for Ethical Doctoral Education in Composition Studies." *College Composition and Communication*, vol. 71, no. 3, 2020, pp. 453–80.

Hensley Owens, Kim, and Derek Van Ittersum. "Writing With(out) Pain: Computing Injuries and the Role of the Body in Writing Activity." *Computers and Composition*, vol. 30, no. 2, 2013, pp. 87–100.

Howard, Rebecca Moore. *Standing in the Shadow of Giants: Plagiarists, Authors, and Collaborators.* Ablex Publishing, 1999.

McPhee, John. *Draft No. 4: On the Writing Process.* Farrar, Straus and Giroux, 2017.

Penn, Joanna, and Euan Lawson. *The Healthy Writer: Reduce Your Pain, Improve Your Health, and Build a Writing Career for the Long Term.* Curl Up Press, 2017.

Pollan, Michael. *In Defense of Food: An Eater's Manifesto.* Penguin, 2008.

"Prediabetes—Your Chance to Prevent Type 2 Diabetes." *Centers for Disease Control and Prevention, Centers for Disease Control and Prevention*, 11 June 2020, www.cdc.gov/diabetes/basics/prediabetes.html.

Scranton, Roy. *We're Doomed. Now What?: Essays on War and Climate Change.* Soho Press, 2018.

Shipka, Jody. "Transmodality in/and Processes of Making: Changing Dispositions and Practice." *College English*, vol. 78, no. 3, 2016, pp. 250–57.

Teicholz, Nina. *The Big Fat Surprise: Why Butter, Meat and Cheese Belong in a Healthy Diet.* Simon and Schuster, 2014.

Vieira, Kate, et al. "Literacy is a Sociohistoric Phenomenon with the Potential to Liberate and Oppress." *(Re)Considering What We Know: Learning Thresholds in Writing, Composition, Rhetoric, and Literacy*, edited by Linda Adler-Kassner and Elizabeth Wardle, Utah State UP, 2020, pp. 36–55.

Walker, Matthew. *Why We Sleep: Unlocking the Power of Sleep and Dreams.* Simon and Schuster, 2017.

Zeevi, David, et al. "Personalized Nutrition by Prediction of Glycemic Responses." *Cell*, vol. 163, no. 5, 2015, pp. 1079–94.

6

SPEAK IN THE TONGUE OF YOUR FATHER

Disentangling "American" Work Ethic and Professional Curiosity

Kate L. Pantelides

Tags: critique, embodiment, identity, productivity

When I was very small, a tour guide yelled at me. Like, really yelled at me. I still remember his red face, the spittle on his lip, the angry movement of his hands. The problem was, I didn't know what he was saying. When spoken fluently (as opposed to my hesitant, broken version), the Cypriot dialect of Greek sounds very loud and very passionate—pretty much all of the time. It is a beautiful language, built for poetry, and the members of my family usually take it up to top volume, with creased brows, busy hands, passionately rolled *r*s, and what—to an untrained observer—looks and sounds like anger. Visitors to our house during my teen years were often scared by my father's phone conversations with his family on the little island across the world. These calls literally rattled the walls. It's likely no accident that many of the friends who stuck around also had passionate, immigrant parents, and they were undeterred by loud, foreign languages. However, this misunderstanding of intention and intonation was not the case for the tour guide. He was mad. He had told me to do something, and because I didn't respond, my father explained to him, "she doesn't speak Greek." Disgusted, the tour guide then uttered the phrase that has stuck with me ever since it was subsequently translated: "Speak in the tongue of your father!"

Since then, I like to think that I have learned to speak in the tongue of my father in numerous ways. When I visit Cyprus, I eat my family's food voraciously, as if doing so can make up for living so far away. In my own home, I push food on people in the way of Mediterranean families. I have also learned to speak Greek with varying success over my lifetime. The pinnacle was when I studied in Athens, Greece for six months; and I'm trying to recapture that near-fluency with Rosetta Stone and

https://doi.org/10.7330/9781646424870.c006

conversation classes. But most of all, I like to think that I've taken up my father's own love language—his work ethic. A theoretical physicist, my father immigrated to the United States at age nineteen, met my American-born mother soon after, and has worked hundred-hour weeks my entire life. I am proud of him deep in my bones.[1] I was raised on Cheerios, raisins, and his experience of the American Dream—its ties to ambition, nose to the grindstone work, and constant drive. When he wasn't technically working, my father was scribbling equations on paper at the breakfast table. We went on family vacation wherever his work was. And when he took "time off"—never for more than hours within a single day, he built a brick wall, wood cabinet, or garden bed (all useful metaphors on their own). He took us to Cyprus, and we worked at learning everything about the island (birthplace of Aphrodite) and our family (analytical and driven).

And I got the message: this is how you work. This is what a good worker looks like. This is how you write. This is how I will write. Advice about how to write effectively in the discipline is similarly, and problematically, tangled up with American notions of morality, worth, and productivity. As the boundaries between work and home have further eroded, the reach of "neoliberal demands of limitlessly increasing personal productivity" (Hensley Owens and Van Ittersum, Introduction) are forcing many, certainly me, to rethink my writing life as distinctly American in beautiful, ugly, and complicated ways. As writing teachers we have an outsize influence on the writing lives of others, so I see this exigency to rethink as both personal and professional.

"The idea of story as theory" is central to feminist and cultural rhetorics practices, and both traditions inform my approach to this project (Novotny). In particular, I use story to marry my embodied experiences as a writer to my theoretical understandings of writing as a discipline. William Banks notes the importance of such work because "regardless of how distant we can get ourselves from the embodied experiences of our lives, if we do not find ways back to those bodies, those experiences, we run the risk of impoverishing our theories and pedagogies" (22). Thus, I "constellate" (Powell et al.) personal narrative with feminist and cultural rhetorical critique to extricate the beautiful things operating in my writing process and work ethic from the racist and troublesome things. The beautiful things: my relationship with my father; my pride in him; my own curiosity. The racist and troublesome things: the bootstraps myth of the American dream; assumptions about equal access to writing time and space. This essay is an effort to write a healthier, more sustainable writing balance into existence, to speak a language that perhaps felt out

Speak in the Tongue of Your Father   91

of reach for my father, so that it can be accessible to my students, to my colleagues, to me, to my children for whom *I* am now modeling work ethic. In the following sections, I try to do this work, dividing my stories, reflections, and recommendations on writing in four-ish sections: Productivity; Embodiment; Identity; and Sustainability. At the start of each section is my attempt to speak in the tongue of my father, drawing on a modern Greek word to orient these ideas, and at the close of the essay is a decision tree, what I hope might function as a collaborative heuristic to invite a new way of speaking about writing for myself and anyone else who would like to try.

PRODUCTIVITY: DISCIPLINARY ADVICE ON WRITING

Παράγω is the Greek verb "I produce," and it never exists on its own. Instead, it must be conjugated, and the pronoun is subsumed into the word itself: I produce (παράγω), you produce (παράγετε), they produce (παράγουν), etc. I think this continuous grammatical reminder that someone is always doing the producing is a useful one. No production without busy people. And although it's not ubiquitous, advice on effective writing processes in writing studies and higher ed has long demonstrated this awareness. It has touted balance, mindfulness, and healthy habits. As Madeleine Elfenbein opined in 2015 about Robert Boice, the oft-quoted social scientist of academe, "The essence of Boice's approach is captured in the title of his 2000 book *Advice for New Faculty: Nihil Nimus*, the Latin phrase for 'everything in moderation.'" She appreciates Boice's humanity and his discussion of the mindfulness and balance necessary for persisting in the professoriate. Boice's advice on how to navigate the university, and particularly scholarly publishing, has continued to shape how we orient to writing projects decades after its first publication. Studies of time-use (Tulley *How Faculty*) and our unequal access to time and support (Pantelides; Marquez) have further complicated our disciplinary understandings, and recent pandemic-induced think pieces in the *Chronicle* and similar venues have been even more gentle and aware of how differently we all have access to the time and attention necessary for writing. For instance, compare Boice's advice in 2000 to "arrange external situations to ensure regular writing productivity" with the more recent, "If you have childcare or other commitments, just try to schedule in a small amount of work per day (1–2 hours, say), and see how you go. . . . If you get any work done at all, you are doing really well" (Taylor). Story certainly influences such revised advice; as Christine Tulley notes:

> I know of a colleague who goes outside and writes in his car so he doesn't have to hear video games blaring. One of my graduate students now writes for 20 minutes before getting out of bed in the morning instead of writing all day on Friday . . . and longer if her children sleep in. Many of us are using time to walk outside as time to think through bigger ideas or problems in our writing. We all are learning to adapt on the fly. ("Resetting")

Although the pandemic and attendant changes to routine have impacted the writing habits of nearly everyone in academia, caregivers in the field have long recognized instability as a primary characteristic of their writing lives. Collections such as *Mama Phd* and *Professor Mommy* offer countless stories of juggling breastfeeding, fertility treatments, miscarriages, manuscript deadlines, and tenure cases—both successful and failed. Such stories were notably absent from our field's *Women's Ways of Making it in Composition*, and numerous subsequent articles took issue with the fact that "several profiled scholars mention twelve-hour work days and/or seven-day work weeks, practices which are generally unsustainable—and undesirable—for mothers of young children" (Cucciarre et al. 42). Yet many parents (including me) concur that "being a mother . . . forces a life balance that in many ways benefits, rather than hinders, my work, insofar as I've had the flexibility to make that possible" (Hensley Owens in Cucciarre et al. 53–54). Christine Tulley's *How She Does It* offers empirical evidence of this flexibility, documenting the writing habits of mothers in the field; such work offers useful nuance to related work in higher education (Mason et al.).

Still, access to balance has long been the province of privilege, as Alice Walker's response to Virginia Woolf's canonical essay, "A Room of One's Own" demonstrates. Woolf famously noted the importance of a woman having a room of her own in order to write (and this really resonated with me during the pandemic, when I didn't have a room of my own). Yet in her subsequent address to a women's group, Woolf describes her privilege, noting that once she had that room and received money for her writing, she was able to not worry about bills. Instead, she purchased a cat with her earnings. Woolf's primary struggle (which is a significant one!) was with gender roles, personified by the idea of the perfect, domestic Angel in the House that stood in the way of her writing. Woolf reflected: "She used to come between me and my paper when I was writing reviews. It was she who bothered me and wasted my time and so tormented me that at last I killed her" (243).

Given Woolf's conclusions, Walker asks us to subsequently make sense of Phyllis Wheatley's talent and her ability to produce, an enslaved woman with neither the room of her own nor the money to support herself that Woolf suggests women need in order to write. Further, Wheatley didn't have the option to *choose* her relationship to the domestic sphere. Walker writes: "How was the creativity of the black woman kept alive, year after year and century after century, when for most of the years black people have been in America, it was a punishable crime for a black person to read or write?" (316). Walker's point is ultimately about access, white privilege, and lack of awareness, but it's also about productivity. She demonstrates that creative composition relies on a special confluence of factors, and sometimes compositions are necessarily delayed, sometimes a generation or more.

For Walker, productivity is something you can pass on to your children. She received the spark of creativity from her mother as well as the delayed gift of productivity because of her mother's hard work and sacrifice in a racist world. She writes, "And so our mothers and grandmothers have, more often than not anonymously, handed on the creative spark, the seed of the flower they themselves never hoped to see: or like a sealed letter they could not plainly read" (320). I certainly don't mean to suggest that the experience of enslaved women and their daughters resembles that of immigrants and their families. Instead, generational sacrifice is also focal to immigrant discourses, though the gardens they tend are often in different circumstances and locales. Or, to return to the Greek verb conjugation that introduces this section, parents may work—λειτουργούν, note that even in the word, parents are subsumed within the action—such that their children may produce (παράγουν).

EMBODIMENT: PERSONAL ORIENTATION TO WRITING

Soma is often glossed as the Greek word for body, but it means more than that. It encompasses all that the body is—the wholeness of the mind-body. Will Banks describes the rhetorical equivalent, a sort of familial embodiment, in which "our bodies, though seemingly whole, are fragmented, because our bodies-as-we-understand-them are conscious (and unconscious) extensions of not only our minds, but also the minds around us. I know the bodies of others by knowing my own body, and vice versa; I read into those bodies as I read into my own; I write those bodies as I write my own" (Banks 23). My father's sacrifices and his work ethic are always operating in the back of my mind and orienting my body toward my work. In beautiful ways, my sister and I have the "embodied knowledge" that comes from being the daughters of an immigrant (Knoblauch 51). Thus, I write in my own body as if it's an extension of the bodies I grew up with. As if writing will tie those bonds tighter and hold those people closer. Both my sister and I work with blinders on, holding ourselves up to the standard that seeped into our bodies through the grape leaves, watermelon, and halloumi we've eaten over the years. Like many daughters of immigrants, we work hard for what seem like complex reasons but are pretty much just to make our parents proud and to make their sacrifices "worth" it.

At nineteen, my father came to the United States to study physics, leaving his home country of Cyprus, an island country a stone's throw from Israel, Lebanon, and Syria, in the conflict-laden eastern corner of the Mediterranean. The majority of Cypriots speak Greek and consider themselves ethnically Greek, though based on my conversations with mainland Greeks, thoughts about the closeness of this relationship are geolocative-dependent. Perhaps most geopolitically unique (and viscerally painful), a third of the island is occupied by Turkey, making it the only country within the European Union to have a divided, occupied capital city. This is the leftover regime from 1974 warfare in which Turkey invaded Cyprus. Since then, the United Nations has maintained a green line between the Republic of Cyprus and occupied territory.[2] My family and I have never crossed the line to see where the homes of some family members once were. Although my father has never openly wrestled with these facts and their impact on his identity—he has always said that as soon as he moved to the United States, he was an American—I continue to wonder how it must have felt to be working in the United States when some of his family members had to flee their houses, when their neighbors were killed. What must it have been like to not be able to call home to know that everyone was safe? To feel so incredibly lucky that our family was safe? I also continue to try to understand how his body is read, particularly in relation to my own.

When we first moved to Nashville, Tennessee, in 1994 I became familiar with a conversation, repeated nearly verbatim through accounts by immigrants of their reception in white-majority homogeneous spaces. A person approaches my father curiously (suspiciously?) in the grocery store/on the street/outside of school and asks, "Where are you from?" "New York." The person scrunches their face disbelievingly, "Originally?" "Cyprus." The conversation would sometimes end there, but often the person wouldn't know what or where Cyprus is, so there would be a brief, usually unsuccessful geography lesson. The primary tension in the conversation is, as Sara Ahmed notes in *Living a Feminist Life* about her own experiences living in Australia and being the daughter of a Pakistani man, the question isn't genuine. The questioner doesn't mean, "Where are you from?" Instead, they mean, "Are you white?" Or, perhaps more precisely, "Tell me why you don't look white so that I can understand my orientation to you." Ahmed notes that in her own conversations, she would ultimately answer that her father is from Pakistan, and then "That's it. The conversation is over. I have given the right answer, the answer [the questioner] was waiting for, even hoping for" (116). Yet, as she explains, the recurrence of such questioning puts the person marked as different as constantly in question: "To be questioned, to be questionable, sometimes can feel like a residence: a question becomes something you reside in. . . . A body can become a question mark" (116–17). Sometimes such a body appears to invite answers to unasked questions. For instance, despite my father's residence in the United States for more than fifty years, he often receives explanations that begin with the corrective: "In this country, we . . ."

Perhaps he got more attention because my mother, sister, and I are pink-skinned, and no one is surprised when I say I'm from New York or Tennessee. My blue eyes, pink skin, and brown hair make my body familiar, something not to be questioned. In most realms my father is "white," but not pink-skinned in the same way as my mother, sister, and I, so this is confusing to some people. I'll never forget when, as a high school student, I accompanied my father to a formal party for the university where he works. I wore my prom dress and twisted my hair up on top of my head. I was proud because I thought I looked grown up, and I was excited to be with my father on such an outing. But everyone gave my dad judgmental, sidelong looks all night, likely not understanding that I was his daughter. Because our skin colors and hair are different, the party-goers couldn't reconcile my presence. We laughed together awkwardly at the relief on their faces when my father introduced me, "This is my daughter, Kate."

As Isabel Wilkerson writes, whiteness in America has much to do with which bodies are accepted, which *somas* are marked, which immigrants are welcome, and which immigrants are perceived as contributing to the American economy. Thus, my father's identity markers and relative whiteness exists on a continuum based on class, global expectation, and immediate environment. He has long dressed in suits and crisply ironed shirts on his many trips to the airport for work because he is, like many immigrants from the Middle East, often the one stopped for "random" inspections. Such encounters are evidence of Eduardo Bonilla-Silva's admonition that "races are indeed invented social categories, but they are *socially real* and reenacted in the everyday life in encounters in all sorts of situations and spaces" ("Color-blind").

THE BEAUTIFUL THINGS IN MY IDENTITY

Την οικογένειά μου, my family. In Greek, all nouns have belonging. There isn't a direct equivalent in English. For instance, when family members call my name, they say "Kate *μου*," which means, my Kate. It's not grammatical to say someone's name without attaching belonging. Thus, in thinking about my identity, its connection to the American dream, and the things I want to further port into my writing life, I think about *η οικογένειά μου*.

My father and his two siblings have a favorite childhood story. Although they are not a regularly gregarious bunch, if they tell the story together, they can barely get the words out for laughing so hard and cutting each other off. The story goes that they were in a village, riding a donkey, and my father kept falling off the back. The poor donkey was only so big, and there were three of them, so *Akis* ("little," my father's nickname at the time, which he quickly outgrew) had to fight to stay on, slip off, and climb back up with nearly every step. He just wouldn't give up; he wanted to see the view from the donkey (or so I imagine), he wanted to see where they were going, and he didn't want to get left behind. This is one of those inside jokes that I don't quite understand—what was so funny? But watching these three serious people, *η οικογένειά μου*, whom I love, crack up, makes me laugh to tears every time. Ultimately, I read this as a story about my father's persistence and curiosity. For better and for worse, he just doesn't give up. He will climb up whatever hill he needs to (even if it's a donkey), and he will struggle to stay there so that he can make it to the end—whatever/ wherever that might be. His curiosity is so passionate that it drives him forward, it wakes him up in the morning, it has driven him to write and research across continents. I too speak this language.

About thirty years later, I found myself similarly in a Cypriot village in the mountains astride a donkey. I was with my sister and cousins, and when we saw the donkey, I just walked toward it without thinking. I didn't ask to ride the poor animal, the donkey's owner simply picked me up, placed me on the donkey, and we trotted off away from my family. We have a picture of me looking back at them, wide-eyed, surprised, but totally into the adventure. My curiosity has certainly carried me away many times. I go in with interest, and I stay on for the ride out of curiosity, stubbornness, and a commitment to the bit. I won't give up, even when I should. This is certainly how I approach writing projects.

Although this is the first time that I've explicitly written about Cyprus and my family, it has always been present in my writing. Throughout my life we have traveled to Cyprus every other summer or so, and my

Speak in the Tongue of Your Father   97

extended family became an invisible piece of my identity—pushing me forward, igniting an interest in rhetoric, solidifying my belief in education. They've also likely driven my stubborn curiosity. This was certainly operating on the eve of my daughter's birth when I desperately tried to meet an article revision deadline. I had never missed a deadline (never do), and I remember pushing aside the stacks of diapers on my table to set up my computer and tweak the works cited. My suitcase for the hospital was open on the floor, half-packed, with a cat cuddled on top of the books, keeping them warm. My almost two-year old was starting to make waking sounds as I did a final quick proofread, attached the manuscript to an email, and pressed send. I did it, but I did it with such anguish and heartache. And the collection didn't come out until my daughter was six years old. I was glad that I could so easily date the article that way, but my big takeaway from that memory is: Why? Why did I push so hard? Why didn't I request an extension? Or why didn't I just pull it from the collection?

In 1967, almost a decade after Cyprus gained its independence from the British, and six years before warfare would tear it up, my father completed his required year of military service and came to the United States on a Fulbright. My *pappou*, or grandfather, a shoemaker, and my *yiayia*, my grandmother, both with fifth-grade educations, gathered their savings and sent *Akis* on a plane with one hundred dollars. His *thia*, aunt Parthonopi, knowing that he would be headed to Illinois with cold weather and snow (virtually unimaginable in hot Cyprus), knit a heavy sweater, which he stuffed in the sleeves of his coat on the plane. In preparation for his trip, he attended orientation sessions, and the American woman who had probably left the United States in the 1950s assured my father that what he really needed was a black suit to prepare for America. Thus, armed with sweaters, a little money, his black suit (that he would never wear), stubbornness, a whole lot of brains (and, likely, "no polish," as Lin-Manuel Miranda sings in *Hamilton*), he came to the United States.

These brains, *η οικογένειά μου*, and this spirit were likely operating when my family and I decided to move across the country for my first tenure-track job. I had a six-week-old baby, and it hadn't occurred to me that I could ask for a semester to recover. Like many, I was never able to take FMLA (Family Medical Leave Act) leave for either of my children because I was working "part-time" as a graduate student. We couldn't afford for me not to work. Thus, I hit the tenure track with a toddler and nursing infant, lucky to be employed, but desperate to prove myself. To others? To myself? I'm still not exactly sure. I continue to feel lucky to

KATE L. PANTELIDES

have gotten that job, to have had the support to go, and the support to stay, but upon reflection I see the cracks in my approach and what I see as that American dream drive forward (in my case, to Michigan, my car stuffed to the brim with countless sweaters).

IDENTITY CRITIQUE: THE RACIST AND TROUBLESOME THINGS

Ενωσις literally means union in Greek, but it's usually discussed in the context of the dream of *Ενωσις*, a political goal within Cypriot diaspora communities that started in the nineteenth century, that they would unite with the Greek state. It was a beautiful dream that inspired poetry, speeches, and art, but it (and many other complex geopolitical factors) contributed to the bloodshed and division of the island in 1974. The American dream has similar beautiful aspirations, similar complications, and, unfortunately, similar consequences. There are so many beautiful things about the American dream. The bravery of moving to a new place without family or friends; the willingness to learn a new place, language, and culture without the requisite maps; the stories of the many immigrants who have come to the United States (the parents of one of my best friends both lived in Iran until they were twenty, came to the United States on the same plane, but didn't meet and fall in love until years later when they were studying at the same American university); the romantic notion of a country constituted of immigrants and Indigenous people, each with such different cuisines, cultures, and stories, where everyone can succeed.

Perhaps this latter component is the most damaging and pervasively written into the fabric of American life (particularly within academic institutions): the colorblind naivety of the bootstraps myth, and the glossing over of the violence at the heart of the country's construction. The myth that "good" Americans will just pick themselves up when they're down on their luck and magically be successful from the force of sheer will and hard work is at the root of American dream discourse. Such expectation is written through our academic writing lives. Wilkerson describes this phenomenon as the importance of the "bottom rung." This discourse suggests that everyone *can* make it in America, but only if someone else isn't succeeding. Of course, this isn't empirically true. The American dream isn't a pie that is finished as soon as a requisite number of people take a piece, but the reliance on the bootstraps myth of individual success reifies the belief in scarcity (which fuels the academic compulsion to compete for resources, publications, positions). I'm doing my best to pick the remnants of this discourse out

Speak in the Tongue of Your Father 99

of my pedagogy, scholarship, and personal expectations for myself and others as writers, but it's everywhere.

Aja Martinez and other scholars of CRT remind us how liberal claims of meritocracy are often rooted in invisible (to white people), misplaced assumptions about equity. The very language that constitutes the idealistic values of the American dream "can converge to restrict social and educational progress for people of color under the linguistic guise of terms like *fairness*, *open access*, and *equal opportunity*. . . . Intentionally and inadvertently, the hegemony has used and can use enfranchising language while, simultaneously, disenfranchising people of color" (Holmes 26). Eduardo Bonilla-Silva writes that the "new racism" that emerged after the Jim Crow era is a much more subtle, systemic, colorblind racism, characterized by an avoidance of direct references to racial categories in policy, discourse, and political agendas (*White*). It's racism that lives in the institutions—like education—that are meant to provide access to achievement and learning across identity markers. It's so insidious that it's in our citation practices (See Cagle and colleagues' "Anti-Racist Scholarly Reviewing Practices" for ways to combat this). Yet both the political left and right have adopted colorblindness as a political tool (Burke), and such rhetoric has significant ideological implications that run counter to collective practice, feminist notions of care, and a realistic understanding of writing processes, which, like all projects, are ultimately distributed and shared.

SUSTAINABILITY: DEVELOPING A "GOOD" WORK ETHIC (WHATEVER THAT MEANS)

Φυσική, physics. My father loves physics. We have had many discussions about how we similarly orient to our disciplines. He argues that physics, like rhetoric and language, is beautiful and elegant. That it describes all phenomena, and that by looking closely, we can better understand our world. When things are out of balance, physics uses math to describe how it will return to a balanced state. Physics offers math to describe what sustainability entails. The purpose of physics as a discipline is to help us understand how the universe behaves. I think this is also what rhetoric does, discursively. And I love my work too: my work with students, my endless questions (and periodic answers) about language and writing, my still dawning understanding (though decades old) of rhetoric, and even (many of) my administrative tasks. It's a privilege to love my work. I reject the constant reminders that "your work doesn't love you back." It doesn't have to. That's not why I work, and that certainly has nothing to do with my understanding of why many immigrants work, certainly not my father. And the love that I have for my work is not the same as the love I have for the people in my life, but we *should* be choosy about where our love is directed. As I and countless other feminist scholars have warned, the gendered labor of love discourse and the glorification of self-sacrifice by woman educators has not served us well in writing studies, and it continues to be the discursive foundation of many of our labor problems.

Like problematic assumptions of access to the American dream and the bootstraps myth, advice on writing is similarly laden with the assumption of equal access to time and the ability to "arrange external situations to ensure regular writing productivity" (Boice). If we're just personally disciplined enough, individually organized enough, and smart enough, we should all find time for writing. Not true. These assumptions are deeply ingrained within higher education and within me. But I am personally trying to work through how I might more equitably and fairly orient to my understandings of writing and work and change my own mentoring practices. I'm trying, as anti-racist activist Chakita Patterson admonishes "allies, co-conspirators, accomplices and activists" to "#DoTheWork On Yourself."

So what is a "good" writing work ethic? And what is "good" motivation for writing? What are racist assumptions of work, and where are the intersections in writing studies' orthodoxy about writing habits? How can I move forward from the pandemic healed (or at least healing) from my self-inflicted wounds about time and my need to write, and theorize a more sustainable practice in my personal and professional life and for those whom I mentor and influence? How can I wrest my commitment to American dream discourse from the racist assumptions of the bootstraps myth? Of course, I don't have generalizable answers (do we ever?), but I take to heart the advice that our colleagues in cultural rhetorics advise as a necessary correlative to critique: "Although we do believe critique of our current disciplinary practices *is* important and necessary, we want to make sure that critique leads to something even more important—*making*. Critique is not the end of the process of decolonization—it's the beginning. We want to make something that people will *use*, rather than to take things apart only to show that they *can* be taken apart" (Powell et al. Act II, Scene 1). With this in mind, I offer a decision tree (Appendix: figure 1) and brief, associated decision-making narrative that I hope to use in the future to help me think through my own work ethic, what drives me, and what projects I will select to work on.

I have been so oriented toward saying yes to work, toward working without stopping—for many reasons—some gendered, some I associate with my identity as the daughter of an immigrant, and some are simply a response to the academic hierarchy. A recent CliftonStrengths assessment admonished me, "You have an internal fire burning inside you. It pushes you to do more, to achieve more. After each accomplishment is reached, the fire dwindles for a moment, but very soon it rekindles itself. . . . Your relentless need for achievement might not be logical. It might not even be focused. But it will always be with you . . . you must learn to live with this whisper of discontent" (Gallup Access). However, I don't know that this is how I want to move forward. As I've thought through these aspects of writing work ethic as they relate to productivity, embodiment, identity, critique, and sustainability, I've realized how important it will be for me to say no going forward. I don't want to write because of my blind adherence to a notion of productivity that I haven't effectively questioned. The decision tree in the appendix demonstrates my effort to be metacognitive about my writing work and, perhaps most importantly, the writing work I invite others to participate in. Hopefully you will find it useful too.

Like many, I hope to move forward from a year of challenge and reflection with a more intentional approach to my work. And, in this polarized political moment, I'm also trying to better understand what being an American means—particularly because my father's role as a new American is so central to my life—and how this intersects with my identity as a writer and an educator. I hope that by slowly speaking my broken Greek and continuing to write with curiosity and persistence, I can speak in the tongue of my father. But as my fluency grows, hopefully so too does my understanding of how to use this language to say something new, to write in more sustainable ways than I have. I hope that, like in one my favorite pictures from my childhood, I can sit on my father's shoulders and offer something new for myself, my students, *my* kids. Maybe you can speak a new language too.

APPENDIX: DECISION TREE

I developed this decision tree to function as a heuristic that guides writers through questions to help them decide whether or not to participate in a writing project. It is meant to facilitate self-talk or conversation with a trusted colleague about whether or not to engage in work, and it mirrors the self-talk that I usually have around such decisions. By developing this decision tree, I attempted to further codify this self-talk

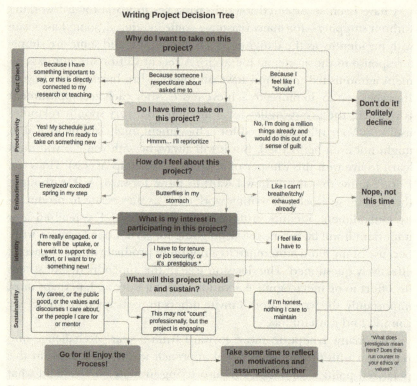

Figure 6.1. Writing Project Dialogic Decision Tree.

in an effort to hear it more clearly and take the final recommendations more to heart. Decisions about whether to take on new projects are rarely simply yes/no decisions, and there are many considerations to take into account. This decision tree only addresses four primary levels of decision-making—concerns related to productivity, embodiment, identity, and sustainability—all addressed in my essay. Others might adapt this decision tree to account for other decision-making factors. The decision tree offers a tool to match the narratives I've offered, and it's an attempt to create rather than simply critique, as colleagues in cultural rhetorics remind us to do. Instead of simply tending toward yes, this decision tree asks writers to mindfully choose their work (as much as possible). I used a form of these questions to help me decide whether or not to propose writing for this collection:

- First, I went to the gut check: Upon reading the Call for Papers (CFP) I was excited. I had so many ideas, and I was eager to start drafting. I actually drafted three totally different proposals because I felt like I had something to say.

Speak in the Tongue of Your Father   103

- In terms of productivity: I was drowning in administrative tasks when I first came across the CFP, but the timeline seemed possible given my other writing. I hesitated but continued to mull my decision.
- Regarding embodiment: I felt energized responding to the CFP. It came in the midst of my own pandemic reflection, and writing was a wonderful respite.
- Identity: I have long wanted to write about my relationship with my father and my "American" work ethic, so this writing opportunity offered me a chance to write through questions I've wanted to address. Increasingly, I'm trying to pick apart my understandings of "prestige," as hinted at in the decision tree, because I see it as very much caught up in problematic academic hierarchies.
- Finally, considering the sustainability of the project: I felt confident in my ability to complete the project, and I hope to "count" it in my publications when I submit my dossier for full professor. Often when I think about the relative sustainability of a project, I think about who it serves. Does the project allow me to work through a question or issue of importance to me? Does the project allow me to work with a graduate student? Does it impact the discipline or conversations in ways that are consistent with my values and theoretical orientations? Does it sustain people or discourses who/that I value?

I invite other writers to work through these questions and perhaps substitute others that make more sense given their immediate writing context. I recognize that _choosing_ to write/not to write can be a privilege, but those under tenure pressure or needing to write for further job security will hopefully use this tool or their own version to select venues more strategically for their efforts. Hopefully you can adopt this tool so that it speaks to you.

NOTES

1. Of course, this work in his career was only possible because my mother worked hundred-hour workweeks in our home and as a parent. I am also proud of her deep in my bones and recognize how work is gendered and constituted with different value as such, but that is for a different essay.
2. Cyprus was under British rule in various forms from 1878–1960, became an independent country in 1963, and then a member of the European Union in 2004. The colonial occupation still has its roots in the island—perhaps most clearly demonstrated in the British military base that stands in the center of the island, sovereign British territory.

WORKS CITED

Ahmed, Sara. _Living a Feminist Life_. Duke UP, 2016.

Ballif, Michelle, Roxanne Mountford, and Diane Davis, Eds. _Women's Ways of Making It in Rhetoric and Composition_. Routledge, 2008.

KATE L. PANTELIDES

Banks, William P. "Written through the Body: Disruptions and 'Personal' Writing." *College English*, vol. 66, no. 1, 2003, pp. 21–40. *JSTOR*, www.jstor.org/stable/3594232.

Boice, Robert. *Advice for New Faculty Members*. Allyn & Bacon, 2000.

Bonilla-Silva, Eduardo. "The Structure of Racism in Color-Blind, 'Post-Racial' America." *American Behavioral Scientist*, vol. 59, no. 11, Oct. 2015, pp. 1358–76. doi:10.1177/0002764215586826.

Bonilla-Silva, Eduardo. *White Supremacy and Racism in the Post-Civil Rights Era*. Rienner, 2001.

Burke, Meghan A. "Racing Left and Right: Color-Blind Racism's Dominance across the U.S. Political Spectrum," *The Sociological Quarterly*, vol. 58, no. 2, pp. 277–94, 2017. DOI :10.1080/00380253.2017.1296335.

Cagle, Lauren E., et al. "Anti-Racist Scholarly Reviewing Practices: A Heuristic for Editors, Reviewers, and Authors." 2021. https://tinyurl.com/reviewheuristic.

Cucciarre, Christine Peters, et al. "Mothers' Ways of Making It—or Making Do?: Making (Over) Academic Lives In Rhetoric and Composition with Children." *Composition Studies*, vol. 39, no. 1, 2011, pp. 41–61.

Elfenbein, Madeleine. "Take It Easy: The Wisdom of Robert Boice: Advice for Practicing Mindfulness During Academic Work." *Inside Higher Ed*, 5 Nov. 2015. https://www.insidehighered.com/blogs/gradhacker/take-it-easy-wisdom-robert-boice.

Gallup Access. "Clifton Strengths." my.gallup.com. Accessed 1 Sept. 2022.

Holmes, David G. "Affirmative Reaction: Kennedy, Nixon, King, and the Evolution of Color-Blind Rhetoric." *Rhetoric Review*, vol. 26, no. 1, 2007, pp. 25–41. DOI:10.1080 /07350190709336684.

Knoblauch, A. Abby. "Bodies of Knowledge: Definitions, Delineations, and Implications of Embodied Writing in the Academy." *Composition Studies*, vol. 40, no. 2, 2012, pp. 50–65. *JSTOR*, www.jstor.org/stable/compstud.40.2.0050.

Marquez, Loren. "Narrating Our Lives: Retelling Mothering and Professional Work in Composition Studies." *Composition Studies*, vol. 39, no. 1, 2011, pp. 73–85.

Martinez, Aja. *Counterstory: The Rhetoric and Writing of Critical Race Theory*. National Council of Teachers of English, 2020.

Mason, Mary Ann, et al. *Do Babies Matter? Gender and Family in the Ivory Tower*. Rutgers UP, 2013.

Novotny, Maria. "Cultural Rhetorics in Precarious Ties." *Writing and Rhetoric MKE*, 7 July 2020.

Pantelides, Kate. "The Joys of WPAhood." *WPAs in Transition*, edited by Jacob Babb, et al., Utah State UP, 2018, pp. 100–10.

Patterson, Chakita. "7 Day Anti Racism Challenge." *7 Day Anti Racism Challenge*, 2020, www.antiracismchallenge.com.

Powell, Malea, et al. "Our Story Begins Here: Constellating Cultural Rhetorics." *Enculturation*, 25 Oct. 2014. http://www.enculturation.net/node/6100.

Taylor, Lucy. "Ten Work–Life Balance Tips for Researchers Based at Home During the Pandemic." *Career Column*, 8 Apr. 2020, https://www.nature.com/articles/d41586-020 -01059-4.

Tulley, Christine E. *How Writing Faculty Write: Strategies for Process, Product, and Productivity*. Utah State UP, 2018.

Tulley, Christine. "Resetting Your Research Agenda." *Inside Higher Ed*, 2 Apr. 2020. https:// www.insidehighered.com/advice/2020/04/02/how-continue-push-your-research -forward-while-staying-home-during-pandemic-opinion.

Walker, Alice. "In Search of Our Mothers' Gardens." *Available Means: An Anthology of Women's Rhetoric*, edited by Joy Ritchie and Kate Ronald. U of Pittsburgh P, 2001, pp. 314–20.

Wilkerson, Isabel. *Caste: The Origins of Our Discontents*. Random House, 2020.

Woolf, Virginia. "Professions For Women." *Available Means: An Anthology of Women's Rhetoric*, edited by Joy Ritchie and Kate Ronald. U of Pittsburgh P, 2001, pp. 241–46.

7

"EMBODIED ACTION" AS PRECARIOUS PROCESS
Writing Productivity at the Intersection of Crip Self-Care and Academic Contingency

Andrew Harnish

Tags: critique, adaptability, embodiment, and productivity

This is a chapter about productivity and writing, about productive, disabled writing. It is about the process and "writing workflow" (Lockridge and Van Ittersum) I've developed to meet the demands on my time and the needs of my disabled body. My method in this project follows Jessica Restaino's call to "blend the personal and the scholarly and to make something new out of each" (6). Consequently, much of my data is auto-ethnographic. In this piece, I narrate how my writing is impinged upon by my impairment. I then turn to the reductive narratives of writing that I drew on in graduate school, narratives that wounded my body. Finally, I put my impaired, academically contingent writing process and workflow in conversation with Bre Garrett's account of "embodied composing" (222) and Louise DeSalvo's vision of "writing as a way of healing" (3).

DeSalvo, a Virginia Woolf scholar and memoirist, offers her account of writerly productivity in her widely praised guide, *Writing as a Way of Healing: How Telling Our Stories Transforms Our Lives.* Her narrative argues that writers ought to engage with painful experiences, and even traumas, yet her prescriptions for how to write about pain seek to bring about "cure," an outcome that is seldom possible or desirable for disabled writers. I read DeSalvo's argument alongside Restaino's inclusive call to bring the body, in all of its complexity and vulnerability, into scholarly projects in writing studies. Restaino's thesis complements Garrett's argument, in "Corporeal Rhetoric as Embodied Action: Composing in/through Bodily Motion," for rhetors to acknowledge that "bodies perform as multimodal places or sites of inter-action," and that "a range of bodily capabilities should be considered among the available means" for expression, whether through physical or linguistic

https://doi.org/10.7330/9781646424870.c007

performance (218). Garrett's account of a movement-based creative workshop has shown me that my disabled productivity can be increased by attention to embodied composing, which I employ while prewriting and preparing my body to write during my yoga practice. In this paper, I use Garrett's, DeSalvo's, and Restaino's work to interrogate my disabled productivity, an approach to composing that troubles traditionalist notions of productivity while insisting that disabled writers are justified in pursuing output during those intervals when our bodyminds allow it.

Ultimately, I conclude that disabled scholars need to develop highly individualized processes and workflows—which include an openness to hybrid genres—as we strive to maintain the output that is required of us in the academy, especially when our positions are contingent.

In academia, productivity is necessary. Yet the pursuit of productivity is also widely, and often rightly, critiqued. The neoliberal university constantly asks more of its employees, and especially of those who are most contingent—adjuncts, visiting professors, and other non-tenure-track faculty. Understandably, academics bemoan these labor expectations, but critiques of productivity go beyond complaints about demanding institutional requirements, and implicate productivity, and productivity rhetoric, in a wide range of structural injustices. As the rhetoric and women's studies scholar Ruth Osorio puts it in a tweet,[1] "productivity rhetoric is racist, ableist, sexist, queerphobic, settler, capitalistic bullshit." Osorio, a tenure-track professor, somewhat playfully posits napping as a subversive alternative to productivity rhetoric and the constellation of injustices that putatively surrounds it. But whimsical as her tweet may seem, it is deeply grounded in the rhetorics of queer theory and disability studies, which are predicated, respectively, on the refusal of cis, heteropatriarchal sociocultural expectations (Edelman; Freeman; Halberstam; Warner) and the contestation of the neoliberal assumption that compensation ought to be indexed to individual economic output (Kafer; McRuer; Piepzna-Samarasinha; Wendell).

As a queer, disabled scholar of writing studies, I have been nourished by the antinormative praxes of queer culture. I'm committed to contesting neoliberal arguments that seek to measure human worth and human culture purely in financial terms. Yet as a contingent academic seeking a stable academic position, I need to be productive as a writer. And as a disabled writer who often enjoys my work, even when it hurts, I'm not as persuaded as Osorio that rhetoric that encourages productivity—in my case, writing—is always unjust or exploitative. I have a limited amount of time to write, and, due to the constraints of my body, limited windows during which I can write. I want to use that time productively.

"Embodied Action" as Precarious Process   107

Given my limited capacity for output, I wish I didn't have to spend so much of my time narrating the story of my impairment. I wish my condition were more immediately obvious and legible, but, as it stands, very few doctors—much less colleagues or academic bureaucracies—have any frame of reference for my embodiment. At seventeen, I underwent an endoscopic cardiothoracic sympathectomy. Like its distant cousin, the lobotomy, a sympathectomy is a brutally simple procedure. It involves the deflation of the lungs and the severing and permanent destruction of certain nerves to the hands and feet.

Why would anyone undergo such a procedure? Why did I undergo it? As a child, I was healthy, if plagued by anxiety. But in my teens, a series of confounding changes took hold. Suddenly, I was six feet tall. Suddenly, my voice deepened. Suddenly, too, like clockwork, every morning, and again every afternoon, the pangs struck my belly. In school, I squirmed in my narrow desk, digging my elbow into my side to try and distract myself from the bloating, spreading pain, praying my guts wouldn't rumble. Mortifying as my digestive troubles were, I didn't fixate upon them—or, at any rate, I didn't dwell on them the way I did my palms. My hyper-sweaty hands, which started acting up at the same time, functioned as the outward marker of all my bodily anxiety and discomfort. Whenever I was nervous, my hands began perspiring uncontrollably. By my late teens, the mere possibility that my hands would sweat was enough to make any impending social engagement seem terrifying.

And then one afternoon, browsing the web, I stumbled onto a site that advertised a procedure that promised to "cure" sweaty palms once and for all. I obsessed about that website. I fantasized about the surgery it advertised: an endoscopic cardiothoracic sympathectomy, which worked by permanently destroying the nerves that control the sweating of the hands and feet.

I underwent the procedure in November, in Philadelphia, an hour and a half from my family's farm. When I awoke after the surgery, I touched my palms. They were warm and blessedly dry. "Thank you," I whispered to my mother, who was seated beside me. "Thank you so much." Loopy with painkillers, I kept repeating my gratitude until I lapsed back into slumber.

Did I notice the changes to my face that first week? The stiffness, the sudden stillness, of my upper body? I can't recall, now. What I do vividly remember is the first day of gym class that spring. When I changed into the thick jersey I always wore, I was shocked by how thickly I sweated beneath it. "Compensatory sweating," it was called on the sympathectomy message board. A common enough side effect, one that I had brushed aside pre-surgery. Only several years after the procedure did I realize what the "compensation" was trying to accomplish. A sympathectomy doesn't merely sever the nerves that control the hands and feet. It destroys the nerves that control the perspiration of the entire upper body—a point that my parents and I either ignored or missed in the list of the surgery's side effects. My head, my neck, my shoulders, arms, and most of my chest have lost the ability to respond to heat. My brain has lost the ability to cool itself efficiently. The compensatory sweat that flows from my lower body in high heat is simply my brain's desperate attempt to cool itself. Always, in the heat, my face tightens. The pressure builds in my temples. My thoughts slide away from me, like the compensatory sweat coursing down my thighs and stomach.

I never received a specific diagnosis for the symptoms that prompted my sympathectomy. Had my parents been more curious about my condition, I might have received the sort of comprehensive workup that would have uncovered the cause of my symptoms. As it was, however, my parents merely accepted my insistent claim that I needed to have the procedure. The better part of a decade passed before I began to speculate about the initial causes of my symptoms. The spark was an unhappy digestive episode at a New Year's party, which prompted a friend to suggest that I try eliminating gluten from my diet. The next day, my digestive symptoms abated. My head felt clearer. And as I stuck to that diet over the course of the next month, my compensatory sweat diminished. My focus continued to improve, at least when my bodymind wasn't being overwhelmed by heat.

I've never been tested for a gluten allergy, following the advice of a physician friend who assured me that since my diet is working, there's no reason to investigate it. Still, it seems possible that a food sensitivity provoked the digestive symptoms that accompanied my persistently sweaty palms. There's no way to be certain; a sympathectomy is irreversible, so it's impossible to try an elimination diet on my body as it was in my teens. All I know is that in the ten years since I stopped consuming wheat and malt and barley, I've felt far better than I did in the gloomy years directly following my sympathectomy. I've become more alert, more intellectually engaged, and more academically productive. But the constraints on my bodymind remain, tightening whenever the temperature rises, disrupting my concentration and warping my posture and spine by forcing me to hunch in the heat. The degree of freedom imparted by my altered diet regularly crashes against the limits of my body, even now that I've developed a more accepting and integrated relationship with my impairment.

"Embodied Action" as Precarious Process   109

Always, as summer approaches, I write rapidly, frantically, doing my best to get my thoughts onto the page before my skin starts to tighten, my mind starts to muddle, and the pain in my hunched back starts to throb. As a contingent academic, I feel I have no choice but to strive for this productivity. And my commitment to output isn't merely the result of the harsh pressures of the academic job market. A part of me enjoys being productive. Now, in my late thirties, I've found a way to balance the imperatives of productivity with the needs and vulnerabilities of my bodymind, most of the time, at least. But my journey to a productive, disabled writing praxis has been circuitous and, at times, actively wounding. I therefore offer the following narrative of my writing process as a graduate student as a cautionary tale, an account of how the headlong pursuit of output can be every bit as dangerous as Osorio, and other critics of productivity rhetoric, argue.

LACERATING PRODUCTIVITY

I entered graduate school in my late twenties. I'd spent the years after my surgery struggling through college, skipping class, sleeping far too much, and working a series of jobs that left me miserable—barista, night janitor, laborer on my parents' farm. Now, freshly free from gluten's destabilizing effects on my digestion and concentration, I felt liberated, and I set about trying to make up for the time I felt I'd lost.

In graduate school, my favorite account of writing was Kurt Vonnegut's claim that there are two kinds of writers: "bashers and swoopers" (Vonnegut qtd. in Campbell). Swoopers, as I understood them, were writers like some of my gifted classmates, who could quickly and efficiently complete the projects they embarked upon. Most swoopers "write a story quickly, higgledy-piggledy, crinkum-crankum, any which way. Then they go over it again painstakingly, fixing everything that is just plain awful or doesn't work" (Vonnegut qtd. in Campbell). And, as Vonnegut argues, there are also "bashers," who "go one sentence at a time, getting it exactly right before they go on to the next one. When they're done, they're done" (Vonnegut qtd. in Campbell). I knew I wasn't a swooper, but I didn't despair. Misreading or misremembering Vonnegut's argument, I decided that bashers are not those who write slowly and methodically, as Vonnegut contends, but writers for whom language doesn't come easily. Gradually, I insisted, by parking at their desks and churning out pages, bashers can produce fine writing.

I internalized my mistaken paraphrase of Vonnegut's narrative about writers in 2011, around the time Malcolm Gladwell's book *Outliers* was

110 ANDREW HARNISH

ubiquitous in the national conversation around productivity. In *Outliers*, Gladwell popularized the idea that creative accomplishment depends on sustained effort, but the notion that writers need to labor diligently to increase their output has a long history in writing studies. In the 1982 article "Increasing the Productivity of 'Blocked' Academics," the behavioral psychologist Robert Boice notes that successful writing is produced "not through flashes of inspiration but by dint of hard and uniform labor" (198). Boice cites the novelist Irving Wallace's regular monitoring of his writerly output as proof that "record keeping and other methodical procedures can be used to treat writers who complain of unproductiveness" (198). Boice's method relies on "stimulus control over writing behaviors . . . enhanced by a suitable (e.g., quiet) locale, a regular schedule of writing, and reinforcements for the completions of writing" (199). Boice argues that this approach can be augmented with techniques that ought to be familiar to all teachers of writing: self-reflection, freewriting (which Boice calls "automatic writing") and an emphasis on the social aspects of the writing process, otherwise known as "the use of social support" (199–200). Ultimately, however, Boice's behavioralist approach is focused on increasing the productivity of already accomplished writers. In *Outliers*, Gladwell goes further. His program promises aspiring writers (among other aspirants) a route to exceptional professional accomplishment. *Outliers* contains the seductive claim, which Gladwell attributes to the neurologist Daniel Levitin, that "ten thousand hours of practice is required to achieve the level of mastery associated with being a *world-class* expert—in anything" (40).

Yes, I thought, the first time I encountered Gladwell's argument. The idea that all writers need is ten thousand hours of labor seemed to confirm Vonnegut's contention about bashers and swoopers. Bashers are writers who are simply trying to get in those ten thousand hours. Once they achieve it, success is inevitable.

In the years since the publication of *Outliers*, the ten-thousand-hours rule that Gladwell relies on has been debunked (Resnick). Still, it is true that if you avoid distraction and write in a routinized way, you will inevitably produce a considerable quantity of writing. But what I failed to realize for far too long is that practice and persistence aren't sufficient. Ability is also required. Capacity of the body. It's not enough to "bash away" as a writer—to suppose, as I did, that quality will somehow emerge out of a sufficient amount of time spent hammering at a piece of writing or a sizable stack of pages. As most writing teachers know, effective composition requires effective revision, "re-seeing" the work, taking time away from it, sharing it with others, and returning to it with a critical perspective. And one's ability to re-envision a piece of writing is tied directly to the capacities of one's bodymind.

Most discussions of the writing process don't linger on the embodied differences of writers, though this is changing as attention to disability increases within writing studies. As scholars of composition and disability (Cedillo; Konrad; Miller; Price; Wood) remind us, our bodyminds remain a determinative variable in our writing. Different bodyminds have different writing processes and styles, different abilities to produce narrative order, and different capacities for the physical toll exacted by the act of writing. Not every writer is equally capable of composing in every genre or genre system. But what many neoliberal rhetorics of productivity refuse to acknowledge is that this difference is a good thing.

Productivity does not need to be constructed and assessed narrowly: it need not operate on an able-bodied time sequence or in corporate spaces where only cis white heterosexual people feel comfortable. It can be pursued in all kinds of ways—a point that the COVID-19 pandemic has clarified. Remote work—work that is more accessible to disabled people and working parents—can be highly productive. And there is value, too, in writing and approaches to writing that acknowledge failure and the need for self-care, and in writing that employs hybrid forms to enact and express disability, pain, and other forms of difference. Indeed, these forms can increase the productivity—the output—of queer, disabled, and other marginalized (and multiply marginalized) scholars. They can provide contingent scholars with additional opportunities to voice their precarious realities.

For much of my time as a graduate student, I failed to acknowledge the potential in inclusive forms and genres. Committed as I was to hiding my abjection, both in my prose and my comportment, I had no respect for hybrid genres that left the chaos of the writing process, and of my embodiment itself, apparent on the page. I never supposed, in the first years after my sympathectomy, that I might pursue writing that embraces what Restaino calls "stillness, passivity . . . a falling away of the structures we always thought we could count on—including ourselves, our bodies, our methods, our texts, perhaps even 'what we (think we) know'" (156). Instead, I bore down harder, spending long hours in my chair, producing hundreds of pages of insufficiently edited work, much of which I ended up discarding, all because I supposed that good prose would magically emerge as I accumulated my Gladwellian ten thousand hours of writing. In the process, I ignored the needs of my body—I ignored my worsening posture; I dismissed the nagging pain I felt as I wrote. To reduce the heat that built in my head while I'm concentrating, I hunched—and still

ANDREW HARNISH

often hunch—forward, to try and encourage heat to rise from my back and neck instead of condensing in my brain. Years of sitting like this have degraded the balance and integrity of my pelvis and spine.

When I did consider my embodiment in those days, I lamented it, bemoaning my sympathectomy and regarding my impairments as implacable obstacles to my productivity. Not until well into my PhD program, when I took a class entitled Body Theory, did I discover that the complexities of embodiment could be a subject, that disability could be generative, both formally and as a topic. Slowly—far too slowly—I've come to accept and even draw comfort from the differences of my bodymind. Having finally traced many of my writerly struggles to my sympathectomy, I've sought to adapt—not to pursue productivity for its own sake but to produce the baseline level of output that I need to remain in conversation with my field and stay eligible for a tenure-track position. I've improved what Lockridge and Van Ittersum call my "workflow thinking," which they define as "the act of reading knowledge work as modular and intertwined with technologies." As part of this effort, I attend to the technology that directly impinges on my writing—I organize my writing projects in individual file folders. I save my work by date, and back it up daily, just in case something goes wrong in "the cloud." I've configured Microsoft Word to eliminate most distractions: I don't display my word count; I hide the tab ribbon. But I'm especially conscious of the aspects of my workflow that touch on my body: my ergonomic position, the temperature of the room, the fan blasting away at my feet. To further improve my focus, I shave my head. I write as much as I can in winter and whenever the weather is comparatively mild. I've also changed my formal approach; I've opened myself to new forms of scholarship, new modes of writing, approaches that make use of "broken methods and contradiction," "creativity and too much feeling," and "blurred genres" (Restaino 12). I've felt the value of the concords and connections that have ensued when I've put the complicated, messy story of my impairment in conversation with my scholarship. And so I keep writing, in all of my incapacity and academic contingency, and despite my pain, drawing inspiration from the workflows and processes of others in an effort to maintain my productivity.

The following tweet from Chicana feminist scholar Maria E. Cotera is meant as a repudiation of neoliberal productivity, but it might also be read as redefinition of productivity, one very much in keeping with my argument here. In a tweet that, like Osorio's, functions as another public critique of productivity rhetoric, Cotera writes, "I want to be generative–not productive–as a scholar." Cotera's binary

"Embodied Action" as Precarious Process   113

positions collaborative, mutually beneficial generativity in opposition to forms of productivity that operate individually, competitively, even colonially—highlighting the problematic aspects of productivity that Osorio also decries. Following Cotera, I endorse the value of generative writing and scholarship, scholarship that strives for connections with others—for utility, rather than volume. Yet I remain invested in output, and in rhetoric that encourages output, so long as productivity is not pursued simply for its own sake, or without regard for the toll it exacts on the bodymind of the laborer/writer. The productivity that interests me is disabled productivity. My understanding of the value of this kind of output is rooted in the conviction that disabled and debilitated scholars need to identify strategies that can increase our output and efficiency as writers, because when opportunities to think clearly and compose lucidly emerge, they need to be acted upon. Disabled productivity is not about satisfying the demands of systems that perpetuate structural violence. It is about enabling disabled people to generate, *pace* Cotera, meaningful work and, in particular, meaningful writing, in keeping with the affordances and limitations of our bodyminds.

In the remainder of this essay, I explore my recent engagement with three generative approaches to writing, all of which have informed my academically contingent, disabled productivity. The first is Bre Garrett's account of "corporeal rhetoric as embodied pedagogical action," (221) a queer-theory-and-disability-studies-informed approach to writing that I've applied to the yoga practice that increases my flexibility and thereby sustains my writing praxis. The second is a more traditionalist approach, namely Louise DeSalvo's vision of "writing as a way of healing," the phrase that provides the title to her acclaimed writing guidebook. Parts of DeSalvo's argument have informed my disabled productivity, but her work is also important because it has helped me clarify what disabled productivity is not. Jessica Restaino's argument, cited throughout this piece, offers a far more accessible approach to disabled productivity. Her work further illuminates the strengths and limitations of DeSalvo's method.

"CORPOREAL RHETORIC" AS A TOOL FOR TRANSFORMING A WRITING ROUTINE

Sundays are always my favorite writing day. Sunday mornings, I rise at my favorite time, somewhere between six and seven o'clock, and amble into the kitchen to make a smoothie and brew coffee. While waiting for the fog of sleep to lift, I sprawl on the recliner, unlock my phone, and check email, scroll through Twitter, and open the LMS app to check how many of my composition students have submitted their latest writing assignments. Around 8:30, I make my way back to the bedroom and park at my desk. I've tried standing while writing as a solution to back pain—my desk has a crank that raises my workstation—but I can only stand while doing work that is comparatively cognitively undemanding. I can lesson plan while standing. I can read and respond to student work, but I cannot compose in a sustained and focused way. The moment I try to bear down, my temples tighten. My focus blurs. So I sit and hunch forward in my chair and strive to concentrate on the words on my screen, balancing my need to focus with my tolerance for discomfort. If the pain is bad in my back and sit bones, I do my best to pick my way around it while remaining focused on my subject, rising every few minutes for breaks.

In this way, I scrabble forward as a writer, or motor forward on the exalted (and mysterious) days when there isn't pain. But always, on Sundays, I am sustained by the promise of yoga. Sundays, for the last year, a few minutes before 11:00 a.m., my husband and I have hurried from our computers and rearranged our living room, pushing the recliner against one wall and the dinner table against another, shifting the coffee table to the front of the room and propping a laptop upon it. We roll out our yoga mats, change into comfortable clothes, and log in to Zoom—usually right at eleven.

At the start of every session, our teacher reminds us of the importance of emptying our minds and leads us through our warmup breathing exercises. Inevitably, my mind refuses to clear. My thoughts wander. When I first began practicing yoga several years ago, I was frustrated by my inability to control my thoughts. I rebuked myself for dwelling on article revisions and job applications when I was supposed to be joining my energy with that of the universe or meditating on an inspiring word or image. But as I've become more experienced, I've taken ownership of my disabled, imperfect yoga practice. I understand it now as operating to serve the needs of my bodymind. It strengthens my abdominal muscles and back and improves the flexibility of my limbs so that I can spend more time at the computer. It also helps me work through writing problems. That wandering attention during moments of meditation—that's prewriting. Physically *and* intellectually, my yoga practice—what Garrett calls an act of "embodied composing" (222)—is an integral part of my writing process.

For Garrett, "embodied composing acknowledges corporeal engagements in writing" and "examines the bodily affordances available in situated composing practice" (222). Garrett developed her account of embodied composing by reflecting on the composing practices in a feminist theory and disability-studies-informed writing workshop led by the disability studies scholar, Petra Kuppers. In that workshop, Kuppers led participants—many of whom were disabled or contending with chronic pain or fatigue—through a series of individual and collective movement exercises, punctuated by moments of writing. Activities included moments of guided touch and collective vocalization.

Much of Garrett's analysis of the workshop is concerned with how its approach to embodied composing might inform academic writing instruction. She argues that "rhetorical activities such as invention, access, and action can be understood as interrelated embodied knowledges, or ways of knowing, located and made available for use via the situated affordances of particular bodies in collaboration with other situated bodies" (218), a point that affirms my approach to yoga—during yoga, my body, and, to some extent, my thoughts, move in response to the instructor's motions and promptings. Garrett further contends that attention to the embodied, situated dimensions of individual writing processes complicates normative assumptions around composing practices, delivery, accepted modalities, and especially what counts as acceptable collaboration. She notes that in embodied composing, "distinction from one body to another becomes less productive than the assemblage, linkage, and overlap among/between different bodies, and the physical inter-action that results from contact across corporeal differences" (224), a claim that has the potential to open up new forms of composition, inside and outside of the classroom.

Pedagogically, the greatest utility of Garrett's intervention is in its attention to the ways embodiment impinges on the writing process. Student writers—and all writers—should feel welcome to explore the embodied dimensions of their composing processes independently, while always being respectful of the needs and stated boundaries of other bodies. Garrett's arguments about the value of multimodal forms of delivery—including vocalized and performance-based forms—affirm the turn toward multimodality in writing studies (Bowen and Whithaus; Palmeri) and are in concord with Jody Shipka's assertion that writing studies needs to acknowledge the "messy, multimodal, and highly distributed dimensions of writers' processes," including their embodied, situated dimensions (34).

As a contingent, disabled writer seeking to sustain my writerly productivity, I've been most inspired by Garrett's arguments around invention. As she notes, traditionalist accounts of invention tend to "position delivery as a predetermined knowledge, a mere packaging and sending-forth process rather than a process implicated in the means by which one invents" (218). Invention, for me, is deeply "implicated" in my body and is sparked by mobility—by walking, stretching, holding poses, and focused breathing. My thoughts refuse to "settle" as I stretch or meditate, and I've accepted this aspect of my process. Indeed, I've come to rely on the connections that emerge during savasana, the final, supine resting pose in most sessions of yoga. The cultivation of the embodied dimensions of invention is a part of my writing process that is transferable, one I carry with me from genre to genre. Holding poses during yoga is as much a part of my workflow as the adjustments I've made to my word-processing program and my posture while writing. Yoga is, to build on Lockridge and Van Ittersum's definition of workflow, as much of a tool as my chair and the ergonomic arrangement of my desk; it is as much an activity of writing as other forms of prewriting, including reading and outlining.

My yoga practice doesn't merely build the strength and flexibility that enable me to spend hours in the chair. The promise of postwriting yoga also helps me cope with the chronic pain that results from my sympathectomy-warped posture. I hasten to add that yoga is not a panacea for everyone with chronic pain or musculoskeletal issues. But it does help me. The anticipation of my practice sustains me as I try to marshal my thoughts while picking my way around and through humming aporias of pain, just as the practice itself offers relief on those days when it's too hot for me to exercise outside. My reconception of meditation as a space for freewheeling invention, rather than focused mindfulness, offers further confirmation of Garrett's claim that the embodied composing "foregrounds differences as spaces for productivity, locating key moments for invention, or reinvention, through unforeseen circumstances" (225). My approach to yoga is not traditional, but it works quite well for me.

Productivity is not the only aim in an embodied composing practice. There is self-care, self-sustenance, often accomplished, as Garrett and Kuppers remind us, in relation to and through others. But there is also the effort to produce writing, output that can make meaningful scholarly and creative interventions, and, for contingent, disabled scholars like me, hopefully lead to stable employment and to conditions that will facilitate more conducive writing environments, improved workflows, and spaces that better enable the exploration of all phases of the embodied composition process.

FINDING CRIP PRODUCTIVITY BY ESCHEWING ORDER AND EMBRACING HYBRIDITY

I came to Louise DeSalvo's *Writing as a Way of Healing* on the recommendation of one of the members of my femin-queer writing group.

"Embodied Action" as Precarious Process   117

As I began reading, DeSalvo's analysis of writing's relationship to pain and trauma immediately reminded me of Restaino's acclaimed monograph *Surrender: Feminist Rhetoric and Ethics in Love and Illness*. The texts follow different methodologies and reach separate conclusions, but both argue persuasively that writers can benefit by carefully composing toward pain and confusion. Yet as valuable as it is, DeSalvo's narrative ultimately reveals how even works that seek to be inclusive of pain and embodied difference can ultimately marginalize disabled writers. By contrast, Restaino's inclusive, hybrid-friendly approach is a keystone text for disabled productivity in the context of writing studies. But there is still value in DeSalvo's approach; although it isn't consistently open to embodied difference, it does engage thoughtfully, if too belatedly and briefly, with the question of how disabled people might maintain their output as writers.

Part of what makes DeSalvo's book worthy of sustained analysis is that it doesn't promise to create "good" writers. Instead, it offers a program by which writing can be used to produce emotional, and in some cases physical, healing. DeSalvo's approach draws its inspiration from the work of the psychologist James W. Pennebaker, whose studies of expressive writing have led him to conclude that writing clearly about experiences, and especially traumas, is the surest route to emotional recovery. Blending Pennebaker's scholarship with accounts of her own writing life, DeSalvo argues that in order to be "healed" by writing, writers ought to "write regularly in a relaxed way" without "fight[ing] our process or try[ing] to force or control it" (85). She adds that "it is essential that we watch with a relaxed awareness what occurs as we write" (85). And just as writers should approach their processes in a calm and patient fashion, so, too, she argues, should writers be calmly thorough and deliberate in describing their subjects.

DeSalvo's argument about the importance of a regular writing routine is consistent with Boice's behavioralist approach to eliminating writing blockages and increasing productivity. But while Boice is most concerned with helping academics improve their output, DeSalvo's claims about the relationship between content and healing are most readily applicable to her primary genre of memoir. Still, given the recent turn in writing studies toward hybrid methodologies that include autobiography and autoethnography, DeSalvo's approach is worthy of attention.

DeSalvo explains that "a healing narrative renders our experience concretely, authentically, explicitly, and with a richness of detail" (57). It "links feelings to events" (59) and is "a balanced narrative. It uses negative words to describe emotions and feelings in moderation; but it uses positive words, too" (59). "A healing narrative reveals the insights we've achieved from our painful experiences" (60). Implicit in all of this is the assumption that the more legible writing becomes to others, the more healing it will enable. DeSalvo approvingly cites Mary Beth Caschetta's claim that "there's really nothing like a crystal clear *plot* to bring back all the meaning in life" (62). This fixation on clarity and legibility separates DeSalvo's project from Restaino's. Yes, both projects offer strategies for narrating truthfully, but DeSalvo's emphasis on legible, accessible writing as the route to psychic catharsis is at odds with Restaino's openness to the possibility that truth and authenticity might be found in failure, paradox, and darkness.

DeSalvo's breezy account of her writing process and workflow is also largely inaccessible to disabled writers. As a disabled writer, I find DeSalvo's prescriptions sensible, appealing, and impossible, in equal parts. I don't point this out to discredit them. They certainly worked for her; the writing in her guide is warm, detailed, and carefully researched. DeSalvo, who died in 2018, had a process and workflow that produced a rich output. But for many writers, it simply isn't possible to write in a "relaxed way." Yes, it is possible for me to eliminate outward distractions—turn off the television, close the blinds, lock myself away in my room. Still, much as I can try to shut out the outside world, I cannot still or silence my body. I hurt. I twitch. And while I wish I could only write when I feel nourished by the process, often, as a contingent academic, I do not have the luxury of controlling my routine. I write because I have work that needs to be done, and I often end up physically depleted by its completion, falling victim to the neoliberal productivity that I deplore, like Osorio.

Late in her narrative, in the chapter entitled "Writing the Wounded Body," DeSalvo begins to grapple with the complicated relationship between illness, impairment, and narrative. She deftly acknowledges the socially constructed dimensions of the widespread hostility toward embodied difference. She approvingly cites approaches to illness that regard it as "an opportunity . . . as something to contemplate" (181). Under this view, illness "invites the sick person to undertake an internal spiritual and healing journey. It provides the possibility for growth. The sick person is a seeker, a voyager, an explorer" (181). But, she adds, revealing her ongoing preference for the escape from illness through composition. "The word can cure" (181).

DeSalvo's persistent emphasis on cure and healing has little to offer those of us with chronic or permanent impairments. As the disability studies scholar Alison Kafer puts it, the "curative imaginary . . . cannot

"*Embodied Action" as Precarious Process* 119

imagine or comprehend anything other than intervention" (27). Kafer clarifies that it is not necessarily wrong to long for cure or healing (27). Many ill and disabled people long for this—I long for it, just as I try to minimize my pain and incapacity and maximize my productivity. But the curative imaginary that Kafer describes assumes that there is no possible value in disability or impairment. Instead of reflecting on the generative perspectives or insights that might arise out of embodied difference, the curative imaginary supposes that the only possible response is the erasure of that difference. DeSalvo's endorsements of cure are embedded in her narrative's framing. Healing is not a synonym for cure, but it does signify the sort of recovery that is (often) at odds with the embrace of embodied difference and anti-normativity.

DeSalvo's argument that healing can be achieved through balanced, well-proportioned writing is also at odds with femin-queer- and disability-informed approaches to embodied composing. As composition scholars as varied as Restaino, Aneil Rallin, Ian Barnard, and Aja Y. Martinez argue, hybrid, fragmented, and other anti-normative forms can help bear witness to suffering that can't be neatly excised—for example, the ongoing trauma produced by the racism and queerphobia that Rallin, a visibly queer Indian American, is regularly confronted with in the United States. For many marginalized people, life in the hypermediated, racially and economically stratified, disaster-prone twenty-first century is an ongoing, sustained trauma, one that cannot be resolved by any program of writing, however deliberate and careful. Again, this doesn't discredit DeSalvo's program or Pennebacker's research; the approach to writing they advocate for surely works for many people. But it is simply one approach to embodied composing. Other valuable approaches that can produce comfort, if not cure or heal, include emergency manifestos; autoethnographies; projects that center uncertainty and failure, like Restaino's monograph; and hybrid works that blend pedagogy and queer rage, like Rallin's *Dreads and Open Mouths: Living/Teaching/Writing Queerly*.

For disabled writers, DeSalvo's argument is most relevant when it reflects directly on the relationship between writing and disability. In the final chapter of her book, DeSalvo notes that when writers' bodies change, "we can write a new story for ourselves, to discover who we are now" (182). Writing, she adds, "helps us assert our individuality, our authority, our own particular style" (183). Here, finally, is an account of writing that acknowledges the value of emotions like rage and unsatisfied longing that affirms the utility of hybrid and anti-normative approaches to writing. In this chapter, as throughout her guide, DeSalvo draws affectingly on her own experience—in this case, with asthma. She notes the fear she initially felt during the onset of her symptoms and lists a series of despairing quotes from her journal at that time (200). In analyzing the writing she used in her memoir about that experience, DeSalvo details how her embodiment affected her formal choices:

> In writing *Breathless*, I discovered I was no longer writing long sentences punctuated by semicolons, containing lots of dependent clauses. I started writing very short sentences. Then fracturing my sentences. Because my body and my writing were different, my writing was different. Sentences that chopped and sputtered were the only ones I could write. (201)

In addition to highlighting the way embodied difference can produce formal changes, DeSalvo also acknowledges the value of "chaos narratives" (195). She complicates Arthur Frank's account of "restitution narratives" by pointing out that restitution doesn't need to mean simplistically "overcoming," but can signify "living with illness, disease, dying and disfigurement" (198). And she concludes the chapter by acknowledging that for ill and disabled people, writing does not need to be about wholeness or healing but can instead be about "resistance" and "reparation" (205), values that are more consonant with the complexities of persistently traumatic and disabled experiences. But compelling as it is, this chapter feels as if it belongs in a different volume. It describes an entirely different approach to writing than the one that is supposed to lead to healing. Perhaps that is DeSalvo's point. Perhaps, for her, writing the wounded body is, if not an afterthought, then something that is inherently connected to endings, to the conclusion of embodiment. But for disabled writers, our wounds and embodied differences are part of our ongoing realities, and it is up to us to integrate them into our workflows and processes.

It's Sunday now, as I write this. I have pain again in my right sit bone, but yoga is only forty-five minutes away. At 10:58 a.m., I'll scurry to the sitting room and help my husband shift the furniture and create our makeshift yoga studio. When the class begins, I'll sink into the poses and feel release, even as I accept that, for my sympathectomy-scarred body, no permanent healing or cure is coming. I'm okay with that. I'm okay with being a writer who produces comparatively little, especially relative to how much I type. My awareness of the complexity and embodied contingency of every act of writing serves me well as a teacher of composition. I understand the difficulty of writing faced by my students. I feel it every day when I sit down to write. I know, too, the complex and variable relationships that obtain between process and genre. The process of every writer is unique, just as the process varies from genre to genre.

"Embodied Action" as Precarious Process   121

One of my commitments as a teacher of first-year writing is to encourage my students to reflect critically on their processes and on the genres they feel the most drawn to. In this way, I hope to help them find their way toward writing practices that are good matches for their embodied literacies. This commitment is drawn from my scholarship in disability studies. Disabled writers and scholars know that we need to create customized, individualized processes and workflows so that our bodies can best sustain the output required of us as academics. This productivity is all the more necessary for those of us who are contingent.

I still don't know if I'll ever find a permanent academic home. In the meantime, I will keep writing, drawing strength from the femin-queer theory and disability studies scholarship that helps me maintain the workload required of me to remain viable as a contingent scholar and teacher. What I do know is that in a few minutes, I'll settle onto my mat and close my eyes, and I'll think about this article while my yoga teacher encourages me to "turn my third eye to the universal light," and I will do so affirmed by Garrett's account of embodied composing. When my routine is finished, I'll have lunch. Perhaps I'll nap—Osorio would be pleased. Then maybe I'll find my way back to my desk. Or, if I'm feeling sore, I'll take the afternoon off and read the novel on my bedside table, or maybe dip back into Ian Barnard's *Upsetting Composition Commonplaces*.

As I move—and hunch—forward as a teacher and scholar, I'll keep drawing inspiration from new guides, new approaches, new programs for writing. Some, like DeSalvo's, will be incomplete (at least for me), but I may still be able to learn from them, as I learned from DeSalvo about process, about workflow, and, in places, about resistant, defiant embodied writing (and biscotti, DeSalvo's favorite snack while writing). And all the while, I'll keep trying to improve my writing workflow and process with the aim of improving my disabled productivity, in order to secure a permanent job and produce the kind of hybrid writing that I, like Restaino, find sustaining, professionally and personally.

NOTE

1.   I've drawn on several tweets in this article because Twitter is an increasingly important genre system for sharing research and academic ideas. Klar et al. point out that part of the appeal of Twitter is that it provides scholars with additional opportunities to actively promote their work and ideas. They position social media in opposition to more traditional, passive forms of publication, arguing that on social media, "it is the researcher who initiates communication with the audience. The possibility that scholars can push their research out, rather than hope that it is pulled in, holds the potential for scholars to draw wide attention to their research" (2).

WORKS CITED

Barnard, Ian. *Upsetting Composition Commonplaces*. Utah State UP, 2014.

Boice, Robert. "Increasing the Productivity of 'Blocked' Academics." *Behaviour Research and Therapy*, vol. 20, no. 3, 1982, pp. 197–207. https://doi.org/10.1016/0005-7967(82)90138-3.

Bowen, Tracey, and Carl Whithaus. *Multimodal Literacy and Emerging Genres*. U of Pittsburgh P, 2013.

Campbell, Ollie. "Bashers and Swoopers: How the Tools We Use for Writing are Letting Us Down." *Medium*, 3 July 2016, https://medium.com/@oliebol/bashers-swoopers-257e9f27fb33.

Cedillo, Christine V. "What Does It Mean to Move?: Race, Disability, and Critical Embodiment Pedagogy." *Composition Forum*, vol. 39, 2018. https://eric.ed.gov/?id=EJ1188979.

Cotera, Maria E [@MECotera]. "I want to be generative—not productive—as a scholar." *Twitter*, 2 May 2021, 8:06 a.m., https://twitter.com/MECotera/status/1388872525682290691.

DeSalvo, Louise. *Writing as a Way of Healing: How Telling Our Stories Transforms Our Lives*. Beacon Press, 2000.

Edelman, Lee. *No Future: Queer Theory and the Death Drive*. Duke UP, 2004.

Freeman, Elizabeth. *Time Binds: Queer Temporalities, Queer Histories*. Duke UP, 2010.

Garrett, Bre. "Corporeal Rhetoric as Embodied Action: Composing in/through Bodily Motion." *Essays in Honor of Sharon Crowley*, edited by Andrea Alden et al., UP of Colorado, Utah State UP, 2019, pp. 210–27.

Gladwell, Malcolm. *Outliers*. Little, Brown, 2008.

Halberstam, Jack. *The Queer Art of Failure*. Duke UP, 2011.

Kafer, Alison. *Feminist, Queer, Crip*. Indiana UP, 2013.

Klar, Samara, et al. "Using Social Media to Promote Academic Research: Identifying the Benefits of Twitter for Sharing Academic Work." *PLOS One*, vol. 15, no. 4, 2020. https://doi.org/10.1371/journal.pone.0229446.

Konrad, Annika. "Access Fatigue: The Rhetorical Work of Disability in Everyday Life." *College English*, vol. 83, no. 3, 2021, pp. 179–99.

Lockridge, Tim, and Derek Van Ittersum. *Writing Workflows: Beyond Word Processing*. E-book, U of Michigan P, 2020. https://doi.org/10.3998/mpub.11657120.

Martinez, Aja Y. *Counterstory: The Rhetoric and Writing of Critical Race Theory*. National Council of Teachers of English, 2020.

McRuer, Robert. *Crip Theory: Cultural Signs of Queerness and Disability*. New York UP, 2006.

Miller, Elisabeth L. "Literate Misfitting: Disability Theory and a Sociomaterial Approach to Literacy." *College English*, vol. 79, no. 1, 2016, pp. 34–56.

Osorio, Ruth [@rorhetorician]. "productivity rhetoric is racist, ableist, sexist, queerphobic, settler, capitalist bullshit! you know what isn't? NAPPING! napping is great! I want to see more people brag about the naps they took! If you need someone to give you permission to nap today, I can be that person!" *Twitter*, 12 Apr. 2021, 11:01 a.m., https://twitter.com/rorhetorician/status/1381668713456312322.

Palmeri, Jason. *Remixing Composition: A History of Multimodal Writing Pedagogy*. National Council of Teachers of English, 2012.

Piepzna-Samarasinha, Leah Lakshmi. *Care Work: Dreaming Disability Justice*. Arsenal Pulp Press, 2018.

Price, Margaret. *Mad at School: Rhetorics of Mental Disability and Academic Life*. U of Michigan P, 2011.

Rallin, Aneil. *Dreads and Open Mouths: Living/Teaching/Writing Queerly*. Litwin Books, 2019.

Resnick, Brian. "The '10,000-hour rule' was debunked again. That's a relief." *Vox*, 23 Aug. 2019. https://www.vox.com/science-and-health/2019/8/23/20828597/the-10000-hour-rule-debunked.

Restaino, Jessica. *Surrender: Feminist Rhetoric and Ethics in Love and Illness.* Southern Illinois UP, 2019.

Shipka, Jody. *Toward a Composition Made Whole.* U of Pittsburgh P, 2011.

Warner, Mark. *The Trouble with Normal: Sex, Politics, and the Ethics of Queer Life.* Harvard UP, 1999.

Wendell, Susan. *The Rejected Body: Feminist Philosophical Reflections on Disability.* Routledge, 1996.

Wood, Tara. "Cripping Time in the College Composition Classroom." *College Composition and Communication,* vol. 69, no. 2, 2017, pp. 260–86.

8

SHOWING UP
Una Manera sobre Writing Process

Zakery R. Muñoz

Tags: identity, critique, embodiment

This is me showing up. This is what I tell myself each day when I write. I'll even write it first before anything else. It's my ritual, my prayer. I go through this writing ceremony because I believe that showing up to the work is what it takes. By *work* I mean writing and by *what it takes* I mean what is necessary to successfully participate in the field of rhetoric and writing studies (RWS). I offer this piece from a place of vulnerability, as a graduate student, as a Burqueño—a dual identity of conqueror and (un)conquered. This chapter offers a narrative on my *manera* (mah-neh-dah), my *way* or manner of writing and writing process. I write from the perspective of "out here," as in *we out here*, from the margins, not quite accepted into the full ethos of RWS but on the fringe, a pre-dissertation PhD student on the *way*, just trying to survive. Despite the many helpful and varied texts on the lives, writing, and writing process from the professoriate (Boice "Contingency," "Professors"; Villanueva; Tulley), less attention has been paid to the nuanced histories of graduate students on the *way* to finding a home in the field (Sword, *Air and Light*, "Writing"; Brooks-Gillies et al.; Madden and Eodice; Prior; Prior and Shipka; Sullivan; Micciche with Carr). This chapter aims to write while in the process—not as a reflection from the gaze of tenure or "having made it." Instead, I interrogate my manera now and my history as a first-generation college student and five-time dropout. I use manera as a methodology, functioning in two ways: process and craft; the two, for me, inseparable. My story interrogates popular writing advice, *los consejos,* (e.g., *stay true to yourself, write what you know, make time to write, writing is hard*), furthering our conversations on writing processes while attending to the manera of writing and the embodied labor involved.

RWS has a long history of discussing writing and writing processes. We know that writing processes are complex and distinct. We know that

https://doi.org/10.7330/9781646424870.c008

writing is situated across time and place and affective embodied experiences. Yet I contend and will develop further that there is more we can do with process. There must be. The book that inspired this chapter, *How Writing Faculty Write* by Christine Tulley, models *Paris Review*'s "Writers at Work" interviews, sharing dialogues from "fifteen rhetoric and composition faculty with significant publications or growing influence in the field about their writing process" (8). Tulley's book, as the title implies, seeks to understand how writing faculty write, what their processes look and feel like, what consejos are followed and valued among the professoriate to get a "composite picture" of some of the leading members of our field (9). The patterns Tulley identified across the interviews represent typical writing advice familiar to most scholars: the professoriate recognizes things like the difficulty of the writing processes, persistence, process, *and* product. The interviewees "think rhetorically" about process and their writing, "they use invention strategies that foreground discovery and organization" (14), and they work on a variety of timetables but "small writing times" are predominant (26). This book shows us many representations of the field, offering us distinct insight into the writing lives of our faculty. Still, the question that has haunted me throughout graduate school remains: how *do* writing faculty write?

In *Writing Workflows: Beyond Word Processing*, Tim Lockridge and Derek Van Ittersum respond to calls for a "return to empirical research into writing processes" (78). Through the lens of *workflow*, they seek to "examine contemporary writing processes without limiting that inquiry to activity in the head or to the contexts alone." "Through a focus on workflows . . . [they] demonstrate the varying ways different applications mediate writing," how our work is both contained-in and contains, but not limited to, writing software and technology (27). In this chapter I hope to acknowledge this move toward considering our writing processes as a site for critical examination. I argue that this ethic needs to be embodied in the graduate writing seminar, that we might take better care in supporting our graduate students and preparing them for the embodied labor of the discipline. I will do this through narrative; being my manera; and offering, for whatever it's worth, some consejos of my own.

I must comment that my text demonstrates a certain paradox, an incongruity, that comes with simultaneously belonging and not belonging, identifying as a dropout and as an emerging scholar, being on the *way* and having made it. I will not apologize if this confuses or invokes an explicative query, for "I will not always give you an experience about

126   ZAKERY R. MUÑOZ

myself then interpret that experience or make sense of it for you" (Inoue 5). Gloria Anzaldúa famously describes this identity paradox in *Borderlands: La Frontera* as the "new *mestiza*," the "consciousness of the Borderlands" (99). This consciousness is inherently incongruous as an identity "plagued by psychic restlessness" as a consequence "from the clash of voices [that] results in mental and emotional states of perplexity" (100). While Anzaldúa conceptualizes the *mestiza* identity as gendered, this consciousness permeates bodies across the borderlands, across my home, at the fringe. This is what it means to be Burqueño and what the Burqueño voice looks and feels like. Instead of resisting the paradoxical moments in my chapter, I write *into* them through storytelling, my method/ology, my manera. My paradox, in part, is a consequence of writing *on the way*, not a post-graduate-school reflection. I invite you, with me, to simultaneously hold this friction, this consciousness, separate and together; I invite you to show up with me.

FIVE-TIME DROPOUT

I've dropped out of school five times—three times in high school and twice in college. At least by my count, it's hard to be sure (it wasn't really something I was counting while I was doing it). One thing is certain, I never graduated high school. My GED is framed next to my MA in my office. Early in my graduate studies at the University of New Mexico (UNM), I might have felt what is frequently described as imposter syndrome. Maybe I wasn't sure I belonged in graduate school, in RWS, that I was faking it until I made it, as they say. This wasn't an abstracted feeling. I had measurable data pointing to why I didn't belong—my GPA wasn't near the minimum to even apply to graduate school. An algorithm could have easily sorted me out of the admission process as "not meeting the minimum requirements for consideration." However, I didn't describe myself as an imposter then and I still don't. After all, the department of English, where RWS was housed at UNM, is situated on "the traditional homelands of the Pueblo of Sandia" where "the original peoples of New Mexico—Pueblo, [Diné], and Apache—since time immemorial, have deep connections to the land" ("Indigenous Peoples'"). If anything, the institution is an imposter to the Indigenous land upon which it sits. I write now from Syracuse, the ancestral lands of the Onondaga Nation, the Central Fire, the Wampum Keepers, who have lived here since time immemorial.

I use this language, *imposter*, to help articulate my feeling of dissociation within RWS. I want to be clear that I didn't feel dissociated from the land and the concrete over that land that is UNM. It is my home; it will always be home. From where I stood, there was not a large representation of *mi gente* (my people) in the discipline of RWS; prose and craft (la manera) received little attention, and I struggled on both fronts: with my inherited identity and my constructed identity, as a Burqueño and a writer who labored over my craft for its own sake. My meaning of the word "writing" seemed incongruous with how writing was/is discussed in the field. It seemed to me that the craft of writing took a backseat to rigor, academic chops, or showing that the homework had been done, the research. The more citations, the better, it seems. But I know and argue there are a lot of ways to persuade, storytelling and narrative being my manera. I imagine some first-generation college students might feel that their maneras tend to go against the grain of what is expected. Students like me. Especially when we are constantly being reminded of this position (sorry if I'm doing it here), first-generation—I even have a shirt that says, "first generation proud," the only free, branded merchandise I've received.

David Russell points out that "disciplines never acquired a conscious knowledge of the rhetorical conventions they used daily and expected their students to use" (17). In other words, this "[un]conscious knowledge" tacitly haunts the expectations of our discourse. And when not explicitly acknowledged, taught, and made seen, this knowledge risks further marginalizing bodies with no predisposition to these expectations. Bodies like mine. Laura R. Micciche with Allison Carr in "Toward Graduate-Level Writing Instruction" remind us that "absent direct instruction, graduate education in English assumes that students learn how to write critically through repeated exposure and an osmosis-like process" (485). I stand by this claim and echo it throughout this chapter. While I know I'm a good (enough) writer, I might not write or participate in a way that is typified, and RWS might say, "That's a good thing." I say, "We'll see." To me, the pleasure of storytelling, the craft, came first—still does. Story is where I'm most comfortable, but I still feel I'm taking great risks every time I do so. This is where the first consejo comes under interrogation, *be true to yourself.*

BE TRUE TO YOURSELF

At least since the 1970s, RWS has been invested in linguistic justice practices in undergraduate writing instruction (see CCCC). In a way, RWS is continually telling students to *stay true* to themselves, especially in first year composition (FYC). I think about this a lot in my writing classroom.

But it isn't enough, *not good enough*, to just think about or even discuss language rights in the classroom. It's an ethic that must be embodied through anti-racist methodologies, through meeting the needs of the students, even if that expressed need is frequently *to be a better writer*. I teach my students to think deeply about how they use language, line by line, as it exists in their minds and reveals itself on the page, as we all do (I hope). I want them to not just feel like their voice has value but to learn how to use their voice in spaces and genres where writing might not be comfortable, to take risks, to understand convention but wander when they can. This is hard work—it demands that we sit together in our difference; it demands that we acknowledge, as Stephanie Kerschbaum urges, "the way categories [of difference] help us negotiate situations while holding those category identifications open for new interpretation and understanding" (92). I teach them to take great care of their words, to offer language that is persuasive and that inspires wonder. We need to take our own consejos and teach our graduate students that their manera matters, too.

Writing this chapter inspired me to design a national study that surveys and interviews graduate students and professors in writing studies, broadly conceived, about their maneras of writing. The study is ongoing; however, the preliminary results show that seventy-one percent of the participants were not required to take a course that focused explicitly on their development as a writer. These early results suggest that we have not made graduate education attentive to the different processes in which graduate writers compose. I write this as someone who has received helpful feedback one-on-one with faculty, yet in the space of the graduate seminar, other writing-related tasks are prioritized over individual craft and writing processes. If writing is a mandatory labor as a scholar, then graduate writing pedagogy needs to be compulsory in graduate curriculum. Otherwise, those privileged with the predisposition of academic rigor rise while the rest of us are left clueless on where to even begin—we become marginalized even further.

I'm writing this now as a graduate student because I don't want to lose sight of where I came from and the many challenges I face every day—we out here. I write now about being dissociated with the field of RWS because it was never imagined for people like me, people who can't spell, who can't grammar, who have troubled tenses because our "tongues are wild," who are dropouts. I don't even feel confident now telling this story because it has been *told so many times before*, as they say. I've been told, to my face, that my "story is nothing new," to "stay in my lane," and that I should read and cite scholars *like* me who *may* have had similar experiences to demonstrate what I already know—a sincere thank you to Victor Villanueva, Felipe Gonzalez, Manuel, Maria, Genevieve García de Mueller, Octaviano Larrazolo, Aja Y. Martinez, Eduardo Lalo, Mario Montoya, Gloria Anzaldúa, Tori Cárdenas, Ralph Cintron, Sylvestre Muñoz, we out here. I was asked to cite things I knew via phronesis like the histories I grew up with and experienced, being born and raised in New Mexico (see scholarship on settler colonialism: Patrick Wolfe, Aimee Carrillo Rowe, Eve Tuck, Andrea Riley-Mukavetz, Malea D. Powell, thank you all). My deliberate use of story was consistently deleted as not scholarly or corrected as grammar mistakes (I can grammar now, look at me). I was constantly asked to remove bits of craft, my narrative, from my work. *Qué feo*, I know. Be sure, this isn't a literacy narrative. If you cite this text, please don't call it a literacy narrative. Please don't call it "blended" or "mixed" scholarship, either—these are settler terms. I am not "blended" or "mixed," neither is my manera. I'm making meaning here the only way I know how.

I hope I am making clear this complication with *stay true to myself* as writing advice. Is my *way* valued or not? Time will tell as my compositions sleep in wait for a chance at publication and acceptance in the field of RWS. While at odds with my manera, craft, and academic expectations, I do feel gentle nudges of encouragement. I mean, I am here with you now, and through this relationship between reader and writer we together are showing up to each other. Keep an eye on me.

MANERA AS METHODOLOGY

Consider this metaphor: We are teaching someone how to drive a car. Should we tell them to drive how they know? Should we tell them to think rhetorically about driving? Should we tell them to make time to drive? Should we tell them driving is hard? Should we show them a lot of different kinds of cars? Or should we first demonstrate how to drive, show them all the nuances, model driving, and then let them get behind the wheel for a try? The action of driving the car is arguably the most important part of the process. It is this part, the actual driving part, of the manera where we might further our discussions about writing and writing processes.

Micciche and Carr remind us how "it's no secret that graduate students (much like faculty) regularly encounter academic writing as an emotionally fraught, privately experienced hardship" (479). In their piece on writing processes, they argue for more intervention into graduate writing instruction at the level of "critical writing workshops."

130   ZAKERY R. MUÑOZ

In other words, Micciche historicized, argued for, and created a system-atized place to make the craft of graduate writing a priority (thank you, Micciche and Carr). I hope to continue this argumentative throughline, similarly avoiding a structuralist or current traditionalist *way* that might presume the professoriate holding a skeleton key, a one-size-fits-all to the academic writing process. There is no singular *way* to write, I think we all might agree, no monolithic process, no step-by-step DIY *way* of becoming a professor of writing, and I like to think my story embodies this ethic—this is part of why I share. But this doesn't change the real-ity that we all must write; this doesn't change the reality that structures of writing exist in RWS, structures practiced by faculty in popular texts, structures that are overlooked in pedagogy because we haven't come to terms with the moves that have been typified in our processes or they have been so engrained in how we do things that these moves are assumed to be learned through exposure, like writing an organized theoretical framework, writing compelling anecdotes from available data, writing an argumentative throughline, writing a grounding meta-phor, to name a few. Micciche writes about, as a graduate student, strug-gling to unpack terminology, for not knowing "*how* to do so" (emphasis in original; 478). These examples aren't exhaustive; I'm simply calling attention to some of the expectations we have for our texts. And since we have these expectations for our texts, I maintain that they need to be explicitly taught in graduate courses—not in office hours but during our time in the classroom, together.

To make clear what I mean when I say craft, I will untangle writing processes into distinct actions: "the craft of writing" and "what sur-rounds writing." Following Prior and Shipka, I recognize that "literate activity is about nothing less than ways of being in the world," and we cannot discount this aspect of literate activity (181). I suggest, however, that we further examine what happens during our "literate activity"—what happens when we write. I want to focus on the type of advice being offered by Tulley and interviewees in her book that tend to focus on "what surrounds writing," the kind of consejo frequently heard by graduate students like myself. "What surrounds writing" is different from inscribing words: it is everything besides the inscription of words. "The craft of writing," for the purposes of this framework, is any *way* or manner a writer might inscribe; where they start writing, how they form sentences, when and how they decide to quote research, when they inscribe claims, and so on. It is important to note that this separation between "the craft of writing" and "what surrounds writing" is artifice because they never exist separately, as all our writing is situated in our

Showing Up   131

embodied experience. Again, these two *ways* of theorizing writing process are not discrete, they are inseparable, and largely depend on each other, as Tulley and others have suggested. Our experiences as humans shape how we show up to our writing, as thoroughly documented in research like that of Prior, Prior and Shipka, and Tulley. The rest of this chapter will consider how we might continue this important insight into our processes with an explicit focus on "the craft of writing." I invite my reader to consider with me how these *ways* are separate and entangled through my framework of manera.

Manera directly translates to *way*. Not to be confused with *camino*, manera is a method or manner of doing something. Consider the sentence, "We all write a certain *way*" or "Nosotros todos escribimos de cierta *manera.*" Manera is not a physical road or path but an abstraction of how things come to be done, the process. I avoid using camino because there is no one road—there is only *way*. Manera as methodology considers process to be literate practices that include craft along with other literate practices and histories that surround writing. Further, manera considers how our words sound and appear off and on the page, how we embody and make seen our writing through our craft. Manera starts with craft; process is entangled with craft. While craft exists in what surrounds writing, in conversations with colleagues (thank you, everyone), in mental notes, marginalia, and everything else done in preparation to show up to the writing space, craft is also embodied through the labor of writing. I advocate for continued pedagogy on this labor for graduate students. Graduate students, like me, find it hard to even begin writing because this manera, "the craft of writing," is often hidden and unseen. How do scholars sit down and draft? How do they move words about the page? How do they type/write out frameworks? How many screens are they working with? How do they navigate the dimensions of windows, tabs, pdfs, paper articles, books, and citations? How do they construct sentences? When do they cite? How do they do *this* labor?

Mainstream graduate course structures, despite well-meaning attempts, risk conditioning *bad writing habits*—binge writing, marathon writing, unread citations, procrastination—or habits that are not easily transferable to the professoriate (Tulley), and the consejos deployed to graduate students offer little insight on manera. Manera is largely trained in coursework. We study texts in class so that we might one day write and be accepted. The labor and "the craft of writing" seems contained to a black box from which projects and drafts emerge. How writing faculty write is only witnessed in its completed form(s). I encourage my reader to consider new graduate writing activities and graduate

ZAKERY R. MUÑOZ

seminar structures, *ways* that make real the consejos that we tell ourselves and our students.

MANERA STARTS WITH CRAFT

I didn't even know what was happening at first, why I was constantly
dropping out. I wasn't a troublemaker—the world frightened me. But
I was a bad student. In middle school I slept on the floor during class,
only getting up when called upon (thank you, Ben, for letting me sleep).
My family said I was unchallenged, the school said I was lazy, but I had
a hard time comprehending anything we were assigned to read or write
about. After my first eye exam, my family realized I couldn't see and
maybe glasses would help me. Glasses helped me *see* the board, but they
didn't help me *see* much of anything. My language didn't seem to work
right either. Not a lot has changed, I'm still a bad student (those who
know me might disagree). In undergrad, I remember my class, Hispanic
Frontiers, with Professor Samuel Truett. I sat front and center, eager to
learn about *why bro* I am the way I am. I fell asleep every class. Despite
struggling as a student, I've always felt compelled to write and read. I
was told that I wouldn't amount to much of anything if I didn't learn to
read and write properly, that I wouldn't get a job, that girls wouldn't be
interested in me because I was lazy—all these problematic and untrue.
My family and I were both sold on the value of literacy. Young Zakery saw
serious stakes for learning to write and read well. At home, I hung big
pieces of glass in my bedroom and used an Expo marker to outline plots
for novels, using writing to make sense out of what I was experiencing in
my life and in the classroom. I was being assimilated. I was raised as an
English speaker in a Spanish-speaking household. The complexities of
language possess(ed) me. I wanted to be a writer and write through my
plight. Literacy both pulled me in, tantalizing me with perceived opportunity, and pushed me away, this story, after all, is *nothing new.*

These questions of language and assimilation were unclear and
unseen to me growing up. Now I have the language to describe my
plight with language. I was persuaded by the literacy myth (Graff; Graff
and Duffy). "Defined broadly, the literacy myth is the abiding belief
that merely acquiring literacy guarantees economic prosperity," and this
myth was embodied by both my family and me as they taught me English
(Harker 14). They said, "Go to school if you want a good job, *mijo*"—if
you see me around, ask me about the concrete story (like cement, not
a metaphor). They spoke English to me because they thought it was
correct, and they spoke Spanish to each other for the same reason. As

Showing Up   133

a result, I ended up between the two languages, with enough English to communicate basic needs but not enough to write and persuade—I had to find this skill set on my own, scouring novels for meaning, looking for representations of myself, highlighting quotes that neared my truth, tattooing them on my body that I might never forget. Language to my *Umpa* (grandfather) was only as good as any tool in his belt, and I realized this on the day I pointed to a windmill and asked him to say it in Spanish and he said, "Windmill."

> And I said, "En Español, Umpa."
> And he said, "Windmill."
> And I said, "You're saying *windmill* en Inglés, ese."
> "Of course, I am, mijo," he said, "I wouldn't call it anything in Spanish. I have no reason to talk Spanish right now."

He understood language in a profoundly different *way* than me, as a tool to be deployed when needed but without creative expression, or so it seemed. He didn't need to move his words around for rhetorical effect. This was his *way* of survival; this was his response to the plight of conquest, immigration, assimilation. He understood language on the level of utility, as a means to an end, not as a site for investigation. This tooling or taming, this disciplining, of language, caused me a great deal of internal strife. I embodied literacy as being a *way* to make it, and I committed my life to reading and writing, fiction at first, but now I'm here making meaning on the fringes of RWS. We out here, and I feel all parts of my life are incongruent. Literacy has offered me a *way*, but I won't say that it is *the way*, just one, even if I didn't feel it growing up. Umpa was a carpenter, my father a cashier. No one in my family had gone to college before I did, just me, *solamente*; I'm alone. Literacy felt like una manera out of the working class, but the continued ends to my literacy story have yet to be realized. As I've said, we'll see.

I've always been a storyteller, but I have been continually haunted by literacy—from conquest—haunted from dropping out. It is incredibly challenging for me to even begin writing, as a kid, as an undergrad, as a graduate in RWS. *Pobrecito*, I know. And for these reasons, I've always felt a strong internal resistance to completing anything. It is clear to me now that manera is entangled with craft. When the *way* a student writes isn't valued, manera suffers and people drop out, become marginalized, feel imposturous, aggregate anger, struggle to start and finish any writing. How can we show up to a place where we are unheard and unseen? Why should we?

I share anecdotes from my dropout story because this is part of my identity that is now unseen, something vulnerable that I carry around, even joke about—feel free to joke about it with me. Dropping out so many times and still continuing the path to literacy has shown me that writing and writing processes are all about showing up to writing. Part of showing up is embodying my manera and being witnessed on the page. The only reason I'm writing this now is because I relentlessly continue to show up. Call it perseverance—I call it tolerance, survival, resistance, plight. This is what it means to be a Burqueño, inheriting trauma from settler colonialism. It needn't be this *way*. Manera can be nourished, interrogated, and seen. Manera can be precious.

THE FIFTEEN-FOOTER

I finished writing my master's portfolio and defense during the winter of 2019–2020, just before the COVID-19 pandemic aggressively brought our lives to a standstill. I carried around a fifteen-foot extension cord with me so I could plug in my laptop just about anywhere. I worked everywhere, at the coffee shop Michael Thomas, at Blake's Lotaburger, at the Frontier Restaurant, out on the curb, never out of reach from an outlet with my extension cord. Colleagues plugged in with me, and we sat out there and wrote together. This is something we lost during the pandemic. I haven't felt comfortable showing up to work in a public place since, not even with my trusty extension cord, not even with my trusty booster shots. My work suffered. It suffered even though there was less time transitioning between the parts of my day, everything on Zoom. We didn't have to get fully dressed or be ready for our days. All we had to do was turn on the computer, pop in and out of meetings and classes, from the *comfort* of our homes. Manera and accessibility were challenged during the most extreme times of isolation and lockdowns.

However, in a lot of ways I was privileged in my working life—my pay wasn't dramatically affected (thank you, Syracuse). I worked in public places before the pandemic because there were fewer things distracting my attention away from the work, my writing. I was putting my body out there, in the public spaces of Albuquerque, to make the writing process less isolating. Not all of us can do this; we all have our embodied *ways*. I now realize how important this embodied experience was to my manera and my identity. It didn't make sense to me, logically, that I gained so much time at home during the pandemic but was unable to stay moti-vated to produce a thing. This is where I place the second consejo, *make time to write*. Being uninspired and unmotivated during the pandemic made me realize that the writing process isn't just an element of hav-ing *time to write*, and this is supported by Tulley when she mentions that "writing in small moments during the day (even in five minutes) is the norm for most interviewees" (22). Five minutes is hardly enough time to do anything. Somehow our prominent scholars in RWS, people with the ethos to dispense consejos, manage to produce significant bodies of work in the tiniest corners of time. How? These maneras seem to go directly against Boice's (in)famous research that urges us to commit portions of our day to writing, using his methodology to carve out blocks of time during our days to sit down and write. This troubles me as a graduate student. When and how am I supposed to write? In small increments, sprints, forcibly through large blocks of time, or worse, *whatever works best for me?* We all must work in and with whatever is best for our bodies, and in this *way*, we do *whatever works best for us.* However, once we have that five minutes, if the craft of our writing was never nourished, how exactly are we supposed to make use of that precious time? It's no surprise that a seasoned faculty member might write whenever time allows, their *way* has revealed to them some typified expectations of the field. I argue that now is the time we make this knowledge compulsory pedagogy, evidenced by degree requirements, course offerings, and writing activities.

MAKING TIME TO WRITE

Making time to write is a frequent concern most writers and scholars have. The reasons why we don't have time to write are inexhaustible, at various levels of our careers come with different kinds of responsibilities that distract from writing. One thing remains constant for all scholars—we all need time to write. Writing is our job, whether we are crafting, researching, teaching, or advocating for writing, our responsibility as members of RWS is to take good care of writing. Tulley writes how many new faculty members, making the transition from student to faculty, "realize that open blocks of writing time they may have had as students no longer exist and/or binge writing episodes to get dissertation chapters completed won't function in a new faculty position" (28). The interviewees have several ways of coping with the lack of time, as we all do. Language like "stealing" parts of the day to write is common, or not having the "leisure" of long days to write, as Selfe comments, "I mean, none of us anymore have long, leisurely, uninterrupted days to write," and so she commits her writing to "small little moments of the day" (35). This language fascinates me because I understand writing to be a full-bodied experience and a large part of the job I signed up for. It is my job to show up to these days of writing. I do not "steal" time from other responsibilities to write, other things "steal" my writing time. These interviews show a clear discrepancy between what we do as graduate students and what we are expected to do as faculty. This discrepancy shows even as we complete coursework. The life of the faculty member is largely a mystery to me. After reading Tulley's book (which, I should mention, I enjoyed; thank you, Tulley), I'm wondering how to attend to manera and "the craft of writing." In short, I respectfully ask, are we training/preparing our graduate students to write or otherwise function as faculty members? What are the consequences if we are not? If new writing faculty are finding that their training is insufficient for the job, I would say no, no we are not being appropriately trained. And I think a large reason why is because "the craft of writing," the kind of writing we need to be doing on the job, is tacit, assumed to be learned through exposure to enough texts and enough *ways*.

I used to sit outside with my Nana and count cars. We each had a color, and we'd count how many cars of that color drove by. Whoever counted the most cars won. It's funny to think about writing this way, showing lots of ways to write, different kinds of writing zooming by. It's funny to think that I learned anything about driving by watching all those cars drive by me. It's funny to think that I learn anything about writing just by being exposed to writing. If we all need to *make time to write*, then we need to make it a priority in the graduate seminar. Teach me to write in the small corners of my day. Teach me how to add one sentence to the next, how to string them along, how to guide the reader through, how to be kind to them that they might not stumble, and, if they do, teach me how to make it intentional. Teach me to think of each sentence as precious, respecting and nurturing it as it grows, help it find its form, find what it's trying to do, and let it.

My admittance into Syracuse was extraordinary. I remember being in my office at UNM, sort of stuck in there for the day and getting a phone call from Brice Nordquist and an invitation to attend this private university in New York. And I said, "Who, me?" *Mira, que* fancy, I know. My family and friends still imagine me taking the subway to classes. They, like me before I moved, have no concept of New York as a state, just an enormous city. I imagine most people in New York have no concept of New Mexico as a state, just an enormous country. I graciously accepted the invitation, eager to see the literacy myth to the end. I had no idea how hard it would be to leave Albuquerque, a first-generation college student, the first Muñoz to leave home. I had no idea how hard it would be to move on from all this during the pandemic. See my home with me: a determined roadrunner, full speed through the yucca, stops and sees, tail at full mast, then back at it, *beep beep*. What do you see? All I see is chiles roasting outside of Smith's, an old, blind Chicano ringing a bell, selling tamales out of a cooler, "*tamale tamale tamale*." All I see are hot air balloons, like lazy castles in the sky. All I see is the Sandias, still setting pink, have been for an eternity. I see *all sick*. All I see is conquest, streets named after conqueror, conquered, unconquered and still resisting conquest, every day. I see her out there in the street, a ghost. She's haunting. She's out there saying *all this land is stolen*. I see everything, *ese*. I see everything.

When it was announced that I was the incoming fellow at Syracuse, I cried. I would be released from two years of my teaching duties. What this means is Syracuse, for some reason (I try not to think about it), is buying me *time to write*. This is a privilege, I know. Now I have double the time, double and double it again—double double. Still, I struggle to write.

REIMAGINING THE GRADUATE SEMINAR

It's easy for me to imagine whole projects; like, the entire thing. For example, I imagined a project about writing processes. I'd name the writing process manera. I'd show that manera has multiple parts, that the field of RWS has given critical attention to "what surrounds writing," that I can make an offering to this research concerning "the craft of writing." How am I doing? I'd end by offering some consejos of my own. I try to then summarize my projects in one sentence; I call it a one-liner—here's mine: the craft of writing is rarely compulsory pedagogy in graduate school, and students' maneras suffer the consequences. I don't take full responsibility for my inability to see projects in parts rather than *complete* wholes. I suspect most graduate students are only presented with entire texts to study, never manera, the *way* of making. Even with our classmates in coursework, sharing drafts and doing peer review, we don't see the true growth of a document. We hear consejos. We may see a draft, even two, but we emerge from our *binges* with (in)complete works, and that's that. What I'm trying to say is we witness projects not growing line by line but exponentially. But writing happens on the page line by line. What I am trying to say is our *way*, our maneras, are complete mysteries because we don't write together. The projects just emerge from a black box and are shared. I believe the purpose of scholarship like Tulley's is to shed some light on the writing process. I heard voices, from scholars I respect a great deal (thank you, Malea Powell, Jacqueline Jones Royster). I learned a lot about how they imagined showing up to the work. At times I felt solidarity, even, and maybe that was the point. The major difference between what I was looking for and what is presented is the *how*—everything that surrounds their writing is different from their craft of writing. How do we write a publishable (hopefully readable) text? The one time I was exposed to pedagogy on craft, how to use my manera and translate it into (scholarly) words on the page, was in an off-brand, hybrid under/graduate, cross-listed, pure elective course titled Analyzing Prose by Jerome Shea (thanks, Shea, we out here). I argue that we need more classes like this; at least, we need to embody this ethic across coursework. If we take the many consejos on writing and reimagine them, we might be able to create something new.

Recently I have been asked what I would change if given the opportunity, concerning the structure of the graduate seminar. And I said, "Who, me?" Here is my offering. I understand the typical graduate seminar to be fourteen to sixteen weeks, each week requires at least one hundred pages of reading, usually more. Our homework is to write a short response to the readings. Every professor is different, but they typically just want to know how we engaged the work in three to five pages. These compositions make up the majority of the writing in the class. We might be asked to produce a few questions inspired by the text for the class answer. We might be asked to read each other's responses online. We show up to class for discussion, and we do it all over again—I call this model response-based pedagogy, the typical seminar. The rest of the class, and our grade, depends on a few more tasks. The first is typically a discussion-led day, where graduate students are given the opportunity to be the professor for a day. The second is a final seminar paper, typically sixteen to twenty pages in length. When it's time to start working on the seminar paper, the readings and responses tend to not let up. And near the end of the semester a diligent graduate student in three to four classes will be reading four hundred pages a week and writing a near eighty pages to end the semester for final projects. If the student is lucky, professors will let them "double-dip" their final projects, using one project for two or more classes, as long as those projects meet the courses' outcomes. This creates a situation where the graduate student must then *binge* write in the end so they might submit something for the final grade because they are keeping up with everything else—not to mention teaching, professional development, and other institutional graduate student expectations. Taking a critical look at this structure, we might begin to understand why students tend to procrastinate (I know I do). More specifically, I want us to think about how this pedagogy is

Showing Up   139

affecting the writing process. This structure of the graduate seminar, the response-based pedagogy, doesn't prioritize our consejo *make time to write.*

For courses on topics, here's an alternative that makes room and prioritizes the craft of writing, inspired in part by a course I took by Michelle Hall Kells (thank you, Michelle): Divide the structure of the class into two parts; the first part of the course is the same as the first model, prioritize readings, even increase them. Front-load the class with reading, response, and discussion. The second part prioritizes teaching craft to the graduate student writer. The graduate student might be encouraged to organize their own reading list, conference with the professor and colleagues, develop a project, and then write and deliver the project. Back-load the class with time to write. This model embodies the ethic of *making time to write* while also staying true to the discipline's body of knowledge.

Consider another offering on some suggestions on how to address "the craft of writing" in the classroom: professors need to be writing with their graduate students. There are a lot of *ways* to go about this. Freewrites are common across all college writing classes. Professors need to be completing this in-class assignment with their students, and most professors do, but they need to be demonstrating (thank you, Aristotle) the professor's writing, as it happens, projected onto the board and shared. This is hard work, I know. It's uncomfortable, I know. I've been embodying this practice with undergraduates for some time now, and I encourage professors of graduates out there to do the same. Virtual classes have only made this suggestion more viable through screensharing software that we already use when presenting and leading discussions. Writing with graduate students this way not only demonstrates how the professor crafts but also embodies an ethic of vulnerability and transparency.

This same model, writing in front of and with graduate students, can additionally be deployed when the time comes to work on the seminar projects. Professors can display the writing they are working on while graduate students work on their final papers. I'd even challenge and encourage graduate students to demonstrate their writing *in process,* on the *way,* through projection or screenshare, live. Instead of leading a discussion day, lead a writing day. Like a workshop for the action of writing, this *way* of writing together creates a space much like the driving instructor teaching someone how to drive a car. We need to be sharing and demonstrating our manera. We need to be writing together. These suggestions fit nicely in the graduate seminar broadly, classes that follow

140   ZAKERY R. MUÑOZ

histories or topics in the field. However, I maintain that we continue to consider a compulsory graduate seminar on the craft of writing, a seminar that embodies the ethic of the typical writing advice we share and hold dear, a seminar that embodies an ethic of transparency through shared literate activities, a seminar that isn't a seminar at all but a practicum, or a workshop, as Micciche and Carr suggest.

In Shea's class on analyzing prose, I remember him saying something like, "If you're stuck, read the last thing you wrote aloud and ask yourself *where next can this sentence go? What are the nouns doing? And what can they do next?*" This might just be another abstract consejo or even something that I proverb. One thing is sure, this advice from Shea is profound—it leans more toward the actual examination of the craft of writing, of the *way* we write and *how* to do it. It is lessons like these that I'm looking for when I read texts on writing and writing processes. It is activities like these that I argue will better prepare graduate students for the job of the professoriate. Let's embody this ethic. How can we show up to writing together? Where next can our graduate pedagogies go?

WORKS CITED

Anzaldúa, Gloria. *Borderlands: La Frontera.* Aunt Lute Books, 1999.

Boice, Robert. "Contingency Management in Writing and the Appearance of Creative Ideas: Implications for the Treatment of Writing Blocks." *Behaviour Research and Therapy,* vol. 21, no. 5, 1983.

Boice, Robert. *Professors as Writers: A Self-Help Guide to Productive Writing.* New Forums, 1990.

Brooks-Gillies, Marilee, et al. *Graduate Writing Across the Disciplines: Identifying, Teaching, and Supporting.* WAC Clearinghouse; UP of Colorado, 2020.

Conference on College Composition and Communication (CCCC). "Students' Right to Their Own Language." *College Composition and Communication,* vol. 25, no. 3, 1974.

Graff, Harvey J. *The Literacy Myth: Cultural Integration and Social Structure in the Nineteenth Century.* Transaction, 1991.

Graff Harvey J., and John Duffy. "Literacy Myths." *Literacies and Language Education,* 3rd ed., edited by Brian V. Street and Stephen May, Encyclopedia of Language and Education, 2014. https://doi.org/10.1007/978-3-319-02321-2_4-1.

Harker, Michael. *The Lure of Literacy: A Critical Reception of the Compulsory Composition Debate.* State U of New York P, 2015.

"Indigenous Peoples' Land and Territory Acknowledgement." *U of New Mexico Division for Equity and Inclusion,* https://diverse.unm.edu/about/land-acknowledgement.html. Accessed 1 Aug. 2022.

Inoue, Asao B. *Above the Well: An Antiracist Literacy Argument from a Boy of Color.* WAC Clearinghouse, Utah State UP, 2021.

Kerschbaum, Stephanie L. *Toward a New Rhetoric of Difference.* Conference on College Composition and Communication, NCTE, 2014.

Lockridge, Tim, and Derek Van Ittersum. *Writing Workflows: Beyond Word Processing.* U of Michigan P, 2020. https://doi.org/10.3998/mpub.11657120.

Madden, Shannon, and Michele Eodice, editors. *Access and Equity in Graduate Writing Support*, special issue of *Praxis*, vol. 14, no. 1, 2016. http://www.praxisuwc.com/141-final.

Micciche, Laura R., with Allison D. Carr. "Toward Graduate-Level Writing Instruction." *College Composition and Communication*, vol. 62, no. 3, 2011, pp. 477–501.

Prior, Paul A. *Writing/Disciplinarity: A Sociohistoric Account of Literate Activity in the Academy*. Routledge, 1998.

Prior, Paul A., and Jody Shipka. "Chronotopic Lamination: Tracing the Contours of Literate Activity." *Writing Selves/Writing Societies: Research from Activity Perspectives*, edited by Charles Bazerman and David R. Russel, WAC Clearinghouse; UP of Colorado, 2003.

Russell, David R. *Writing in the Academic Disciplines: A Curricular History*. 2nd ed., Southern Illinois UP, 2002.

Sullivan, Patricia A. "Writing in the Graduate Curriculum: Literacy Criticism as Composition." *Journal of Advanced Composition*, vol. 11, no. 2, 1991, pp. 283–99.

Sword, Helen. *Air and Light and Time and Space: How Successful Academics Write*. Harvard UP, 2017.

Sword, Helen. "Writing Higher Education Differently: A Manifesto on Style." *Studies in Higher Education*, vol. 34, no. 3, pp. 319–36, 2009. doi: 10.1080/03075070802597101.

Tulley, Christine. *How Writing Faculty Write*, Utah State UP, 2018.

Wolfe, Patrick. "Nation and MiscegeNation: Discursive Continuity in the Post-Mabo Era." *Social Analysis: The International Journal of Social and Cultural Practice*, no. 36, 1994, pp. 93–152. *JSTOR*, www.jstor.org/stable/23171805.

Villanueva, Victor Jr. *Bootstraps: From an American Academic of Color*. NCTE, 1993.

9

WRITING QUEERLY
Honoring Fragmented and Embodied Identities in Composition

Beth Buyserie

Tags: identity, productivity, embodiment

Over the past few years, I have attended more specifically to aspects of mental health in my composition classes: ensuring students are aware of our campus resources, conducting in-class mental-health checks, and openly talking about the importance of self-care to destigmatize mental illness. Yet recently I have begun questioning how our composition classrooms and the writing process itself might explicitly, even if unintentionally, contribute to poor mental health. Each semester, I begin my composition courses by asking students to draw their relationship to writing. While many students range from enjoying writing to being relatively ambivalent about the process, some students draw fairly desperate images. "I hate writing," they confess, embarrassed to be in the class, certain that something is wrong with them.

I have a similar confession. Although I have been teaching composition for nearly twenty years, writing has never been a smooth process for me. My complicated relationship to writing is particularly disheartening and uncomfortable because of my professional identity. I have been a WPA and writing teacher, mainly on the contingent faculty track, for nearly twenty years. I am a teacher of teachers, instructing new graduate students and mentoring experienced teachers in the teaching of writing. Yet I, too, have often said that I hate writing. To clarify, I love *teaching* writing, and I particularly thrive when introducing new teachers to the profession. I am energized by the passion they often develop for their new craft, their dedication in working with students, the way they question how writing can be both a practice of liberation and, simultaneously, a means of reinforcing power. I am drawn to the complexity of writing, and I strive to explore the connections between language and power—to challenge, as guided by scholars such as April Baker-Bell and Stacey Waite, the whiteness and normativity embedded within discourse

https://doi.org/10.7330/9781646424870.c009

and our smallest units of language. As Baker-Bell emphasizes, engaging in writing practices that de-center whiteness and privilege counternarratives of communities of color must be central to our work as teachers committed to social change and anti-racism. As a composition teacher dedicated to equity, I believe writing is both a calling and what we are called to question.

Therefore, the teaching of writing, though admittedly a challenging task, is as necessary to me as breathing; talking about writing is my oxygen. Yet there are so many times, often when I am alone and trying to convince myself I have the authority to write, that I simply can't breathe. I have a longstanding, deep-seated anxiety and depression around writing, and the pressure of creating a scholarly finished product results in such extreme stress that I wonder how I can continue. To state it bluntly, in the "publish or perish" world of academia, I equate my own writing with perishing. As I continue to write for publication, the physical embodiment of this writing-related stress only grows worse. What, I desperately wonder, is wrong with me? Why is my writing process so steeped in doubt? Why does it enhance my depression? How can I contribute to the scholarly conversations I care about if I experience this much stress in the process? And how can I claim to be a writing teacher if I am this frozen by my own writing?

These questions are relatively new for me, as I was able to avoid writing for a public audience for a long time. My long-term position as a non-tenure-track WPA allowed me to focus on teaching composition rather than its scholarly production. During this time as a proud contingent faculty member, I also received many messages that the university did not value someone in my position producing academic writing. When I began my PhD, I struggled with the expectation that I would soon need to produce the type of writing I was reading for class. Despite that I inherently knew these exceptional articles had been revised multiple times, our class analysis stressed the importance of the *finished* product—not the fragments central to the process. Overwhelmed by academic expectations of the coherent and complete, I wrestled with deep-seated internalized messages that I was not qualified for this work.

My transition to academic writing during grad school was further complicated by the fact that my sexuality had also recently shifted: an unexpected twist to my identity that, though life-affirming in many ways, augmented the tension I experienced with writing. As I drafted my dissertation, writing became an embodied part of my identity as I navigated the process of coming out to myself. Each page of writing represented—and still represents—deep sacrifice and many hours of self-doubt, punctuated by moments of frantic composing. I was, in between writing, desperately trying to discern how I could communicate the shift in my identity with my husband, children, and close friends without my life falling apart. For a time, my life not only fell apart, it shattered. And I had to write about it. As I was earning my PhD in cultural studies, writing about my identity and positionality was an expected part of both the process and product. Therefore, writing soon became the equivalent of coming out, and each time I wrote I had decisions to make: could I come out to my audience? Should I? Given that I was completely new to my sexuality, would anyone accept my insights on queerness and queer pedagogy? More importantly, did I acknowledge my own embodied ethos as a queer person coming out later in life?

Accepting my ethos as a writer was tested again these past few years as I shifted from the contingent ranks to a WPA tenure-track position. The transition to the tenure track was not smooth. Suddenly, I was expected to devote large swaths of time to writing—to *producing*—publishable and research-based writing almost instantly. Once my tenure clock began relentlessly ticking, I was encouraged to work from home at least once a week to remove all distractions. To be alone. My heart broke each time I had to choose between my family and my profession, knowing I had to keep writing to advance in my field. Yet my depression and WPA work made writing for long chunks of time almost impossible. The erratic time I had for writing caused deep stress as I—despite what I taught my students—privileged the finished product that would count for tenure rather than honoring the fragments so critical to the process: the time spent thinking, the unfinished paragraphs, the discarded ideas, the emotional energy necessary to process my shifting identities. In other words, when I refer to fragments, I mean fragmented writing not only in terms of time but in terms of shattering the certainty of what we presume to know. Our writing, as Stacey Waite might argue, becomes fragmented when we question what we know as well as what we *don't* know—which takes considerable emotional labor. Yet the academy does not often hold space for this embodied and emotional work. Instead, only the CV line proclaiming the work has been published counts. Fragmented writing, I am implicitly told, is not valued in this space. And I am often one more person devaluing it.

Because my graduate research highlighted queer composition scholarship, my tenure-track research agenda—and hence my job—now became, in my mind, dependent on publicly writing about an identity that was new to me. The shift in both my sexuality and my faculty role also changed all the structures I depended on to write: I became a single mother, moved to a new state, left behind friend networks for me and my children, began a new job, adjusted to a single income, and struggled to connect with a new community during a pandemic. After so many changes, I began to understand why my writing felt fragmented: each time I wrote, I had to pause to process the emotional backlash of what I was describing. To cope, I started working with a counselor specifically to attend to these intertwining identities of being both newly tenure-track and newly queer in midlife—for both positions required me to navigate and question my jagged relationship with writing.

My counselor taught me techniques that I strive to apply to both my own writing and my teaching: honor the fragments, reject the need to be accepted by others, and seek moments of failure. In this chapter, I explore how these lessons provide new insight into both my own writing process and the teaching of composition. I question what writing might encompass when we emphasize just how fragmented the writing process can be—and honor the possibilities for writers to seek and embrace those disconnects. In this discussion, I seek composing approaches that do not implicitly expect writers/people to be whole but acknowledge our unfinished selves as integral to the writing process. To do so, I weave in my lived experience with queer scholarship and disability studies in composition, as these frameworks honor incomplete selves and reject normative timeframes for completion. Overall, this chapter examines possibilities for honoring the fragmented nature of writing as we navigate transitions in our lives—and for creating something new out of the pieces of our lives as we write.

LESSONS FROM MY COUNSELOR: QUEERING THE STORY MY BRAIN TELLS ME

The story your brain tells you does not have to be your only story.
—A lesson from my counselor

For years the story my brain has told me about writing has been one of deficit and solitude, negating my self-worth. I have wondered if the reason I struggle with writing is because I do not—I cannot—follow the accepted advice on writing: write a little bit each day, have a quiet space to write, protect large amounts of time for your writing. Although I yearn to simply ease into a writing routine, thinking about writing fills me with tension, and despite how hard I try to be calm, I find my body doing whatever it can to avoid the process. There is much at stake in this struggle. In *Dreads and Open Mouths: Living/Teaching/Writing Queerly*, Aneil Rallin writes, "You must teach that writing can be collaborative, need not be a solitary, suicidal act" (69)—and I have clung to both the pain and the comfort in these words as I try to rewrite the story my brain tells me. Slowly I am coming to learn that approaching writing as a series of behavioral tasks may not fully address my issues with writing, for even when I follow this advice, the anxiety still remains. In "Self-Authorship and Faculty Writers' Trajectories of Becoming," Sandra L. Tarabochia clarifies that the typical advice for writing has focused on our behaviors. For example, when we provide models of proficient writers, Tarabochia notes, we often highlight the strategies they employ to complete their writing. These strategies, such as writing for fifteen minutes a day, can certainly be helpful and on initial review would appear to honor fragmented writing. Yet Tarabochia, based on her longitudinal study of faculty writers from a variety of disciplines, critiques these behavioral-based strategies as insufficient: without context, they do not acknowledge individual faculty members' embodied experiences, their relationship to writing, or their identities.

Tarabochia argues that focusing on behavior-based strategies might actually hinder faculty writers' composing processes. For example, Tarabochia describes the insufficiencies of behavior-based writing advice for Mandy, a participant who researches connections between LGBTQ identities and religion. Tarabochia claims, "The common advice to simply write more and feel less might not only fail to meaningfully sponsor but actually impede Mandy's trajectory of becoming by forcing her to compare her rocky path with the seemingly smooth paths of her successful colleagues" ("Self-Authorship" 26). In other words, the advice to simply keep writing, Tarabochia suggests, does not develop faculty writers' self-authorship or identity as a writer. Moreover, in "From Resilience to Resistance: Repurposing Faculty Writers' Survival Strategies," Tarabochia argues that if we advise faculty to keep writing despite the obstacles, we are actually promoting a problematic form of resiliency, one that encourages faculty to dismiss the systems of oppression that might affect their writing—advice that is particularly harmful to those marginalized by and within academia.

Rather than focusing on behavioral strategies, Tarabochia promotes a better understanding of our emotional connection to writing. Acknowledging our emotions is a key aspect of honoring, rather than despairing over, fragmented writing. Acknowledging my own emotions in this process, however, took some time. After many years of intense anxiety and depression connected to my writing, self, and identity, I finally decided to talk to a counselor again. I perhaps should have gone sooner, but I was trying to address my issues on my own with (free) behavior-based approaches—and while I try to destigmatize mental health support for my students, I had a harder time deciding to seek counseling for my struggles with writing. After all, I was a writing teacher and WPA, and I had successfully (yet with much pain) written a dissertation. I knew my concerns stemmed not from my inability to craft quality writing but from my inexplicable aversion to doing so: the unshaking belief that I could not do this work. Additionally, I hoped that once I had published a few articles, I would have the confidence to continue publishing. Instead, the anxiety deepened, and the maxim to publish or perish became a very real command to my brain. I was not surviving.

Eventually I began counseling, both to address my anxiety around writing and to discern how my shifting identities connected to my writing anxieties. I recognize that counseling is not a panacea, and while I promote mental health and self-care, I want to note that professional counseling is not inherently equitable. Indeed, many marginalized groups have difficulty finding the support they need through professional counseling, due to the fact that a predominantly white and otherwise normative counseling staff is often ill-equipped to recognize and understand how deep stressors connect to structural oppressions such as racism (Ridley). As a white woman, I have access to counseling that always affirms my racial identity, a basic need not afforded to all people of color; this segregated access to healthcare continues to widen the rifts in mental health between racial groups, even as the awareness about the importance of mental health increases (Ridley). As a queer woman, however, I was hesitant to attend therapy. Given the highly conservative nature of my location, I could not be certain a counselor would be accepting of my sexuality or knowledgeable about queer identities. Fortunately, my university had recently formed a counseling program designed for LGBTQ-identified people. From the beginning, I could talk openly about how coming out later in life intersected with my transition from contingent faculty to tenure-track faculty—and how my anxiety around writing encircled both identities like a knot.

My counselor and I began working with a therapy called Acceptance and Commitment Therapy, or ACT. ACT emphasizes psychological flexibility or "the ability to fully connect with the present moment," identify our core values, and ultimately act more consistently with these values (Bennet and Oliver 57). Rather than pretending we can make our thoughts and feelings disappear, ACT guides us in examining and making space for those feelings—to acknowledge their presence, without judgment. ACT, according to my counselor, does not promise that we will feel *better*, but that we will *feel* better, allowing us to more successfully navigate the legitimate stressors around us. My intent here is not

148 BETH BUYSERIE

to describe ACT fully, nor to promote ACT as the ideal approach to counseling (in fact, some aspects of ACT did not work for me). Rather, I highlight some lessons I learned that are helping me untangle my torrid relationship to writing and publishing.

Lesson 1: Change the story my brain tells me. That narrative is not the only story.
I admit, for several years I tried very hard to dismiss how important my sexuality was to me. I was not embarrassed about my sexuality—the shift in many ways felt completely right—but I had for several years tried to pretend that it did not matter, that I could continue to live my life as it always had been. I was not thriving in my old life, but there was a sense of responsibility and stability that was comforting to cling to. Similarly, I have tried hard to dismiss the reality that I experience deep anxiety and depression around my writing. While critical disability scholars such as Margaret Price challenge rhetorics that associate depression and anxiety with brokenness, I did want to be "fixed," to no longer feel shame with writing. This chapter is my opportunity to revise my relationship with writing while still honoring the embodied life of writing as a queer woman who experiences anxiety and depression. Rather than avoid writing, I want to be able to hold space for all the emotions that accompany writing.

In "For the Love of Writing: Writing as a Form of (Self-) Love," Gabrielle Isabel Kelenyi provides an emotion-based model of how to rewrite the story that my brain tells me about writing. Kelenyi also experiences anxiety around writing, and she says, "I've needed to flip the stereotypical script about the act of writing from one that is punishing and painful to one that is safe, empowering, and loving" (17). In this, Kelenyi intentionally connects writing to a form of self-love. As Kelenyi notes, "Coming to this realization that love undergirds all my writing doesn't make writing easier" (20), so Kelenyi seeks ways in which writing manifests as a form of love, both for self and others. Kelenyi says:

> In this way, I embrace the idea that everything I write is an act of love. . . . My writing process protects me from anxiety and helps me stay productive—it loves me. It is kind to me because it enacts the idea that what I must write is important and impactful, that somehow some way it will enact and spread more love through demonstrating care, commitment, responsibility, and trust, and through sharing knowledge. (20)

I am not yet in this space with my writing process, but reaffirming that my writing can be a form of self-love and a way to offer my heart to others has helped me more consciously notice my negative emotions and maintain a level of calmness when despondency threatens to overtake me.

I want to associate my writing with joy. To do so, I have turned to queer compositionists who challenge normative expectations of writing. In *Dreads and Open Mouths: Living/Teaching/Writing Queerly*, Aneil Rallin maintains that finding joy in writing can be a radical and queer act. Rallin, who identifies as a "queer of color writer/thinker/scholar/activist/ teacher/immigrant" (5), argues that in predominantly white and normative academic contexts, "Writing is not tolerated as a questioning, but only as an answer, as something fixed and not as something that is uncertain in its movement . . . something that is unfinished" (22). Rallin contests that joyful writing can challenge oppressive structures: "There may be value or joy in writing that is not clear, writing that is emotional, undisciplined, that it is possible and necessary to imagine forms and configurations of thinking/writing outside and beyond the confines of patriarchal logics and disciplinary directives" (65–66). For me, this embodies the act of writing queerly: of questioning normative forms, as well as writing in ways that are playful, that make room for unfinished thoughts and moments of joy.

Joyful writing, I have found, can also be deeply personal. As I composed this chapter, I had the rare chance to visit a good friend from the town I lived in and loved for seventeen years. My friend shared how she, after teaching for twenty years, is starting to lose joy for her craft. What, we asked ourselves, brings us joy? Writing doesn't yet or always bring me joy, so I try to squeeze in little bits of joy between my writing. Once I returned home from my visit, I assembled a bookshelf and finally unpacked a box of books. Now I sit in my grandmother's blue recliner chair, gazing at my bookshelf and smiling. Creating this happy space to write brings me joy. I have also taken many breaks to water my garden, which, despite the fact that it is being eaten by grasshoppers, and even my zucchini is wilting in the hot sun, brings me joy. I have ridden scooters down the sidewalk with my nine-year-old son in pursuit of a lemonade stand. And I have stayed up past midnight sitting on my front porch to watch and listen to and feel a rare rainstorm provide the gift of water to our parched landscape. Attending to the rain, taking the time to be thankful for its presence during our deeply concerning heat and drought, was joyful. These are distractions and necessary tasks that fragment my writing, but that, if I am intentional about the process, allow me to create new pathways that connect writing with life-affirming emotions.

Importantly, I have also found joy and affirmation during the writing process itself, particularly when writing about concepts that challenge normative structures: exploring life-giving literacy practices for

150   BETH BUYSERIE

later-in-life queers, expanding on the possibilities of queer pedagogies, and exploring the problems and potential of resilient pedagogies. As I read Rallin, I am drawn to passages that highlight the decadence of writing, such as, "His lover reminds him to remember the pleasures of language, of words, of writing" (Rallin, 66). I have for so long associated writing with depression and solitude, and as I start to rewrite the narrative my brain tells me about writing, I am trying to honor the fragments as a valid part of my process—and to associate writing with life and joy.

Lesson 2: Honor the fragments and accept my present emotions without judgment.

Like many, I have lived a fragmented life, one where the sharp pieces of my embodied experiences don't always fit together neatly. Writing is one way to examine and make sense of the pieces. However, queer composition scholars like Rallin and Waite resist the notion that our writing, our composing process, should actually compose, or order, our lives. Instead, they advocate for queer approaches to writing that disregard normalcy as an unquestioned good. As I read and write my embodied self as queer later in life, I have had to question my own assumptions of normalcy in regard to writing: the assumption that publishing means that you are smart and that struggling to compose means you are not; that if I try hard enough, I can write without anxiety or depression creeping in; that my resistance to writing means that I am not a writer; that if only I were more dedicated or organized, I would be a writer; that if I direct a composition program, writing should come naturally. In fact, the opposite is often true: I deeply struggle with writing. Writing queerly—or questioning power and normalcy in the writing process—is, I posit, a form of mental health. It allows me to pause when I begin to judge my relationship with writing. Writing queerly is a way for me to honor the fragments of my life and resist a normative narrative that expects me to be whole.

Lesson 3: Seek moments of failure.

There is pressure to be a mythical perfect self. During my counseling sessions, I identified one of my greatest fears to be the fear of rejection. Many academic journals proudly maintain their prestige by ensuring a high rejection rate. I am trying to understand that rejection in writing does not equate to failure of self. Yet at the same time, my counselor suggested that I intentionally fail in order to ease the tension between perfection in writing and inherent self-worth. With this lesson, I am learning that writing queerly can be a way of sustaining and nurturing mental health. For example, in *Teaching Queer*, Waite emphasizes the importance of seeking failure. In citing J. Jack Halberstam, Waite explains that queer failure allows us to "dismantle the logics of success" (qtd. in Waite 57). Such dismantling of normative definitions of success suggests a number of questions. If academic success equates to frequent publishing of notable essays in top-tier journals, what might it mean to fail at writing? How might queer writing failures sustain me in ways less valued by the academy? What might be ways to fail at a normative expectation to publish or perish? And how can I accept moments of failure as necessary to my mental health?

I would be remiss if I even unintentionally suggested that counseling, mindfulness, or individual behavior might completely address tensions that I and many others experience with writing. Rather than promote the narrative that, with enough work, an individual can overcome any obstacle (Price), in the next section I examine the structures that promote such a negative connection to writing—and present several models for revising that narrative.

PROMOTING FACULTY MENTAL HEALTH: DECONSTRUCTING THE PUBLISH OR PERISH BINARY

> *To earn tenure, you will be expected to publish and engage in scholarly productivity in an ever-increasing upward trajectory.*
> —Paraphrased language from my tenure-track contract

Signing my tenure contract, committing to a perpetual research agenda despite the fact that writing has incited depression and anxiety, was incredibly challenging. I am still not certain that I made the right decision. Yet I have learned I am not alone in my tenuous relationship with writing. In "Self-Authorship," Tarabochia critiques the environment of academic writing that almost casually uses the term "publish or perish" without acknowledging the perilous position that binary represents, particularly for faculty marginalized by the academy. In her longitudinal study of faculty writers from various disciplines, Tarabochia finds that faculty are frustrated by the expectation to continually publish at the expense of one's mental health. Moreover, Tarabochia validates that faculty, particularly those of us new to publishing or marginalized by the academy, need more than a directive to publish in order to thrive in the process. Instead, Tarabochia urges the discipline of composition

152   BETH BUYSERIE

to actively encourage and support faculty self-authorship. As Tarabochia emphasizes, writing connects not only to our profession but to faculty identities and lived experiences. As such, "struggles with meaning making, shifting relationships and identity negotiation are, indeed, entangled in writing lives and must be addressed as part of a holistic approach to faculty writer support" ("Self-Authorship" 17). Therefore, Tarabochia insists we need critical mentoring strategies that sustain faculty writers as they write and navigate changes in their embodied selves. I assert that such critical mentoring is also a way for universities to actively promote and support faculty mental health.

As writing teachers, how can we create spaces where students' fragmented writing is valued and enhances learning if our own writing context promotes rapid publishing over faculty development and self-authorship? While I have experienced extreme stress at publishing on the tenure clock, I am fortunate to be at a research-intensive university that recognizes, promotes, and funds the scholarship of teaching. Various administrators have told me that they value my work as a teacher and as director of composition—and they would rather I attend to my mental health and model reflective teaching than produce an abundance of articles simply for the sake of publishing. Furthermore, they adjusted my teaching statement so that teaching, including my administrative work supporting teaching at the program level, is my area of emphasis for tenure. Far from devaluing my scholarly writing, this process provided me with the space and reassurance to focus on projects that are meaningful to me—and to make space for the fragments in my thinking.

Tarabochia advocates that faculty writers receive intentional mentoring designed for faculty development, saying, "Building a healthy writing life can inspire important identity work as faculty decide who they want to be as scholars and people" ("Self-Authorship" 18). While I did not initially know how to seek the mentorship I required to navigate the intensified writing expectations, I am now receiving more support. The models my university employs to guide faculty in their writing do much to relieve my particular anxieties around composing. For example, in a recent teaching portfolio workshop, participants worked closely with mentors to review a short portion of our ten-to-twelve-page teaching portfolio before beginning another short piece of writing that day. The following morning, we would meet again to review the draft and discuss further revisions. This model worked exceptionally well because I had the consistent guidance of someone who cared about my writing—and about my professional and personal identities—coupled with frequent, low-stakes deadlines. Next semester, I will participate in a teaching academy where participants, again guided by mentors, research and write on a project over the course of a year. This model makes my anxiety manageable as I know I will not be alone in the process. As Mays Imad, a neurobiologist who specializes in trauma-informed and inclusive pedagogies, emphasizes, faculty working together can "use writing as a bridge to connect and heal" ("Transcending Adversity"). And so, yes, my writing continues to be fragmented—but supported. More importantly, my identities as both a new assistant professor as well as a later-in-life queer person, are both valued. While more models exist, I highlight these as possibilities for revising the academic writing process in ways that attend to embodied identities—and that rewrite the narrative so that faculty might publish *and* thrive.

A FRAGMENTED PEDAGOGY

I am a queer person seeking stability. Those processes and identities are at odds with each other. I need to honor the fragments, the shifts, the instability, the unknowability, the lack of assurance. I want to enact a pedagogy that allows students space to do the same.
— A fragment from an earlier draft

The unknowability of writing has always been a danger to me. Imad notes in her work on trauma-informed pedagogy that "because we are not quite equipped to handle ambiguity, our brains are interpreting unanswered questions as a source of danger" ("Leveraging the Neuroscience"). As composition teachers respond more intentionally to mental wellbeing in the classroom, I am increasingly interested in the students whose anxiety, depression, and other mental health concerns affect both their writing and their experiences in our classrooms. Since I know how taxing writing can be, how can I arrange my course so students can navigate potential challenges they might have with writing? Imad underscores that many students may have experienced trauma. Teachers, Imad suggests, can best support students if we design our pedagogies with the assumption that many students are experiencing some form of trauma—rather than adjusting only when students disclose a trauma ("Leveraging the Neuroscience"). During the initial year of COVID-19, teachers and universities were often more flexible, as the assumption was that life was challenging for most people. With the expectation to "return to normal" comes the possibility that teachers will return to less flexible teaching methods. In pushing against this normative expectation, I am instead trying to enact a pedagogy that honors the fragments in students' lives and explores possibilities for encouraging

154   BETH BUYSERIE

fragmented writing in the classroom. While I do not pretend that these approaches will magically address the various and unique needs of all my students, I believe that honoring the fragments in our teaching can help both students and teachers gain new insights about writing, as well as allow us to associate writing with life-affirming thoughts.

Honoring the Fragments: Encouraging Unfinished Writing

In this section, I provide a few brief thoughts on what a fragmented pedagogy might entail. In creating a fragmented pedagogy, I suggest not simply that teachers create more time for fragmented writing but that we create opportunities to examine how the fragments of our writing might ask us and our students to examine what we don't know about our research—to learn as we write rather than write to finish. And to learn more about our embodied selves in the process. For example, when reading published articles, teachers and students often focus on the finished product rather than imagine the fragments that evoked the draft. To question the normative process that privileges the finished product, teachers might instead seek models of professional writers' fragmented writing to frame discussions of process. For example, Tarabochia intentionally made her research data into a poem, removing key phrases from participants' interviews and writing in fragments to expose the heart of the concept:

> *Writing's like a road trip: trying to get to the next stop*
> *this factory process of keeping things moving. . . .*
> Those months that I didn't do much
> *hurry, think of a project*
> Where I was just sad
> *I don't see the end of it.* (Tarabochia, "From Resilience to Resistance")

In another approach to fragmented writing, Rallin creates a series of contradictory sentences, thoughts that explore the complex nature of writing and teaching, of race, sexuality, and language, that encourage us to pause . . . and consider how multiple sets of contradictory statements and competing embodied identities might simultaneously be true:

> You must teach as if your life depended on it.
> You must recognize your life does not depend on it.
> You must teach as if some of your students' lives may depend on it.
> You must recognize that your teaching is or may be peripheral to the lives
>   of your students. . . .
> You must teach that writing may save lives.
> But writing can also kill. That, too, you must teach. (Rallin 67, 69)

Writing Queerly 155

Changing the Narrative: Audience and Peer Review

Multiple times, I have experienced severe anxiety when I think of who might be reading (and judging) my arguments. Every sentence that I compose screams that I am not done, that the piece is not good enough to be read by others. In composition, we emphasize that writing for a specific audience allows us to more intentionally craft our message. Yet I also wonder how our teaching of audience—the emphasis that someone else will actually read our writing—might impede the writing process for some writers. Rallin stresses that considering an audience might not always enact a radical pedagogy, particularly when we ask students whose identities are marginalized by the university to persuade an oppressive audience. After all, for some students, the "opposing" side might literally debate the students' right to exist. Rallin asks quite pointedly, "If we have to think always of mollifying our opposition, would anyone be able to write?" (64). In contrast, Baker-Bell highlights the social media practices of Black communities who intentionally write for a Black audience and utilize writing to foreground life-giving linguistic practices that advocate for racial justice and social change. Together, Rallin and Baker-Bell provide teachers with reasons to question the ways we teach audience in rhetoric and writing.

Finally, in applying Kelenyi's process of writing as a form of self- and community love, I ponder how students might respond if we asked them to select an audience that they loved and cared for rather than ask them to select a generic audience that has a stake in the issue (though the two audiences need not be contrary). As Kelenyi emphasizes, "Love can also transform the practice of writing from one that is viewed as harmful, tedious, and painful . . . into one that is transformative, worthy, positive, and healing. This is because writing is a way to understand and be understood, to feel and be felt, to commune, to connect" (17). I love the possibility that fragment writing might allow us to more intentionally connect with an audience—and with ourselves.

CONCLUSION: CONTINUOUS RESHAPING AND ACCEPTANCE

I don't know what this piece will be when I finish. Knowing the final product is not the goal.

I am learning that it is okay to feel anxious about my writing, to consciously release my need for stability and knowing. As a teacher, I have started sharing my challenges with writing with the students and teachers in my program. While I do not believe that the classroom is a

156   BETH BUYSERIE

counseling session, I want to provide opportunities to discuss the emotional aspects of writing with students, to intentionally dispel normative myths of linear and "easy" writing processes. I try hard not to project my own emotions and experiences with writing onto my students—some of them truly love writing and feel great freedom in expressing themselves in writing—but I do want to acknowledge that, like me, some students struggle with writing in ways that have nothing to do with their ability to write. These are the students that I am interested in supporting through this particular project.

As Kelenyi emphasizes in her essay on writing and love, "As writers and writing educators, we must rethink the function of writing and reclaim what kind of writing is productive: writing for/as love is functional and relational; it is a radical act" (17). My goal in this chapter, in addition to providing what I hope are meaningful thoughts for my audience to ponder, has been to reshape my relationship with writing. I admit, I was yearning for a completely new writing experience, one where I could consistently hold space for my anxious thoughts and compose a draft without avoiding the task. Not surprisingly, that did not happen. But in the spirit of honoring fragments, I tried to be more mindful of any feelings of despondency, to acknowledge their presence, and to keep writing (punctuated by many naps). Ultimately, I am coming to a greater appreciation of how fragmented writing, rather than being a sign of failure, can frame a more positive relationship to writing. Fragmented writing allows me a way to navigate my anxiety with writing, to intentionally seek and honor the slivers of thought rather than the finished product. Fragmented writing, therefore, is more than simply writing in short bursts of time: fragmented writing also involves the time required to navigate our embodied identities as writers and people. In other words, fragmented writing can be an intentional strategy and augment mental health if framed in ways that honor who we are—and are becoming.

WORKS CITED

Baker-Bell, April. "We Been Knowin: Toward an Antiracist Language & Literacy Education." *Journal of Language and Literacy Education*, vol. 16, no. 1, 2020, pp. 1–12.

Bennett, Richard, and Joseph E. Oliver. *Acceptance and Commitment Therapy: 100 Key Points and Techniques*. Routledge, 2019.

Imad, Mays. "Leveraging the Neuroscience of Now." *Inside Higher Ed*, 3 June 2020, https://www.insidehighered.com/advice/2020/06/03/seven-recommendations-helping-students-thrive-times-trauma.

Imad, Mays. "Transcending Adversity: Trauma-Informed Educational Development." *Educational Development in the Time of Crises*, vol. 39, no. 3, 2021. https://doi.org/10.3998/tia.17063888.0039.301.

Kelenyi, Gabrielle Isabel. "For the Love of Writing: Writing as a Form of (Self-) Love." *Writers: Craft & Context*, vol. 2, no. 1, 2021, pp. 16–24.

Price, Margaret. *Mad at School: Rhetorics of Mental Disability and Academic Life.* U of Michigan P, 2011.

Rallin, Aneil. *Dreads and Open Mouths: Living/Teaching/Writing Queerly.* Litwin Books, 2019.

Ridley, Charles R. *Overcoming Unintentional Racism in Counseling and Therapy: A Practitioner's Guide to Intentional Intervention.* 2nd ed., Sage, 2005.

Tarabochia, Sandra L. "From Resilience to Resistance: Repurposing Faculty Writers' Survival Strategies." *Peitho Journal*, vol. 23, no. 3, 2021. https://cfshrc.org/article/from-resilience-to-resistance-repurposing-faculty-writers-survival-strategies/.

Tarabochia, Sandra L. "Self-Authorship and Faculty Writers' Trajectories." *Composition Studies*, vol. 48, no.1, 2020, pp. 16–33.

Waite, Stacey. *Teaching Queer: Radical Possibilities for Writing and Knowing.* U of Pittsburgh P, 2017.

10

TRANSFORMATIVE PRACTICES
Black Women Exist Beyond Our Ability to Produce

Tatiana Benjamin

Tags: identity, productivity, critique, embodiment

As a Black disabled woman in academia, I am constantly thinking about what it means to be productive in this space. Am I doing enough? This question is sobering because it cannot be quantified. Yet I feel the weight of this question often. Higher education rewards productivity at the expense of our mental, emotional, and physical health. However, I do not want to perpetuate systems that continuously ask Black women to put themselves last. I am unsure whether or not I can escape all the ways academia upholds a fixed definition of productivity. The university operates like a two-sided coin. On one side there is the face value of the diversity model and on the other side is the normativity model of hyperproductivity and elitism. Both models are two sides of the same coin that only find you valuable based on what you can do for the university and not what the university can do for you. The nexus of my identities does not align with either model. I desire to succeed as an academic but not based on hyperproductivity or accepting the disposability of Black disabled bodies.

As I write this chapter, I keep thinking about the following words: productivity and disposability. Our contribution to society is associated with our usefulness. Unfortunately, it is tied to output. One is not valued unless their body and mind can fit within normative systems of production. This is the core of capitalism: how much you can produce. Capitalism is not concerned with your humanity, dignity, or your pains. There is a focus on working hard. There is emphasis placed on "pulling yourself up by your bootstraps." Everyone has the same opportunity, which only absolves blame and reinforces normative ideas of being. However, what happens when we take a step back and realize that this system was never created for Black, non-male, disabled bodies? Capitalism is inherently tied to white supremacy and patriarchy. It is meant to benefit those who are white, wealthy, and able-bodied. Naming

https://doi.org/10.7330/9781646424870.c010

and acknowledging this system pushes us to critique, dismantle, reimagine, and implement new practices on how to live and be.

My blackness, my womanhood, my disabilities all enter academia with me. They stand in the tension of what it means to succeed in an institutional structure that perpetuates inequality. I want to dismantle this system while building a career. The question becomes: How can I reimagine academia as the liberatory and inclusive space I want it to be? Institutional structures can only be transformed to a point because we exist in a capitalist society. However, we do what we can until we get to the place of total liberation. All change has to begin somewhere; for me that change comes from within me and the experiences I have as a Black disabled woman. I am learning how to create and embrace transformative practices rooted in love and community. Through this autoethnographic essay, I demonstrate how community building and care are tools of resistance that place my Black disabled body at the center.

CONTEXT: ALWAYS IN TRANSITION

Managing multiple transitions, research expectations, publications, and writing during the last several years has required a shift in how I care for myself as I navigate research, teaching, and writing. I have also reflected on the responsibility that academia has to me as a scholar. Academia upholds the belief that we are indebted to the institution. This reproduces the normative idea that I am solely responsible for the marginalization I experience as a Black disabled woman inside academia.

I am an early career scholar who is a cisgender Black woman living with chronic illnesses. This autoethnographic essay will focus on the past four years of my life before and during a global pandemic. Through my narratives I engage the paradoxes of being Black, disabled, and a woman within an institutional structure that is not set up for me to "operate at [my] fullest potential" (Bell 1). I do this by connecting my experiences to those of other BIPOC scholars navigating academia. In what follows, I narrate what I am doing to navigate the contradictions of being an early career academic. These strategies include reframing productivity, creating a writing process, prioritizing health, and building in-person and digital communities that allow me to accomplish my goals of writing more without compromising my overall welfare.

Through narrative storytelling I am sharing the challenges of productivity in academia as a Black woman with multiple chronic illnesses. Of course, I cannot speak for all people who identify as Black, disabled, and women. But I want to engage strategies and resources that can aid

160   TATIANA BENJAMIN

another scholar who may face similar issues. It is my way of telling some-one else that they are not alone. That we can work together to ensure that ableism, anti-Blackness, and sexism are not normalized in aca-demia. That it can look different if we build a beloved community; one that mentors, increases women of color faculty, staff, and administrators, and prioritizes their retention in higher education.

BEING BLACK, DISABLED, AND A WOMAN

Expanding the theory of intersectionality to include disabilities opens new ways of exploring the experiences of Black people. Black feminist and disability scholars Moya Bailey and Izetta Mobley argue for a theory of intersectionality that includes disability. Similar to Bell, they note that race scholars will mention the race of people but not their disabilities. This takes away from the depth of the field and the opportunity to fur-ther engage identities and their relationships to power. Including disabil-ity within intersectionality asks for justice that also advocates for Black dis-abled bodies and pushes for a restructuring of our relationship to labor and the politics of care (Black women are more likely to care for disabled people). Bailey and Mobley state, "Race–and specifically Blackness–has been used to mark disability, while disability has inherently 'Blackened' those perceived as unfit" (24). This highlights the violence that Black disabled people experience as well as the erasure of naming disability.

A consistent battle that is fought at every intersection of my identity as a Black woman with chronic illnesses is whether or not I am fit to be an academic. My right to be part of the elite "ivory tower" is inherently tied to race, gender, and disability. Black people's relationship to capitalism is one of laborers not of intellectual thinkers. Our bodies are always at the center of how we can be used to further capitalism. Black women academics experience the violences of capitalism in the microaggres-sions, emotional labor, increased service, and unequal compensation within the "ivory tower." The emphasis on a white supremacist and anti-Black academic space marks Black and disabled bodies as disposable. This makes me critical of ableism but also hyper-aware of disclosing my illnesses for fear of being seen as inept. The scenarios that follow recount my journey as a Black woman living with chronic illnesses.

SCENARIO 1: OHIO

Through the narratives of my mentors, I entered academia aware of what it meant to be a woman of color in this profession, but I had no idea what it meant to be a disabled woman of color. This is the violence of erasing disability. I had no model for my Black disabled body as a scholar. Sociologist Nicole Brown explains this well: "Academics with chronic illness, disabilities or neurodiversity are practically unseen and starkly under-represented in comparison to students with disabilities or disabled people in the general public" (Brown and Leigh 5). I have been navigating the paradox of being a scholar of social justice within an institutional structure that continuously erases my Black disabled body.

My first year as a visiting assistant professor (VAP) placed me face-to-face with being a Black woman scholar living with chronic illness. In the fall of 2018, I started my position as a VAP at Miami University in Oxford, Ohio. It was the first time I experienced a partial complex seizure while teaching. This type of seizure can last between thirty seconds and two minutes. One of the main effects of partial seizures is the lack of awareness. I am aware before and after partial seizures but not during. It can look like I am daydreaming. During that class session, my students were doing in-class activities. I was walking around to each group answering questions. I recall beginning to answer a question. I knew somewhere in there I stopped responding. When I became aware, the students in the group were anxious and confused as to why I did not respond quickly. They were unaware of what was going on, so I brushed it off. I did not want them to find out or be frightened. I held it together and finished out the class session. I stayed composed and hid my own fears.

I centered the well-being of my students over myself. I was fearful of losing my job because of my disability. I feared that my Black disabled body marked me as incompetent. I feared that my disabilities would discount me from a career. These previous statements speak to the way that ableism and racism are institutionalized. I had been working toward becoming a scholar-practitioner for almost a decade. I did not want that to be taken away from me because of my disabilities. These fears could be avoided if systems in academia provided resources and support for faculty living with disabilities. Although there are offices of disability services (ODS) on campuses, there is minimal representation for faculty. For me this has meant a lack of community and limited resources. I also know that being a faculty member with illnesses comes with risk if I disclose my status. Unfortunately, higher education is similar to our larger society—ableist.

Looking back, I can now see how my relationship to power in academia contributed to the erasure of my experiences. My overlapping identities and the precarity of a VAP position stopped me from even acknowledging the importance of my disabilities. At that time, I

162   TATIANA BENJAMIN

accepted the erasure from an institutional system that contributed to my seizures. Hyperproductivity produces stress; stress and anxiety are triggers for seizures. It is a conundrum to push for productivity while being erased and viewed as inept. I learned to hide my disability instead of advocating for systems that are inclusive of disability. This is the unfortunate consequence of institutionalized systems of oppression. I rationalized my health problems as a deficit that I needed to fix by myself. I was fearful of exposing myself and my illnesses.

SCENARIO 2: NEW YORK

Unfortunately, as a Black woman scholar managing chronic illnesses, I am constantly asked to choose between my health and my career. We are expected to be productive in spaces that are hostile to our welfare. Academia's diversity, equity, and inclusion (DEI) initiatives are slowly increasing diversity without efficient systems in place. Faculty also need access to services that can care for our health. The decision to move during a pandemic provided me with health insurance. A necessity for someone who needs medications and other healthcare services so that I can be productive in my writing process. Writing is difficult when you are hospitalized or experiencing frequent seizures and muscle fatigue. Again, I return to the idea of productivity when in reality the access to medication should be the focus. The lack of access to medications and health insurance is tied to socioeconomics. My employment is necessary for me to access the resources I need to continue being. Overall, balancing my health as an early career scholar is an area I am still navigating.

In the fall of 2020, I moved to Brooklyn, NY for a remote postdoctoral fellowship. At first glance this would be a great option for someone living with disabilities. An intersectional analysis looks beyond remote access and finds what remains hidden. Remote access offers benefits, but it did not offer me out-of-state health insurance. A lack of health insurance increases medical cost and bodily impact. The health insurance offered would not cover my health needs. Although I am considered high risk for COVID-19, I still found myself in transition during a pandemic. I moved to New York during a global pandemic because I needed health insurance. I needed the medical services and could not afford to pay the extra fees of being out-of-network. I did everything within my power to avoid moving during a pandemic. I spent hours on the phone with human resources. Then I spoke with the network that provided my insurance to find alternatives to payment and access. It left me feeling hopeless and frustrated. All I wanted was to be protected because of my

Transformative Practices 163

illnesses, yet I felt dismissed. Throughout the phone calls there was a failure to understand the need for my coverage. Having access to health insurance is critical to my overall well-being, which I believe is critical to my overall well-being. Having access and adequate health care should never be tied to a career or productivity.

THE INAPPROPRIATE BODY

If you fall outside of this standard, then you are not seen as fully human (Campbell). I exist in this body that is not "normal," yet the workplace is designed with a standard body in mind. Although I never had another onset seizure while teaching, it would not be the last time that my chronic illnesses intersected with my life as a scholar. Epilepsy is still part of my life. I also have an autoimmune disorder, myasthenia gravis, which presents itself in extreme muscle fatigue. Staying up until the early hours of the morning means limited motion for the next few days. It takes more time for my body to recover. The frequent doctor appointments combined with chronic fatigue and uncontrolled seizures limits the time I could give to writing and other activities. Large blocks of time sitting at a computer were not and are not conducive to my health.

Christine Miserandino's spoon theory explains that people living with chronic illnesses have a limited number of spoons per day. I have had days where I thought I was going to be early but, after showering, doing my hair, doing my makeup, and getting dressed I had only six spoons left. Now I have to walk to campus or the bus stop. Then teach my class. By the time I get home I have zero spoons. I can barely make it up the front steps to get into my house. I am thinking to myself: Where am I going to find the spoons to lesson prep for tomorrow, let alone research and write an article? I do not have as many spoons as someone who is non-disabled. A key component for continuing my scholarly writing is acknowledging what it means to live with chronic illness. I am working on limits and boundaries when it comes to writing and research.

My body requires accommodations, and it cannot adhere to the forty-hour work week. Academia requires even more hours than a standard work week. Although presented as a flexible working environment, teaching, research, and writing goes well beyond forty hours a week. There are times when I work on weekends in order to get some writing done. I also have to make time for multiple doctor appointments that cut into my workday. There are many requests concerning my health that, as an early career scholar, I have avoided asking administrators. When I was a VAP, I accepted the schedule offered to me. This included

8:00 a.m. classes. At first, this can appear to be a small matter. However, I am learning the ebbs and flows of my body's energy. When I will have the most energy determines what I can give to each day. I have learned that early morning classes will hinder the time I can give to writing and research. An 8:00 a.m. class means getting up at least two hours earlier so that I am not rushing to get ready. Rushing will only increase my fatigue. Many people feel exhausted after an eight-hour-plus day. Consider how your body feels after a long day, then double that feeling—that is how I feel. It is through trial and error and the concept of spoon theory that I have learned what times of the day work best for me. Now I request classes that work around my body's abilities.

Academia is currently advocating for my diversity while overlooking the disability and chronic illness among faculty and staff. This continues the erasure of disability in academia. I rarely disclose my health conditions to colleagues, but nondisclosure of my health poses a threat to my life. The fear of sharing means that my colleagues will not know what to do if I have a flare-up or seizure. I am not advocating that anyone has to vocalize their health issues. Instead, I am asking that space be made available to faculty to share without negative consequences. Additionally, we should create a system where placing breaks or canceling class does not become a negative. Even in the midst of health flares I held classes when I was in pain. My own internalized ideas of productivity upheld the idea of returning to business as usual. By voicing my experiences as a Black woman living with disabilities, I am pushing against erasure in academia. I refuse to be erased within an institution that extracts from me.

I am advocating for both representation and the unlearning of the tools of oppression. During the last year I had to ask myself, am I loving myself well? For true social change I need to do the internal work that a politics of care requires. Resistance means moving away from a model of white supremacy that is entrenched in labor. Hyperproductivity as the way to success is a fallacy of white supremacy. It is a tool that works us into the ground in the name of capitalism. As a Black woman living with chronic illness, producing more does not result in the same level of access or success as my white able-bodied counterparts. I have internalized productivity and output at the expense of my own health. This combined with controlling images (Collins 69) that frame Black women in America as unintelligent, inadequate, and lazy push me into hyperproductivity. My internalization of these images has led to me accepting lack of sleep and the failure to care for myself as normal and inevitable. With each new year I am resisting academic grind culture by prioritizing my Black disabled body.

TEACHING AND WRITING

In this section I address the dichotomy of choosing between writing more and caring for oneself as always being a point of tension within academia. From the beginning of our graduate indoctrination, we are taught that writing and research is the priority; then teaching, with little emphasis placed on the self. This becomes even more entrenched when BIPOC scholars hold onto this hegemonic structure. We hold onto this narrative from institutions that benefit from our exhaustion while deeming us incompetent. I navigate this paradox by acknowledging that the ideologies of white supremacy are embedded in academia. We are not going to escape it by adhering to standards that never considered us. With this in mind, I challenge myself to implement a politics of care that values my Black womanhood and disabilities. This does not mean less rigor but prioritizes community care. My first year as a tenure-track assistant professor is helping define what this means for me.

The best description I have for my first semester as an assistant professor on the tenure track is quicksand. I felt like I was sinking, and even when I tried to escape, I could not. I just kept sinking further. I arrived in Virginia in August 2021, just three weeks before the start of fall semester. Of course, as a new faculty member I needed to attend multiple orientations and meetings. Roughly a week full of meetings. Where was I supposed to find the time to unpack and prepare for new classes? I felt like I was always running behind myself. Adding writing time seemed impossible. Trying to keep up with grading and lectures felt like quicksand. Again, I kept asking myself, how am I going to edit the articles I have been working on? It was the help of a Black woman mentor and co-author that provided some relief in terms of writing. The article we co-authored required a final round of edits, and she volunteered to complete this round of edits. As a full professor and Black woman in academia she knew the intensity of the first year. This act of kindness provided me a moment of reprieve that allowed me to breathe and re-center myself so that I could focus on another writing project.

Fall 2021 was an intense semester with lack of sleep and feeling constantly overwhelmed. It was a learning curve for me. Entering spring semester, I decided to find ways to protect my time and care for myself better. It began with admitting to myself that these are not "normal" times. This is a global pandemic, and I am not obligated to operate in the name of business as usual. This is reflected in my decision-making around conferences, writing, and other presentation formats. I have limited the number of conferences I applied for and will attend.

I am also adamant about protecting my writing time. I am still working it out, but through the formation of writing groups I have accountability. Writing groups provide me with blocks of time dedicated only to writing. It improves my productivity, but its most beneficial component is the release of inadequacy. Whether or not I write a thousand words during that time, I know that I made the effort. I am able to extend grace to myself. I can rest afterward without the looming belief that I did not do enough. I did what I could do in that space and time. I have been cognizant of what events and opportunities I accepted or attended. The goals I have set for advancement can happen at a slower pace. There is no way to always be on top of things. The best thing to do is reject the idea that we are superhuman or deficient because we cannot keep up with systems that have been designed to ensure our failure.

How do I write, teach, and research in a system set up for me to fail? Higher education fails to offer the resources Black, disabled, women, and other BIPOC scholars need to navigate academia. Obtaining a degree did not magically stop all the ways my daily life is put face-to-face with America's failing healthcare system, state violence, and economic inequalities. Hiring Black women and asking us to not only do our jobs well but to "grind" for a system that does not care for us well is a setup. My response to "grind culture" and a higher education system that fails Black women faculty has been to unlearn hyperproductivity. My models for reorienting my relationship to work and productivity came through Black feminist praxis, disability scholarship, community building, and mentorship.

I refuse to participate in "grind culture." More specifically, I am not going to overwork at the expense of my physical and mental health. I am at my best when I am rested and well cared for. Being at my best is not only about academia but my right to be as a Black disabled woman. Even the resistance against "grind culture" can be co-opted by the university. This returns to the paradox of whether or not we can escape the system we are critiquing. I am arguing for rest as a right that is not tied to producing for the institution. My body has a right to leisure outside of what my rest will produce for the university.

My rest during this pandemic came through small gatherings, virtual online spaces created by Black women academics and professionals, mentoring, and check-ins that remind me to rest. In this context rest is both individual and structural. It is an act of resistance that defies racism, sexism, and ableism, which are the tools that further capitalism. This brings me back to my question, Am I doing enough? This question cannot be separated from my identity and the systems of power I navigate daily. Our current constructions of productivity are biased, ableist, classist, and anti-Black. These biases are embedded in viewing the work of Black academics as less rigorous. There is also a failure to acknowledge invisible labor. Prior to this global pandemic there were few accommodations for people living with disabilities. Little has changed; academia continues to ask for high rates of output at the expense of ourselves. I am now reframing the question of am I doing enough; my new questions are: How can I reassess my relationship to productivity? How can I access and create new resources at my university that will support a balanced writing process?

bell hooks's phrase "white supremacist capitalist patriarchy" continues to push me to think about how I am reproducing these paradoxes inside of academia. My redefining of productivity in my writing and research is tied to my overall well-being. As a race and justice studies scholar my work is both personal and political. My criterion for productivity is not only based on completion. I want to ensure that my writing adequately reflects the experiences and voices of marginalized people. As Black women we have a life force within ourselves that can empower us to full liberation and freedom (Lorde, *Uses*). I am learning how to home in on the power within me to create new ways of being as a Black disabled woman.

IMPLEMENTING PRACTICES OF CARE TO FURTHER MY WRITING

Mentorship is a key component in furthering my practices of care and shaping how I engage with academia. My academic mentors reminded me not to follow their acts of long hours, late nights, and lack of sleep. This encouraged me to carve my own path that insisted I not be a "burnt out" scholar. My daily reminder is that it will get done. There will always be work. I allow myself to just lie down for an hour when I get home. If my body is asking for more rest, then I let her. It is not easy. My own self-critique can make me feel bad that all I did when I left campus was eat and sleep. But then I ask myself, What is wrong with this option? I am human, not superhuman. I am not the capitalist, racist, sexist stereotype of the strong Black woman. It is okay to rest and let tomorrow's trouble be just that, tomorrow's trouble.

Creating virtual writing groups was a key solution to staying afloat. I first used this accountability method as a graduate student and still find it valuable as an early career scholar. One method I use is setting aside two hours each day for research and writing. It is easy to get swallowed up by lesson prep and other duties. By protecting these two hours a day, I can read an article, outline, write a couple of paragraphs or edit a document. This can feel like a slow process but before I know it, I hit my writing goals. My former doctoral advisor and I would use a Google Doc to log our daily hours. After implementing either of these options, my anxiety decreases, and I am able to increase balance in my schedule. Breaking up writing into small blocks removes the mental weight of whether or not I am doing enough.

I also participate in multiple writing groups at JMU. This includes the weekly College of Arts (CAL) writing group at JMU that meets via Zoom. The group meets on Fridays for three hours. This space provides me with the opportunity to share projects, ask for advice, and write. I also have my sister-friends who write with me and hold me accountable. On Saturdays, my friend and I will hold a Zoom session for a couple of hours. For the CAL writing session and the one on Saturday we log in on Zoom. During the first fifteen minutes we check in and share what we are working on for that day. Then we turn our cameras off and continue working on our projects. Then we return about ten minutes before the end of the session and close out. During the closing we share what we did or did not get through during our writing session. There are times when I get a lot of writing done and other moments where that writing time turns into grading. Overall, these virtual sessions have kept me on top of my writing. It is a great feeling to have the rest of the day for other things, which include resting my body. All in all, I have learned to fiercely protect my writing time.

Taking the time to step away is important. Combatting my anxiety is no easy feat. That small voice that asks "Am I doing this well?" or "Is this enough?" creeps in so easily. This doubt is from the microaggressions I experienced within the "ivory tower." The elitism of academia that refuses to acknowledge the quality of scholarship by Black people that centers Black people. As a graduate student, I had a faculty member share her surprise at the quality of my work. It came through as a backhanded compliment. The "oh wow" that you know in your gut is rooted in not believing in the quality of Black women's work. Another faculty member pushed back on my argument about the anti-Blackness of the current immigrant rights movement. She did not accept my positionality of engaging with both the immigration system and the prison system as a Black woman and child of immigrants. I spent a lot of time having to prove both myself and the importance of my research. These experiences were microaggressions that came from white women and non-Black women of color. A reminder that Black women in higher education have few places to rest when pushing against daily microaggressions. This rest is both physical and mental.

Black and women of color faculty, staff, and administrators at James Madison University created a group called Sisters in Session (SIS). This group has aided me since the beginning of my career at JMU. My questions about moving, finding a loctician to style my hair, medical doctors, and community have come out of this group. There is an email listserv as well as a Slack workspace for us to connect and share information, as well as our successes and frustrations. The leaders of the group hold multiple gatherings throughout the semester. These social events have allowed me to connect with different Black women and other women of color that I would not meet otherwise. It is difficult to meet other faculty of color on a large campus. Plus, we are often in our offices all day and then gone when our classes are over. These gatherings have allowed for laughter and opportunities for future collaborations. I am not an artist, but I want to have more artistic and unconventional assignments within my courses. I will be collaborating with one of my colleagues in the Art Department at JMU. Another important collective has been my social justice cohort. I was hired as part of a social justice cohort at JMU. We are all BIPOC faculty whose research, teaching, and writing center social justice and activism. As a cohort we are sharing triumphs and losses. We are also building community by having outings together to explore Harrisonburg, Virginia. I have also created panels with my cohort members this year. I look forward to future research and writing collaborations.

These opportunities were not given to BIPOC scholars. All of these spaces and collaborations were created from the ground up. The writing group, digital spaces, and mentorship occur within and outside of the university. Although we never truly escape all of the ways academia extracts from us, we can still resist. This resistance is rooted in community building.

COMMUNITY, DIGITAL SPACES, AND MY WRITING PROCESS

The space that is being forged and created by Black women through social media cannot be dismissed. The digital space is an alternate form of community that offers support on writing, publishing, and navigating the world of academia as a Black, disabled, woman scholar. The digital space has allowed Black women in academia to hold each other, grieve together, as well as celebrate and experience Black joy. It was through digital spaces and forming a community with other Black and Indigenous people of color (BIPOC) scholars that I survived.

I belong to groups on Facebook that are specifically designed for Black women and nonbinary people in academia. I also follow other

Black academics and women of color on Twitter and Instagram. Facebook, Twitter, and Instagram have become important digital spaces that help me to reassess and evaluate my relationship to academia. The Facebook groups I belong to are by invite only. My invite came from another friend who is also in academia. Once accepted, there is a set of ground rules for how we want to respect each other in addition to not sharing details about what is shared within the group. This is important to protect ourselves within higher education. While I was in the interview process for my current position, I asked questions about what to ask the dean of the college. I have also gained information on writing groups to join.

Twitter is another online platform for academic resources. Academic Twitter and Black Twitter are informal but have been built out over time by following specific accounts such as @academicchatter or using the hashtags #BlackAcademic and #AcademicTwitter. I have found GIFs that state, "I have no idea what I'm doing, but I know I'm doing it really, really well." This is a funny GIF that speaks to the fact that no academic truly knows what they are doing. It is a big relief to be reminded of that fact. Last week, I asked the following question, "When you were an early career scholar, what support do you wish your department/ university provided?" The responses I received helped me prepare for my first-year review with my academic unit head (AUH). I asked about a pre-tenure sabbatical that will give me time to write and research before my tenure review.

Then there is the digital platform Instagram, which offers the option to follow a diverse array of people and influencers. The influencers I follow address topics that are both comedic and activist oriented. The influencers I follow include a focus on body positivity, immigration, and other social-justice-related issues. Instagram's platform is based on posting pictures, stories, and live recordings. Instagram provides snippets and sound bites that can lead you to websites, blogs, and podcasts that further explain the ideas and concepts being presented. Instagram is where I found the account The Nap Ministry by Tricia Hersey. The account's mini biography reads, "We examine the liberating power of naps. We believe rest is a form of resistance and reparations. We install Nap Experiences. Founded in 2016." I have viewed time as a social construction for a while. Her Instagram account pushed me to think beyond time to my body and the importance of rest.

Tricia Hersey is a Black woman who is committed to pushing against grind culture. A culture that pushes the ideology that nonstop, twenty-hours-a-day working will get us status and success. Hersey shares posts such as: "You are not a machine. Stop grinding. The Nap Ministry." Her organization uses their digital platforms to share their framework of "Rest is Resistance." Through her programming that fuses the arts with political resistance she is helping thousands of people understand the power of rest beyond just a physical nap. I view Hersey's frameworks of resistance and reparations as not only liberatory but part of an abolitionist movement. One that is rooted in both praxis and theory. The practice of napping unravels the model of grind culture that only sees our bodies as valuable if we perform the function of work. Hersey states that "[Her] rest as a Black woman in America suffering from generational exhaustion and racial trauma always was a political refusal and social justice uprising within [her] body." Hersey's commitment to rest is about deprogramming our bodies from capitalist models of extraction. I have found this to be powerful because it is breaking away from ideologies. It is a Black feminist praxis that addresses both the physical, mental, and structural battles we face every day. Heresy's Instagram platform has been influential for me. Pausing and assessing our physical and mental wellness is part of this rest. Rest is both spiritual and political (Hersey).

Hersey reminds me that as a Black woman with disabilities I do not have to normalize grind culture. I redress the toll that hyperproductivity takes on my body by making choices that center my disabilities. This looks like moving away from a writing process tied to restless nights. My reprogramming of rest showed up when I decided that last fall I did not have to work on weekends. The majority of my first semester at James Madison University was all-consuming; toward the end, I created a model for myself that insisted on the weekend being my own time to just be. I did not respond to student emails, I slept in, and I enjoyed my favorite shows. Over winter break I leaned further into this rest. My rest is no longer tied to producing for the institution. This is one way of navigating being within the institution but not upholding ableism.

Now it is spring semester, and I am almost through with my first year on the tenure track. This semester I crafted a schedule where I teach Monday through Wednesday. I made Thursdays and Fridays my writing days. On some Saturdays I will do two hours of work. The majority of my weekend is committed to my rest. Of course, this is not a foolproof process. I am not always on top of grading and there are some Thursdays and Fridays I get little writing done. I have accepted that I will fall behind in grading, writing, or researching as I continue my career as a scholar. More importantly, I am making more time to pause and breathe. I will not allow capitalistic structures to take away the joy of laughter and being. My writing process will change each semester or

172 TATIANA BENJAMIN

year. It will continue to be refined and rooted in my needs as a Black cisgender woman living with chronic illnesses.

CONCLUSION

Building a career as a Black woman living with disabilities is a continuous cycle of unlearning ideologies that label me inept and disposable. Just existing in the world of academia is no easy task. Navigating writing as an early career scholar is a process of trial and error that has as many lows as it does highs. Even then the highs seem few and far between. Everything comes back to managing time when there is no way to stop time. Finding the time to write when my body aches, my awareness leaves me, grades are piling up, all while living during a pandemic feels like an impossible task. Quite frankly it is nerve-racking, but as the saying states, hindsight is twenty-twenty. Looking back at the last four years as a cisgender Black woman with chronic illness in academia, I have stopped, failed, and succeeded when it comes to writing and research. It is through mentorship, community building, and digital spaces that I am learning how to exist within academia while not reproducing white supremacist ideologies. These academic and digital communities are created from the ground up by and for scholars who sit at the margins.

The goal is not to return to a pre-pandemic idea of academia as normal. We must deconstruct grind culture. This begins with unlearning the tools of white supremacy. In the words of the great Audre Lorde, "The master's tools will never dismantle the master's house." My call to action is to remind ourselves that as Black women we are not indebted to academia. There is no need to carry the burden of whether or not we belong. I am not accepting the "strong Black woman" trope. I refuse to allow capitalism by another name to perpetuate the strong Black woman who can do it all. Being Black, disabled, and a woman, I had to learn that long hours are not adequately rewarded, nor should my body or rest be tied to money. Lastly, let us live the liberatory work that we do. If we place our value in our productivity, we will truly never be happy. We will not know how to enjoy the fruits of our labor. It will never be enough. Capitalism will always be whispering to us that there is still more to achieve.

My act of resistance against the reproduction of capitalism and white supremacy inside academia is centering my experiences as a Black woman with disabilities. I want to live to continue my writing and as a scholar practitioner who is committed to liberation for *all*. Unfortunately, Black women have a low life expectancy. To combat this,

I am seeking new ways to be both productive and healthy. My writing process consists of chunks or blocks of time. I am also working on resisting the belief that taking a pause in writing means my project will not be finished. Academia is a machine, so it is not going to willfully give me the balance I seek. I must create it for myself. In the words of activist and scholar Angela Davis, "You have to act as if it were possible to radically transform the world. And you have to do it all the time." I have an image of Angela Davis and this quote on my office door. I keep it there every day to remind myself that I can radically change the world by unlearning systems and ideologies of oppression.

WORKS CITED

Bailey, Moya, and Izetta Autumn Mobley. "Work in the Intersections: A Black Feminist Disability Framework." *Gender & Society*, vol. 33, no. 1, Feb. 2019, pp. 19–40.

Bell, Christopher M. *Blackness and Disability : Critical Examinations and Cultural Interventions.* Michigan State UP, 2011.

Brown, Nicole, and Jennifer Leigh. *Ableism in Academia: Theorising Experiences of Disabilities and Chronic Illness in Higher Education.* U College London P, 2020.

Campbell, Fiona. "Inciting Legal Fictions: 'Disability' Date with Ontology and the Ableist Body of the Law." *Griffith Law Review*, vol 10, no. 1, 2011.

Collins, Patricia Hill. *Black Feminist Thought : Knowledge, Consciousness, and the Politics of Empowerment.* 2nd ed., Routledge, 2000.

Davis, Angela. Lecture. Black History Month 2014: Civil Rights in America. 13 Feb. 2014. Shyrock Auditorium, Southern Illinois University, Carbondale, Illinois.

Hersey, Tricia. "Rest Is Anything That Connects Your Mind to Your Body." *The Nap Ministry*, Feb. 2022, https://thenapministry.wordpress.com.

Hersey, Tricia. "About." *Tricia Hersey*, http://www.triciahersey.com/about.html. Accessed Apr. 2022.

hooks, bell. *Writing Beyond Race Living Theory and Practice.* 1st ed., Routledge, 2013.

Lorde, Audre. "Uses of the Erotic, the Erotic as Power." Fourth Berkshire Conference on the History of Women, Mount Holyoke College. South Hadley, Massachusetts. 25 Aug. 1978.

Lorde, Audre. "The Master's Tools Will Never Dismantle the Master's House (Comments at the 'The Personal and the Political Panel,' Second Sex Conference, New York, 29 Sept. 1979)." *Sister Outsider Essays and Speeches.* Crossing Press, 1984, pp. 110–13.

Miserandino, Christine. "The Spoon Theory." butyoudontlooksick.com, 2003.

11

UNDERGRADUATES AND FACULTY WRITING AS PARTNERS

Kellie Keeling, Emily Pridgen, and J. Michael Rifenburg

Tags: collaboration, productivity

A pecan tree lives outside the building where we work and learn. Its crown spreads across the north Georgia sky, casting shade in summer and dropping pecans in autumn. The pecan tree stands alone; the live oaks and water oaks on our campus make their homes fifty or so yards away. But beneath the surface, according to forest sciences scholars, a vast fungal network transmits signals between the pecan tree and the oaks. Despite biological theories that place species in competition against each other, researchers are following data that suggests trees use underground fungal networks to "exchange news about insects, drought, and other dangers" (Wohlleben 10). In *Nature*, Suzanne Simard and colleagues outline the net transfer of carbon between three different tree species, leading *Nature* to coin the term "wood wide web" as a catchy slogan for this research. Publications—popular press and scholarly—have flowed forth since. Simard's *Finding the Mother Tree* encapsulates her career-long research, and Simard found herself the focus of a *New York Times Magazine* article (Jabr).

As we reflect on our undergraduate and faculty writing partnership, we think of the pecan tree we have walked beneath for many years. Individually, we see ourselves as this tree: growing and learning and trying to thrive in a field of study (i.e., English studies) that often privileges the individual over the collective. Our field largely bestows tenure and promotion on single-authored books and articles, gives out awards to individual students, and places grades on individual student essays. Sure, we have thrived in this environment. One of us received tenure; one of us received her bachelor's degree while we drafted this chapter; one of us graduated when we worked on editorial revisions to this chapter. To be fair, within English studies broadly and writing studies more specifically, we do note examples of collaboration. Research teams

https://doi.org/10.7330/9781646424870.c011

win competitive grants from the Conference on College Composition and Communication, and co-authored books receive awards from the National Council of Teachers of English. We acknowledge the work of scholars like Lisa Ede and Andrea Lunsford and Kami Day and Michele Eodice, who, in their co-authored work, outline paths forward for co-authoring in English studies. We note this edited collection itself—a partnership between co-editors. We see faculty co-authoring with faculty; we see faculty co-authoring with graduate students.

In our chapter, we aim to expand understandings and practices of collaboration in writing studies by pointing to our collaborative story of undergraduate students and a faculty member researching and writing together. We research together; we co-author together. Like the pecan tree on our campus, we do not labor alone. We are a part of a larger network. When our country and state experienced lockdown during the global pandemic, we were at work on our co-research. To continue our work, we sent resources to each other when possible, not through fungal networks but through fiber optic cables.

This is our story of sharing and partnering, of accepting coordination over competition. We describe how we developed a faculty and under-graduate writing partnership and how we continued this partnership during lockdown. We highlight outputs of our partnership and position our writing partnership as one that seeks to disrupt neoliberal forces of marketplace competition within US higher education by encouraging all of us to slow down and seek coordination over competition. At the close, we offer a note of caution for undergraduates and faculty who seek to enter a writing partnership. We note how faculty-student partnerships carry potential for labor exploitation because, to return to our guiding arboreal metaphor, students and faculty are not the same tree species. The existing hierarchical structure between undergraduate students and faculty allows opportunities for faculty to exploit students' labor by dictating content, offloading mundane tasks like double-checking references onto students, and lording over decisions like when to meet and how long to meet. Therefore, we engage with how to establish equitable working conditions.

Throughout this chapter, we toggle between multiple voices. We offer a collective voice—like we do in this paragraph. We also offer the perspectives of Michael and Emily, who worked on a yearlong project together; we offer the perspective of Kellie and Michael, who also worked on a yearlong project together. We offer our individual perspectives offset from the main text. We determined author order based on guidance on authorship and author order from the Committee on Publication Ethics and the International Committee of Medical Journal

KELLIE KEELING, EMILY PRIDGEN, AND J. MICHAEL RIFENBURG

Editors, the latter providing clear criteria for authorship. Our author order is alphabetical and does not indicate one person contributing to this chapter more than another.

GROUNDING OUR PARTNERSHIP

In describing our work to audiences, we use *partnership*, not *collaboration*, intentionally. The word "partnership" describes our coordinated efforts to learn and write together and signals our commitment to students-as-partners (SaP) (e.g., Curtis and Anderson; Mercer-Mapstone and Abbot). SaP, also termed *pedagogical partnerships* in some literature (Cook-Sather et al.), has roots in the undergraduate research movement. Like undergraduate research, SaP is built on faculty-student relationships and the committed belief that undergraduate students can contribute to scholarly conversations and should have a voice in the knowledge-making of any field. In an extensive literature review of SaP praxis, Lucy Mercer-Mapstone and colleagues write that by grounding SaP labor in a "values-based ethos," students and faculty shift to "co-teachers, co-inquirers, curriculum co-creators, and co-learners across all facets of the educational enterprise" (2). Such an ethos helps faculty *and* students contribute meaningfully to scholarship on curriculum development, assessment, and writing instruction.

To speak more concretely of what SaP looks like, we point readers to faculty in the chemistry department at Creighton University, who involved students in backward course design over the course of two years and tracked the results five years later (Duda and Danielson); faculty at Massey University in New Zealand, who worked with students to develop an assessment plan for an internship program connected to an educational psychology internship program (Bourke et al.). We point readers to a faculty member at Georgia State University, who partnered with graduate students to define a collaborative public project in a class titled Public Rhetorics for Social Change (Holmes). We also should note the important work coming from within writing studies that, while not directly responsive to SaP theory and practice and not published in SaP-focused journals, espouses the SaP ethos. Here we think of Joyce Kinkead's partnership with undergraduate students to assess elements of a general education curriculum; we think of Joe Cirio's pedagogical practice of inviting students to help design an assessment rubric. Though both Kinkead and Cirio are listed as single authors on their respective publications, practices like these that invite students into teaching and learning practices exemplify core principles of SaP.

Inspired by SaP praxis, Emily and Michael and Kellie and Michael undertook two separate yearlong projects. Chronologically, Emily and Michael completed their project when Kellie and Michael were in the early stages of their project.

Michael and Emily developed and implemented an assessment plan for redesigned first-year writing courses at our home institution, the University of North Georgia (UNG). UNG is a multicampus regional university with roughly twenty thousand undergraduate students. It's a primarily white institution, a federally designated senior military college, and the state-appointed leadership institution. Both Emily and Michael work and learn in the English Department, and Michael serves as co-director of first-year writing and co-chaired the faculty-only committee tasked with redesigning this first-year writing course. For three years, Michael worked with this committee. Changes were made, adopted, piloted, and assessed through a dizzying array of metrics, spreadsheets, and percentages. To add to this quantitative data, Michael partnered with Emily, who, at the time, was an undergraduate English major. Emily and Michael developed a qualitative assessment plan designed to hear from students who took these redesigned courses and to hear from faculty who taught these redesigned courses. Emily and Michael wrote an Institutional Research Board (IRB) application together, presented a poster of their work at an international conference, drafted blog posts for their local center for teaching and learning website, and wrote a blog post for the American Association of Colleges and Universities (AAC&U). Michael and Emily wrote emails to English faculty about their work and wrote emails to upper administrators about the importance of involving undergraduate students in large-scale curricular assessment efforts.

Michael carried the momentum he developed with Emily into redesigning an English capstone course he regularly teaches. He connected with Kellie, who, like Emily, was an English major at the time; they read about research on the importance of capstone courses; they read about the importance of inserting what the AAC&U calls "signature experiences" in capstone courses. Together, they dreamed up what it would look like to implement a signature experience in this discipline-specific capstone course. They developed an assignment that invited students to integrate knowledge from across their undergraduate experiences—curricular, co-curricular, and extra-curricular experiences—and to bring this integrated knowledge to bear on a pressing issue: the decline of the liberal arts through enrollment numbers and budgets and reallocation of resources. Kellie and Michael shared their newly designed course with upper administrators at UNG; with two other student authors, they published a blog post on their local center for teaching and learning website (Green et al.); they designed Spanish-language infographics on SaP to connect with the large Spanish-speaking population at UNG and created brochures about their work. They presented at a local teaching and learning conference and an international teaching and learning conference. With an additional undergraduate student author, they placed an article in an international teaching and learning journal (Keeling et al.).

In sum, the partnerships we developed led us to write in multiple genres, for multiple audiences, and for multiple purposes. We offer our individual perspectives on why we undertook the challenging work of partnering together to write together.

> KELLIE: This project stood out to me because of my personal struggle with obtaining my undergraduate degree. This project created the opportunity—after eight years at three different schools with seven different majors—for me to feel connected to my own learning experience; it has shown that teachers and students can offer one another their own invaluable perspective to create a curriculum that is effective, engaging, and sustainable, relying on the expertise of the teacher and the needs of the students.
>
> During my lengthy college career, I often felt alone. I felt that I was growing and trying to learn in a barren wasteland with no one around me to help. The previous universities I attended never felt like home; the degree I was working towards felt like an obligation, not a way to improve myself. I imagined myself a lone tree, defying the desolate desert that continued to amass around me. No network to rely on for seeing the dangers to come, no elder trees to provide wisdom and guidance, and no companions to motivate and encourage me to continue on. This lack of support led me to quit college for four long years. I felt there was no reason for me to suffer through this, no one cared if I stayed or not. A tree needs its network like a struggling college student needs support. I found this support at UNG and through my work in this partnership.

> EMILY: At first, this working partnership filled a need for me. I needed an internship to graduate and doing this project with Dr. Rifenburg filled that need. However, when I really started the work of assessing students' experiences with the pilot English 1101 course, I found meaning in the work I was doing and became more invested in the project. Working on this project as a student partner gave me valuable experience that I was able to translate into a professional life post-college.
>
> I think the fact that this partnership existed was valuable outside of the work we did, too. From the beginning, I felt that having a student's perspective on a project that affects students was important. I was proud that my department and Dr. Rifenburg felt the same way.

MICHAEL: I struggle to answer this question: Why did I look to form partnerships with undergraduate students? I am more able to answer a similar question: Why do I form these partnerships? I am unsure where the idea-seeds came from. I remember wanting to get undergraduate input into our faculty-only committee tasked with redesigning a first-year writing course. I remember presenting at a conference—alone, of course—about wanting to bring undergraduate students on board this work, and a colleague in the audience introducing me to SaP. Maybe why I did it is the same as why I do it: to build knowledge with others, to have my ideas and perspectives challenged, to offer findings that don't just advance my career but have meaningful impact for the students with whom I share a campus.

As we rarely meet in person, our writing is mediated across scores of screens, apps, and sites. We describe this mediation in the next section.

OUR PARTNERSHIP MEDIATED BY DIGITAL TECHNOLOGY

We planted the seeds for our partnership pre-pandemic, but our partnership flourished during lockdown. The COVID-19 pandemic is too close to us; we do not feel comfortable making bold claims about how our writing partnership changed, how our thinking changed, and how our findings changed because of the global pandemic. What we can offer, however, is concrete statements about how we worked during lockdown and how faculty members and undergraduate students seeking to develop similar partnerships may use digital technology to mediate these partnerships.

Michael and Emily met multiple times in person early in their partnership. They sat outside the library in the shade or found a spot on the third floor of the library. Kellie and Michael have never met in person to work on their project. Even though their project is ongoing as we type this chapter, they do not anticipate meeting in person.

Our partnership was driven by three digital tools: Zoom, Microsoft Teams, and Google Docs. We talked over Zoom, and we authored over Google Docs. To be more concrete, here is how we wrote the first draft of this chapter during the hot Georgia summer days. Before we met on Zoom, Michael emailed a list of questions he wanted all three of us to individually answer during our initial meeting—based on the proposal we authored in response to the call for papers for this edited collection: *What can you individually contribute to this chapter? What is a story or idea that is unique to you and fits for this chapter? What have we collectively done that fits for this chapter?* These questions toggled between the individual and the collective, looking for space for all of us to enter this writing project from our different perspectives. Our initial meeting was the first time Kellie and Emily met. They shared their experiences with each other. We answered our two questions aloud. Michael typed notes. Michael shared his screen. He showed the proposal we authored, and we collectively broke the proposal into an outline. We then assigned sections to each other. Eventually, we arrived at the outline below, with names assigned to each section:

Open with metaphor of trees. Connect to writing together: Michael
Grounding our partnership in SaP: Kellie
How our partnership was mediated by technology: Emily
Benefits of our partnership—pushed against neoliberal demands: Emily
BUT: dangers of unpaid work and exploring labor: Kellie
End with trees?

Michael agreed to receive the individual written sections from Emily and Kellie and assemble them together. Because we knew we wanted to offer our own perspectives alongside our collective perspective, we assigned vignettes. We wrote on Google Docs, which populated a shared folder. We agreed on a date to upload our writing. We met the date. We did not meet again on Zoom before submitting the first draft of this chapter. Michael shared drafts over email. We made changes over email. Our revisions, too, occurred asynchronously. We received news that our proposal was accepted in early 2021 and completed rounds of revisions in late 2022. At that point, two of us had graduated away from campus—one of us to Italy!

Our partnership, mediated through these places and tools, reminded us how physical and virtual writing spaces shape one's writing processes and practices. In *Situating Writing Practices*, Hannah Rule invites readers to consider the situatedness of writing. Rule describes how writing processes "can never be nowhere—processes only unfold through particular bodies; in specific locations, rooms, spaces, or places; with varying tools, objects, and ambient artifacts; and with others near and distant. Processes, in other words, are always already and chiefly physical" (3). The constraints and affordances of composing on Microsoft Word online and Google Docs shaped our writing processes through synchronous and asynchronous opportunities to brainstorm and draft prose; Zoom shaped how we communicated and collaborated, causing us to slow our conversation, not talk over one another, listen hard for verbal and nonverbal cues that signaled one person was ending their speech utterance or preparing to begin one, muting ourselves (literally). Our situated writing processes and practices, as Rule notes, unfolded

Undergraduates and Faculty Writing as Partners 181

through these digital technologies but also unfolded through our interaction with external objects that populated our personal writing spaces. No longer were we gathering in a public space to write—like a library or local coffee shop. But we wrote (together) alone in spaces that we lived in, that we literally designed and staged and decorated—our personal offices and kitchens and bedrooms. We wrote surrounded by external objects that we placed and used and liked. We offer individual vignettes on our writing spaces:

KELLIE: Most of my writing occurred on my couch; I was gifted a lap desk from a close friend, and I would push my ottoman up against my couch, set my laptop on top of my new desk, open my windows, and write. I have never been a desk person; I like to fold my legs up into my chest while I work, pure comfort yields my best work. Most of my writing was fragmented in an extreme way. I am a stay-at-home mom, and my daughter needs my attention above all else. She will frequently crawl up in my lap as I work and try to help mommy type.

EMILY: My writing took place at a small wooden desk in my bedroom for the majority of our time together. I sat in a swivel chair, turned on my lamp, and typed on my laptop. I sold all of my furniture during my last move, so now I write on my parents' couch.

MICHAEL: I write in my home office at a wooden desk my neighbor helped me build. My wife and I have three young kids, and my home office does not have a door. So, interruptions come often. I wear a pair of Bluetooth headphones to block out the sounds of my kids and sometimes relocate to the garage to write. I set up a plastic folding table and type away. Overall, my writing space is sparse. A blue pen, one notepad, a coaster with a drink, my laptop. Sometimes, I light a soy candle.

Laura Micciche's *Acknowledging Writing Partners* helps us investigate how our relationship with and to external objects facilitates or even shapes our writing processes and practices. Micciche uses the phrase "indebted partnerships" to signal this relationship. As we step back from our writing partnership and take stock of the tools we leveraged to write and the wheres and whens of our writing, we note but are not yet ready to explain how offloading our work onto solely digital tools and relocating our workspace from shared communal spaces to personal, private spheres shaped the exigence for our partnerships, the work we undertook, and how we circulated our findings.

The two sections above offer the frame for our partnership. We now shift to the outcomes of our partnership with a focus on what partnership allows and the potential pitfalls that come with faculty and undergraduates laboring together to investigate teaching and learning. We

182   KELLIE KEELING, EMILY PRIDGEN, AND J. MICHAEL RIFENBURG

focus on how partnerships help fight against neoliberal imperatives and issues of labor exploitation within faculty-student partnerships.

SLOWING DOWN TO COUNTER NEOLIBERALISM

Slowing down, working together, and writing together are not natural activities for us, particularly as we find ourselves working and learning within a higher education moment that privileges speed and more and more and more publications and grants. We take seriously ideas about slowing down that are articulated in books like *The Slow Professor: Challenging the Culture of Speed in the Academy* (Seeber and Berg). We came together to learn together. But two outputs of our work, we have happily discovered, are the act of slowing down and the act of coordinating resources. We place slowness and coordination in direct opposition to the privileging of speed and competition that we see as traits of neoliberalism in US higher education. We use the term "neoliberal" with a definition in mind and attributes in mind. The definition comes from legal scholar Malcolm Voyce, who defines neoliberalism as "policies of competition, deregulation and privatization" (2055). Sociologist Teguh Wijaya Mulya offers three hallmarks of neoliberalism: "marketisation, competitiveness, and standardisation" (p. 87). Both Voyce and Mulya highlight the central role of competition. The additional traits characterizing neoliberalism, we argue, rotate around the idea of increasing productivity. Deregulation as a method for increasing productivity; outsourcing to private companies as a method for increasing productivity; standardizing as a method for increasing productivity. US higher education is experiencing a push toward increasing worker productivity and seeing the use of competition (faculty against faculty; student against student) as a vehicle for arriving at this productivity. A concrete example of increased competition is the single-authored research article. According to teaching and learning scholars Vivienne Bozalek and colleagues, "Sole-authored articles are the most highly prized by [higher education institutes] due to neoliberal imperatives such as funding formulae for research incentives and rewards" (2). We counter policies privileging competition. We slow down. We come together not in quest of research incentives and rewards but to build community and knowledge together.

We come to SaP labor because, as Mulya argues, faculty-student partnerships "might contest" (86) "marketisation, competitiveness, and standardisation" (87). For example, he states that by focusing on "knowledge and skills needed for personal growth" (87), SaP practitioners

Undergraduates and Faculty Writing as Partners   183

combat the drive toward market demand; by focusing on "community and belonging," we combat drives toward individualism that are inherent in neoliberal forces (88). We held Mulya's words close as we began and continued our partnership. We came together to develop meaningful spaces for relationships and slow conversations amid increasing moves toward neoliberalism that shuns spaces for relationships and conversations and privileges rapid output for the sake of competition and advancement.

We found that the SaP structure encouraged slowness, slowing down because we committed to community over competition. SaP is labor intensive, time intensive. A faculty member does not add lines and lines and lines to the peer-reviewed-articles section of a CV quite readily through SaP practices. An undergraduate may struggle to find time for such work amid the other demands of the undergraduate experience. We had to slow down to coordinate our schedules so that we could gather on Zoom. We had to slow down so that we could begin work with some shared knowledge about curriculum development and assessment and the academic publishing world. We had to slow down to give each other time and space to write an assignment sheet or respond to new edits on our chapter—especially when we began working across multiple time zones. But through slowing down, we found more time for reflection. We found more time for planning, and when it was time to move forward with data collection or data analysis or writing implications, we moved forward more intentionally, more confidently, and more collectively. Just as physical activity, like running, is improved by, at times, resting, the work of the mind is improved by, at times, waiting and slowing.

Writing from her undergraduate student perspective, Emily describes how slowing down in this partnership benefited her as a student. For the remainder of this section, the "I" refers to Emily:

> I never thought about how our partnership differed from most by pushing against neoliberal demands for more until 2020. Dr. Rifenburg and I had always taken a slow and methodical approach to our work. We did not rush into research, nor did he push me to produce more work than I was comfortably able to do. The way we approached our partnership compelled us to slow things down. In the beginning, we met up to brainstorm and write. We both could have worked more efficiently and produced more if we decided to work individually, but because we chose to work alongside one another, our work was richer.
>
> I was more accustomed to writing with a partner because I was part of group projects each semester, but Dr. Rifenburg had been writing individually for a long time. Navigating how to work together as partners while being conscious of the student-professor power

dynamic also slowed our work progress. Dr. Rifenburg could have easily called me a partner but treated me like an inferior. Delegating tasks to me would have been more efficient, but Dr. Rifenburg chose to take the slow approach and think and discuss how we could work together. Specifically, Dr. Rifenburg constantly provided me with extra resources, articles, and books to read. These materials gave me a deeper understanding of the context surrounding our project. They gave me more knowledge that Dr. Rifenburg already had. This made our partnership more equal by lessening the gap between my experience and Dr. Rifenburg's.

With the amount of perceived free time we experienced in 2020, there was a push to use that time creatively and productively. People seemed to not understand that most of us were trying to survive during the worst parts and were emotionally exhausted once the state of the world began to normalize again. Many of my professors assigned more work than normal because they said we had more time to complete it. During this time, our work through this partnership felt refreshing.

CONCERNS OF LABOR IN FACULTY-STUDENT PARTNERSHIPS

While slowing down encourages community building, we also note how slowing down and coming together in partnership can open space for exploitative labor practices. An overarching concern in our work is building equitable labor conditions for all three of us. We acknowledge the embedded hierarchy at play with a tenured, white, male writing program administrator and two female undergraduate students. We acknowledge how such a hierarchy can facilitate exploitive student labor practices. Moreover, as Emily noted, this partnership was categorized by our university as an unpaid internship. Both Emily and Kellie were English majors with a concentration in writing and publication. All writing and publication students are required to complete a two-hundred-hour internship. To complete this internship, they work both with UNG's career services and the English Department's internship coordinator. Students receive three credit hours for their internship. Michael pitched this partnership as a method for completing the internship to career services, the internship coordinator, and Kellie and Emily. All agreed.

Unpaid internships are fraught with pitfalls. Ross Perlin's *Intern Nation: How to Earn Nothing and Learn Little in the Brave New Economy* criticizes higher education and internship host organizations for providing students with low-quality internship opportunities. According to Perlin, the push on the part of parents, state legislatures, and other key stakeholders to instill workplace readiness in college graduates has led institutions to ramp up internship opportunities, often unpaid ones.

Students pay tuition dollars for these internships, as was the case with the internship Emily and Kellie completed. But Perlin argues students walk away with little value. Katherine Durack offers similar critiques after examining unpaid internships from a writing studies perspective. Durack poses a powerful query: "At what point do our [writing studies faculty] actions cross the line from seeing to our students' professional development to pimping desirable first-time workers who lack the experience to question the circumstances of their employment and who may not yet have developed the judgment to recognize and the courage to report an exploitive opportunity and walk away?" (257). We acknowledge Perlin's broad arguments, and we acknowledge the challenging question Durack offers directed toward us in writing studies. Both push faculty and staff to attend to equitable labor conditions for all students. Yet we believe in the value of internships, as does Durack. Charles Westerberg and Carol Wickersham write that well-designed and well-implemented internships have value, even if they are unpaid. Janet Eyler reminds us of the benefit of well-designed internship opportunities, whether unpaid or paid: close working relationship with the site supervisor, clear responsibilities for the student, and continuous, well-structured reflective opportunities for the student (20). As we move forward ethically and legally with our partnership, we will continue to look toward scholarship on how to design and implement a high-quality internship and how internships can function as what George Kuh refers to as high-impact practice. We will also look to US federal government documents like the US Department of Labor "Fact Sheet #71: Internships Under the Fair Labor Standards Act." This fact sheet clarifies aspects of the 1938 Fair Labor Standards Act by outlining six requirements derived from a 1947 Supreme Court decision that must be met for an unpaid internship to be legal.

But we do not just want to stand on firm legal ground; we also want to stand on firm ethical and moral ground. We will also look to documents released by professional organizations like the National Association of Colleges and Employers' position statement on US internships. We are particularly intrigued by NACE's statement designed to assess the quality of an internship: "At the foundation of such an assessment is the tenet that the internship is a legitimate learning experience benefitting the student and not simply an operational work experience that just happens to be conducted by a student." Within our local context, we define, even capture in learning outcomes, key words in this statement like *legitimate, learning experience,* and *benefitting.* We can ensure that our internship opportunities, like all high-impact practices, are student-focused, legal, and on firm ethical ground.

Kellie provides her perspective as an undergraduate student who completed an unpaid internship. For the remainder of this section, the "I" refers to Kellie:

> The issues surrounding unpaid internships concern the exploitation of students due to their inexperience in the workforce. However, the built-in internship program at UNG allows students to gain professional work experience in their desired field while obtaining their degree. As our internship here at UNG is built into our degree program, a required course just like the [first-year writing] requirements, we are given the resources to locate, secure, and complete an internship in our field as we would complete any other course in our specific program. Administrative advisors will sit down with students and provide a list of popular internships in the community undertaken by previous students; they provide the contact information and a short synopsis of what the work is like in each position. Additionally, the university's English department is eager to engage its students in internships right on campus.

Kellie continues by writing directly about the partnership she and Michael established:

> Dr. Rifenburg was always up front about what he wanted out of our partnership. He came to me after class in the spring of 2019. I was taking a course with him, pre-pandemic, and he approached me, interested in my English major and graphic design minor. He expressed how he saw a lot of value in that combination and asked if I would be interested in working with him for my required internship. After I agreed, he asked me what I wanted to do. He made it a priority to learn what was important to me and the kind of work I was interested in pursuing. During our work, he was also very conscious of our other obligations. He was understanding when life interfered with our scheduled meeting, and he consistently asked if we, Kellie and Emily, were comfortable with the amount of work he requested from us. These factors alone prove that Dr. Rifenburg valued us as partners and felt we provided useful information to contribute to the work he wanted to accomplish. He respected us as scholars with our own skills to offer, and he directed us with his expertise and experience in writing by providing opportunities usually unavailable to undergraduate students—like publishing an article in a teaching and learning journal and another in this collection. Through these professional work opportunities, Dr. Rifenburg provided mentorship by explaining the process of publishing academic written work. He detailed the proposal process for an academic writing project and what was included in that piece of writing, then he led us through the outlining and drafting phases as a collective and encouraged us to write separately from our individual perspectives. He also introduced us to the academic peer review process, demonstrating the value in the process itself and how

Undergraduates and Faculty Writing as Partners   187

to react and revise our work in response to that feedback. These were professional skills we achieved through his expertise, and thanks to his mentorship, we can take these skills with us into our professional careers post-graduation.

Kellie's words remind us of the importance of respect in partnerships. As we move forward with our partnership, we understand the challenges of designing equitable labor conditions within unpaid student internships and within faculty-undergraduate student partnerships.

Emily and Kellie reflect on labor within this partnership:

KELLIE: I do not feel my work was exploited during this internship. During the internship, I strengthened my writing skills and got a peek into what it takes to publish academic writing. I also flexed my graphic design skills by creating brochures, posters, infographics, and presentation materials to detail and share our work with other instructors and administrators. Though these were time-consuming tasks, I am glad it was an internship through my undergraduate degree because an internship like this would be extremely hard to acquire in the professional world and would likely still be an unpaid position. We have been given opportunities that undergraduate students can only imagine, and the work I have done alongside my faculty and student partners have become the crowning jewels to my resume, work I am truly proud to be a part of, work that will help me land a paid position in my post-graduate job hunting because I now possess practical professional work experience.

EMILY: Dr. Rifenburg and I attended ISSOTL [the International Society for the Scholarship of Teaching and Learning] conference in October of 2019. We presented our work and current findings through a poster presentation. People would walk around to different posters and ask questions about the presenter's work. One person came up to me, asked about our poster, and then they asked about my experience in our project. I told the person I was working with Dr. Rifenburg for an internship. The next question she asked was if I was being paid. Until this point, being paid for the work I was doing had not been a concern. I was doing the internship, and in turn the project, because it fulfilled a required college credit. Technically, I was paying to do the project.

I explained this to the person, but they said in Canada, where they were from, unpaid internships are uncommon, and I should look into being paid. The person left, and Dr. Rifenburg turned to me to apologize and explain why I couldn't get paid. I told him I didn't mind, and I still don't mind doing the work and not being paid for it. I wanted to be a part of this project, and the fact that it fulfills a college credit is a perk.

Although I don't hold anything against Dr. Rifenburg, the UNG English Department, or anyone else involved in the internship, I still think about that person's shock when I told them it was an unpaid internship.

CONCLUSION

The north Georgia mountains are home to millions of deciduous trees like our pecan tree. These trees bloom and flourish as spring begins, and they maintain their greenery throughout the summer. As fall comes, they begin to change. The lively green gives way to a variety of oranges, yellows, and reds until they fall, one by one, to the ground, leaving barren trunks that reach for the sky. The trees need the winter to rest, to change, and to grow; as the world turns and warmth returns, they burst with life, changed for the better, stronger, healthier, and ready for the season of rebirth. Education should be thought of in the same way.

How we learn, what we learn, and when we learn are ever evolving, like our society. We are not the same society of people we were five years ago, ten years ago, or twenty years ago; we have grown, and we have changed. With this in mind, we should frequently be revisiting, re-examining, and redesigning education practices and pedagogy to match the needs of the new generations of students and faculty entering academia each year. For our English department, this means understanding and sharing the importance of humanities and liberal arts degrees in the face of reprioritization, encouraging students and faculty to engage in partnerships with one another with the goal of open, productive dialogue to create more meaningful, engaging courses within higher education.

SaP praxis disrupts neoliberal imperatives in higher education. The fast-paced environment of our current society seeps into academia, but in SaP partnerships, students and faculty members alike can slow down, just as the deciduous trees in the winter. Partners can hibernate and reflect on what has come before them, slow down enough to create "the space somewhere else" (Rice 130), which Jeff Rice describes in his contribution to a *College English* symposium on "What College English Should Be." Rice positions this space as a space in English studies wherein "multiple writers [are] engaging with multiple ideas in multiple media at multiple moments" (130). He locates this space somewhere else in the network and offers it as a counter to the focus on the individual author working within a single discipline. We, too, speak against this myopic perspective of oneness and singleness. For us, working off Rice, we imagine a space somewhere else where faculty and students discuss wants and needs and how they could be achieved.

The changes we felt writing together became central change moments driving our work. According to Pat Hutchings, Mary T. Huber, and Anthony Ciccone, change moments are times to do something new: "Educational innovation today invites, even requires, levels of

Undergraduates and Faculty Writing as Partners   189

preparation, imagination, collaboration, and support that are not always a good fit . . . with the inherited routines of academic life" (6). This argument inspired us to lean into our change moment and to push against the drive for more and more and more publishing by sitting together and taking time to build knowledge collectively. We wrote in a space together, for a time together, and look to take what we learned together about the processes and practices of writing into our future writing encounters.

We close with two reflective vignettes—one by Michael and one by Emily.

> MICHAEL: As the three of us drafted and revised this chapter, my thoughts often turned to a line in Mick Healey, Kelly E. Matthews, and Alison Cook-Sather's *Writing about Learning and Teaching in Higher Education*. In a section titled "Academics and Students Writing Together," the author team reminds faculty that "for undergraduate students, writing for publication is often an add-on for which there is not necessarily any benefit beyond the experience and satisfaction of co-authoring with a faculty member" (72). This chapter before you carries currency, an economic benefit for me as a faculty member, when I list this publication on my annual review. I will list this chapter in my post-tenure review portfolio and my CV. I derive literal economic benefit from typing these words on the screen and seeing them make their way into a published edited collection. Emily and Kellie? No. They can derive lessons from this experience that they can describe in job interviews or in job application materials. But neither seeks an academic career as an academic, and seven-thousand-word co-authored chapters on faculty-student partnerships don't carry the same currency outside higher education as they do inside higher education. The three of us all benefit from this partnership, but we do so in different ways.
>
> I derive economic benefit from our partnership, but the many partnerships I have established with undergraduate students have jolted me awake from the doldrums that is the mid-career academic life. James Mulholland describes midcareer burnout and the importance of slowing down to counter this pervasive problem. I'm thankful for the serendipitous turns of events that led me to finding literature on faculty-student partnerships; I am thankful for institutional structures that allowed these partnerships to take root and grow into outcomes like this chapter. After years of laboring alone on single-authored publications about student-writers, I'm thankful to research and write and work with student-writers to continue learning how best to support student-writers.

We close with Emily reflecting on this partnership. As we work on another round of revisions to this chapter, Emily has graduated, married, and started a life post-graduation in Italy with her husband. She is three years removed from her experience working with Michael to assess a redesigned first-year composition course. She writes from this vantage point, looking back on a meaningful undergraduate experience:

> Assessing the curricular redesign of the first-year English course at the University of North Georgia with Dr. Rifenburg and co-writing all the papers, blog articles, and journal articles that came after was the most unique and collaborative aspect of my undergraduate program. I was treated as a partner in a space where that was abnormal. The responsibility I was given helped me grow as a student, writer, and research partner, and for that I am thankful.
>
> Another unique aspect of our project's partnership is that it did not end when I graduated. I began working with Dr. Rifenburg in 2019 as part of a required internship. Now it is 2021, I have graduated, gotten married, and started my career, but I am still working with Dr. Rifenburg. To me, our willingness to continue working together after my graduation speaks to the meaningfulness of student and professor collaborations.
>
> Our project and partnership ultimately centered around writing. We wrote together physically before COVID-19 protocol, and we wrote together virtually during and after the change. We used different technologies like email, Google Docs, Zoom, and Microsoft Word to connect and write for months.
>
> During and especially after our project, our writing focus shifted. We felt that our project and our partnership were worth telling others about, so we wrote for conferences, journals, and blogs. Through all our writing, we reviewed and edited each other's contributions. We asked for advice and feedback on different ideas, so our writing was truly a collaborative effort.
>
> One of the books Dr. Rifenburg gave me to read was *The Meaningful Writing Project*, written by Michele Eodice, Anne Ellen Geller, and Neal Lerner. From this book, I learned what makes writing projects enriching and worthwhile for students. After reading the book and reflecting on my work with Dr. Rifenburg, I can confidently say our partnership, project, and writing were meaningful.

WORKS CITED

Bourke, Roseann, et al. "Assessment and Learning Together in Higher Education." *Teaching and Learning Together in Higher Education*, vol. 25, 2018. https://repository.brynmawr.edu/tlthe/vol1/iss25/2.

Bozalek, Vivienne, et al. "Developing Scholarship of Teaching and Learning through a Community of Enquiry." *Critical Studies in Teaching and Learning*, vol. 5, no. 2, 2017, pp. 1–15.

Cirio, Joe. "Meeting the Promise of Negotiation: Situating Negotiated Rubrics with Students' Prior Experiences." *WPA: Writing Program Administrator*, vol. 42, no. 2, 2019, pp. 100–19.

Cook-Sather, Alison, et al. *Pedagogical Partnerships: A How-To Guide for Faculty, Students, and Academic Developers in Higher Education*. Elon University's Center for Engaged Learning Open Access Book Series, 2019. https://www.centerforengagedlearning.org/books/pedagogical-partnerships/.

Curtis, Nicholas, and Robin Anderson. *A Framework for Developing Student-Faculty Partnerships in Program-Level Student Learning Outcome Assessment* (Occasional Paper No. 53). University of Illinois and Indiana University, National Institute for Learning Outcomes Assessment (NILOA), May 2021.

Day, Kami, and Michele Eodice. *(First Person)²: A Study of Co-Authoring in the Academy*. Utah State UP, 2001.

Duda, Gintaras Kazimieras, and Mary Ann Danielson. "Collaborative Curricular (Re)Construction: Tracking Faculty and Student Learning Impacts and Outcomes Five Years Later." *International Journal for Students as Partners*, vol. 2, no. 2, 2018, pp. 39–52.

Durack, Katherine T. "Sweating Employment: Ethical and Legal Issues with Unpaid Student Internships." *College Composition and Communication*, vol. 65, no. 2, 2013, pp. 245–72.

Ede, Lisa, and Andrea A. Lunsford. "Collaboration and Concepts of Authorship." *PMLA*, vol. 116, no. 2, 2001, pp. 354–69.

Eodice, Michele, et al. *The Meaningful Writing Project: Learning, Teaching, and Writing in Higher Education*. Utah State UP, 2016.

Eyler, Janet. "The Power of Experiential Education." *Liberal Education*, vol. 95, no. 4, 2009, pp. 24–31.

Fact Sheet 71: Internship Programs Under the Fair Labor Standards Act. United States Department of Labor, 2010. http://www.dol.gov/whd/regs/compliance/whdfs71.htm.

Green, Faith, et al. "Partnering with Students to Improve Teaching and Learning." *Teaching Academic: A CTLL Blog*, 22 Oct. 2020. https://ung.edu/center-teaching-learning-leadership/blog/teaching-and-learning/2020/partnering-with-students-to-improve-teaching-and-learning.php.

Healey, Mick, et al. *Writing About Learning and Teaching in Higher Education: Creating and Contributing to Scholarly Conversations across a Range of Genres*. Elon University's Center for Engaged Learning Open Access Book Series, 2020. https://www.centerforengaged learning.org/books/writing-about-learning/.

Holmes, Ashley. " 'Being Patient Through the Quiet': Partnering in Problem-Based Learning in a Graduate Seminar." *International Journal for Students as Partners*, vol. 4, no. 1, 2020.

Hutchings, Pat, et al. *Scholarship of Teaching and Learning Reconsidered*. Jossey-Bass, 2011.

Jabr, Ferris. "The Social Life of Forests." *New York Times Magazine*, 4 Dec. 2020. https://www.nytimes.com/interactive/2020/12/02/magazine/tree-communication-mycorrhiza.html.

Keeling, Kellie, et al. "Redesigning a Sustainable English Capstone through a Virtual Student-Faculty Partnership." *Journal of University Teaching & Learning Practice*, vol. 18, no. 7, 2021, pp. 244–57.

Kinkead, Joyce. "Engaging Undergraduate Researchers in the Assessment of Communication Across the Curriculum Courses." *Across the Disciplines*, vol. 15, no. 2, 2018. https://wac.colostate.edu/docs/atd/articles/kinkead2018.pdf.

Kuh, George D. "High-Impact Educational Practices." *High-Impact Educational Practices: What They Are, Who Has Them, And Why They Matter*, edited by George D. Kuh, Association of American Colleges and Universities, 2008, pp. 13–30.

Mercer-Mapstone, Lucy, and Sophia Abbot. *The Power of Partnership: Students, Staff, and Faculty Revolutionizing Higher Education*. Elon University's Center for Engaged Learning Open Access Book Series, 2020. https://www.centerforengagedlearning.org/books/power-of-partnership/.

Mercer-Mapstone, Lucy, et al. "A Systematic Literature Review of Students as Partners in Higher Education." *International Journal for Students as Partners*, vol. 1, no. 1, 2017. https://mulpress.mcmaster.ca/ijsap/article/view/3119.

Micciche, Laura R. *Acknowledging Writing Partners*. Perspectives on Writing. The WAC Clearinghouse; UP of Colorado, 2017. https://doi.org/10.37514/PER-B.2017.0872.

Mulholland, James. "Slow Down: On Dealing with Midcareer Burnout." *MLA: Profession*, Winter 2020. https://profession.mla.org/slow-down-on-dealing-with-midcareer-burnout/.

Mulya, Teguh Wijaya. "Contesting the Neoliberalism of Higher Education through Student-Faculty Partnership." *International Journal for Academic Development*, vol. 24, no. 1, 2019, pp. 86–90.

National Association of Colleges and Employers. "Position Statement: U.S. Internships." *NACE*, Aug. 2018, https://www.naceweb.org/about-us/advocacy/position-statements/position-statement-us-internships/.

Perlin, Ross. *Intern Nation: How to Earn Nothing and Learn Little in the Brave New Economy*. Verso, 2012.

Rice, Jeff. "Networks and New Media." *College English*, vol. 69, no. 2, 2006, pp. 127–33.

Rule, Hannah J. *Situating Writing Processes*. Perspectives on Writing. The WAC Clearinghouse; UP of Colorado, 2020. https://doi.org/10.37514/PER-B.2019.0193.

Seeber, Barbara K., and Maggie Berg. *The Slow Professor: Challenging the Culture of Speed in the Academy*. U of Toronto P, 2016.

Simard, Suzanne. *Finding the Mother Tree: Discovering the Wisdom of the Forest*. Knopf, 2021.

Simard, Suzanne, et al. "Net Transfer of Carbon between Ectomycorrhizal Tree Species in the Field." *Nature*, vol. 388, 1997, pp. 579–82.

Voyce, Malcolm. "Shopping Malls in India: New Social 'Dividing Practices.'" *Economic and Political Weekly*, vol. 42, no. 22, 2007, pp. 2055–62.

Westerberg, Charles, and Carol Wickersham. "Internships Have Value, Whether or Not Students Are Paid." *Chronicle of Higher Education*. 24 Apr. 2011. https://www.chronicle.com/article/internships-have-value-whether-or-not-students-are-paid/.

Wohlleben, Peter. *The Hidden Life of Trees: What They Feel, How They Communicate—Discoveries from A Secret World*. Greystone Books, 2016.

12
THE SCHOOL BUS NEVER CAME
How Crisis Shapes Writing Time
Melissa Dinsman and Heather Robinson

Tags: identity, collaboration, productivity

The writing lives of women with children are often built on the assumption that, as Donald Hall writes, "time is predictable, subdividable and regular" (qtd. in Berg and Seeber 24). Many narratives of mothers who are writers—especially mothers of school-aged children—show just how fundamental predictable time is. Barbara Kingsolver, for instance, describes the school bus as a muse, in the ways that it punctuated her workdays when her children were young (Charney). For mothers of younger children, too, time away from their children is vital for professional survival. Rachel Connelly and Kristen Ghodsee write, "In terms of its role in facilitating employment, you need consistent, dependable childcare. You need childcare that is available when you need it. The best care imaginable won't do you any good if it is only available from 9:00–11:30" (35). But what happens to women writers when the school bus stops coming, and time is no longer "predictable, subdividable and regular"? What happens to writing productivity when the days become endless and time loses all punctuation beyond the rising and the setting of the sun, and when childcare becomes not merely inconsistent or unreliable, but completely unavailable? What happens to our writerly identities when all our other identities collide into them, forced into the same space and always competing for attention?

Our relationships with time and writing shifted drastically and suddenly in the early days of the COVID-19 pandemic due to the mitigation strategies adopted by the Centers for Disease Control and Prevention. In order to "flatten the curve" of viral infection, schools and workplaces closed, public gatherings were prohibited, and we lived under "shelter-in-place" directives. The pandemic's endless days involved parenting our school-aged children, housekeeping, and work, all in the same space, with the same people around all the time. There were few

https://doi.org/10.7330/9781646424870.c012

meaningful hand-offs between parents because there was nowhere to go that wasn't still in our homes, and the uncertainty of the pandemic's early days meant that our kids needed us around. Writing about New York City's "shelter in place" rules and its impact on her writing, Zadie Smith describes how she had to reinvent her understanding of how her life worked now that there was nowhere to go and so much time to fill. She writes of the yearning to be alone that accompanied the early pandemic days for artists and writers, so used to unstructured and yet predictable time: "The married human, in the country place with partner and children, dreams of isolation within isolation. All the artists with children—who treasured isolation as the most precious thing they owned—find out what it is to live without privacy and without time" (Smith 29).

To work in isolation is, of course, a kind of privilege many women don't have and more lost during the pandemic. We, the authors of this essay, also acknowledge that our ability to work from home and maintain our incomes, which enabled us to protect ourselves and our families from the Coronavirus that began to spread rapidly in our New York City region in March and April 2020, was a privilege as well. But this privilege was not without its challenges, which included the daily competition for psychic space, and the drain on our physical and emotional energies from writing and parenting in a crisis, often at the same time. In order to explore our experiences of writing through COVID-19, we consider the stories and practices of other women who have written through engulfing, slow-rolling crises—war, cancer, pandemic—where the individual impacts are not always felt acutely. For us, as for other women writers, including Virginia Woolf, Mollie Panter-Downes, Nina Riggs, and Zadie Smith, the drive to keep writing remained necessary in the face of an all-consuming crisis, whether global or personal.

This essay is about our stories of finding ways to sustain our writerly identities—without fetishizing productivity—against a backdrop of anxiety, disease, and unpredictable change. As academics, we had relied upon social support structures to make our lives as writers, parents, teachers, and partners possible. The slow-rolling crisis of the pandemic meant that suddenly everyone was home all the time and so work was always around us. That is somewhat the case for writing and academic work in general, but the pandemic exacerbated the worst aspects of the "always on" nature of academic labor. Batsheva Guy and Brittany Arthur describe the feeling of constantly working because there is no distinction between "at work," "at home," "at school," et cetera; Arthur also describes the intense feelings of loneliness that were brought on by working at home, with her very small child, alongside feeling "ashamed, embarrassed and angry" that the falling away of the structures that she had put in place to ensure her productivity, even after becoming a parent, had meant that she of course became much less "productive" (894). Productivity is very much tied to academic identity, but the pandemic has forced us to find new ways to balance our identities as parents, partners, academics, teachers, and writers.

The questions that we grappled with during the early pandemic days still confound us now, since, although the pandemic is receding, the instability and unpredictability of time remain, accompanied by pressure from our institution to get "back to normal," even when we don't know what normal looks like anymore. In this essay, we try to describe how we kept writing during the pandemic, and how we created structures that made it possible to sustain our writing careers alongside the other obligations of our lives. For us, managing writing in the pandemic required finding ways to integrate writing into our day-to-day pandemic routines and establishing strong support structures at home and via collaboration and writing partners, whether for relief, for accountability, for company, or to maintain momentum. We wanted to still be *seen* as writers, and this was made possible by becoming responsible to someone other than ourselves.

CHALLENGING ORTHODOXIES OF WRITING AND TIME

There is a vast how-to-write industry for academics (e.g., Boice; Tulley, *How*; Sword; Silvia). Many focus on managing time, exhorting faculty writers to structure their time deliberately and consistently in order to maintain and increase their productivity, with external accountability structures keeping them on track. Maggie Berg and Barbara Seeber, in *The Slow Professor*, write about the necessity for "timeless time" in order to be creative and produce good work: They entreat us to look to the "environmental factors [that] facilitate or interfere with creative thinking" so that we can "protect a time and place for timeless time" (28). Laura Micciche, too, states that "writing seems to require a destabilized present. Writers lose track of time; writing exerts weightlessness even as reality thumps all around" (64). Robert Boice's research, on the other hand, shows that, to be maximally productive in terms of pages written, short, regular sessions of writing time, with check-ins from others to create accountability, are more effective than long blocks of writing time. But many of the tenets of these "how to write" orthodoxies fell apart, or had to be adapted during the pandemic, when the "consistent and predictable childcare" that Connelly and Ghodsee place at the center of mothers' ability to do their academic work also disappeared.

Firm divisions between work and home are essential for many academic mothers to manage the demands of both job and family. Connelly and Ghodsee write that "Maryellen Giger, a professor of radiology at the University of Chicago and mother of four, suggests that we need to establish a finely tuned on/off switch, turning off home life when we're at work and vice versa. 'You have to be able to turn the switch so you can focus on where you're at'" (120). Without these divisions—these separate spaces—the experience of trying to write with children around resembles what Adrienne Rich describes in "Of Woman Born": "The child (or children) might be absorbed in busyness, in his own dream-world; but as soon as he felt me gliding into a world which did not include him, he would come to pull at my hand, ask for help, punch at the typewriter keys. And I would feel his wants at such a moment as fraudulent, as an attempt moreover to defraud me of living even for fifteen minutes as myself" (qtd. in Micciche 64). Even in noncrisis moments, the interruptions Rich describes are all too familiar to women scholars and writers. But during a pandemic, when everyone is always home, these interruptions become the norm. As Sara Ahmed notes, "For some, having time for writing, which means time to face the table upon which writing happens, becomes an orientation that is not available given the ongoing labor of other attachments, which literally pull them away" (250). Thus, it isn't just time but also space that is essential for writing. Women need the writing table and the space to "orient" or locate themselves and their writing in relation to and away from their other responsibilities; to live, as Rich suggests, as ourselves, as *writers*.

Living on Long Island, New York (Melissa) and in central New Jersey (Heather), "shelter-in-place" started early and lasted for what seemed like endless months. We both have no local family, and even if we did, the fear of infecting others would have kept us from asking for help. (In the early days of the pandemic, so much was unknown about virus transmission that every form of contact beyond our immediate households seemed too risky.) Thankfully, our spouses, both of whom also work at local colleges, were home and we equally shared both childcare and domestic responsibilities. During school hours we each helped our children with online school while sneaking moments of work. Melissa's husband took phone calls and wrote data reports as their fourth grader independently read and took screen breaks; Melissa wrote sections of articles as her first grader completed math worksheets and colored. Heather's wife helped their second grader through four hours of online schoolwork, while Heather shifted her own teaching online for the very first time. Heather's kindergartener watched storytellers perform fairytales and learned to type with British cartoon characters while Heather prepared and taught her classes and attended meetings. Throughout spring 2020, we authors spent hours riding bikes, watching movies, going on neighborhood walks, and doing puzzles together and when we weren't doing this, or when the children slept and our houses were quiet, we wrote. Again, we acknowledge our extreme privilege: not only did we have spouses at home but they are also equal partners in parenting our children. And yet we constantly felt our identities as writers being threatened by all these other demands on our time. Our drive to write remained, but the time we needed to write kept threatening to slip away.

Christine Tulley's analysis of the writing practices of "rhet-comp moms" gets closest to anticipating our experience of writing in the pandemic. Tulley identifies two key structures that academic mothers use and labels them "time blocks" and "time scraps." Time blocks are negotiated stretches of time where all other obligations are cleared out; time scraps are those stretches of time that mothers find at the interstices of their days. In her study, Tulley shows that research and writing mostly gets done in the "time blocks," though sometimes these time blocks might occur with family members around ("Rhet-Comp Moms"). In photos that show the process of writing her forthcoming book, *Rhet-Comp Moms*, Tulley gestures to the impact of the COVID-19 pandemic, during which she was writing her manuscript. Tulley's observation about the importance of "time blocks" for research is borne out by other studies on the pandemic's impact on academic mothers. For instance, Fulwiler and colleagues write that "Child rearing during this global pandemic has left academic mothers with even smaller units of time, which makes deep intellectual thought and writing, which are required for both publications and grants, next to impossible" (2). We quickly found that the structures we had put in place to sustain our writing lives could not withstand the realities of the pandemic; as much as we wanted to write, our drive to write alone was not enough to maintain our writing practice in the face of the new pressures the crisis created. We had to create new strategies and develop new habits in order for our identities as writers to endure. (It is worth noting that, while not the scope of this essay, extensive cross-disciplinary research has shown not only that the pandemic had a negative effect on the research productivity of academics who identify as women and who have children, but that academics who identify as men—even men with children—experienced an increase in their rate of publications and scholarly productivity. See, for example, Squazzoni et al.; Elinas et al.; Deryugina et al.; and many more.)

In the remaining sections of this chapter, we explore two strategies that helped keep us writing during the first year of the COVID-19 pandemic. Specifically, we discuss how we made writing a part of day-to-day life via detailed scheduling of the "endless days" and how we created collaboration and accountability structures, including joint publications, writing or co-writing groups, and accountability partners in order to sustain our work practices and our writerly identities. The toll of living through a pandemic without physical or mental space to work meant that many writing goals went unmet. But since for both of us writing is a large part of our identities as academics, we needed new structures to make writing possible. To explore these strategies and structures, we offer our own narratives interwoven with narratives of the experiences of other women writing through crisis.

STRATEGY ONE: SCHEDULING ENDLESS DAYS

Virginia Woolf famously preached the necessity of a private room for women writers in *A Room of One's Own*. But this advocacy for a space to write is also a symbol of a woman's need for *time* to write. Woolf knew that without privacy, finding time to write—away from family and domestic responsibilities—was a near impossibility. With the outbreak of World War II, a decade after *A Room* was published, private spaces and writing time became scarce, as the chaos and destruction of war infiltrated the British domestic sphere. Woolf spent much of the war's early years in Monk House, her home in Rodmell, Sussex, writing in a private room. By all accounts, the early war years up until Woolf's death in 1941 were extremely productive ones, in part due to her domestic support systems and her own sheer determination. Yet she still describes the war, and in particular the Blitz, as an impediment to creative thought. As Woolf writes in her wartime essay "Thoughts on Peace in an Air Raid," "The drone of the planes is now like the sawing of a branch overhead. Round and round it goes, sawing and sawing at a branch directly above the house. Another sound begins sawing its way into the brain" (243). Throughout the essay, war sounds interrupt her thoughts; they pierce the walls of her writing room, disrupting not only her space, but also her time to write. The war—an always looming presence—is similar to the COVID-19 pandemic in that the threat of outside danger infiltrates the home and with it the mental space of the writer. What were once writing days are now fragmented and interrupted by the constant reminder of danger and, in our case, disease.

But Woolf, who had no children and who also had the support of domestic workers and her husband and editor, Leonard Woolf, didn't lack for a quiet place to work in quite the same way as many women during the COVID-19 pandemic and, indeed, even some of her contemporaries. For example, Mollie Panter-Downes, who wrote her "Letter from London" column about wartime Britain for *The New Yorker*, had to write with two children frequently at home. Like Woolf, Panter-Downes secluded herself in her writing room, a transformed garden hut in her Haslemere, Surrey, home. She also had domestic support, including a nanny to help with her two daughters. In a September 10, 1942, letter to her *New Yorker* editor, Panter-Downes makes clear how significant domestic workers were to her writing productivity: "Life has'nt [sic] been very encouraging for literary composition lately, as my Nannie, prop of my household, has been whisked into hospital for an operation, and I've been combining darts to town with children, cooking, and domestic chores in general! In consequence the output of ideas and results has been pretty thin, but I hope it will improve soon." The absence of her nanny due to a medical emergency means that all "domestic chores," and not just childcare, fall to Panter-Downes, effectively putting a halt to not only her writing but her very ability to come up with new "ideas" for her editors. This creative halt due to domestic support structures falling away was shared by countless women in 2020. As it did for Panter-Downes, who continued to make research trips "to town [London] with children," the disruption to creative time altered the way we approached our work. No longer privileged with reliable "blocks" of writing time, we made use of what we had, which amounted to, in Woolfian terms, "scraps, orts and fragments" (*Between the Acts* 189).

But seeing writing as integrated in our personal lives, and not separate from it, is, according to Laura Micciche, what writing looks like: "Writing cannot be bracketed from the moments and events that define us; it is part of the bundle" (72). This observation, made in the context of Micciche's discussion about how writers inhabit time, describes our reality of writing in the pandemic. Writing, if it was going to happen, had to be a part of every day, rather than something that we set aside until conditions improved, until the kids were back in school, until we felt better, less scared, less stressed. We had to make "time blocks" when we could set ourselves up for sustained writing while our families slept, and, otherwise, use the "time scraps" of the day as they became available (Tulley, "Rhet Comp Moms"). Using our time as well as we could meant planning and always knowing what the next step in our writing was. And because of the strange unpredictability of the endless days of crisis, we couldn't wait for time to open up; writing in time scraps had to be expected, planned, squeezed in among the noise of the day if it was to become sustainable practice.

Nina Riggs's memoir of living with and dying of cancer helps explain how, in a slow-rolling crisis, whether personal or global, finding ways to live and write in the present becomes essential, rather than fixing all hopes on that moment, at some time in the future, when things go "back to normal" again. Early in the narrative of her illness, when she and her husband were both trying to understand what the cancer meant for their present and future lives, Riggs relates a conversation in which her husband referred to the time "when this is over." Riggs replies to him that living for that unknown place and time in the future "invalidates her whole life right now;" she says, instead, "I have to love these days, the same as any other" (Riggs 73). Living in the present, making each day work within the conditions set by her cancer, resembles the work of mothering and writing during the pandemic. Writing was how to make the days mean something for us as they happened, rather than just waiting for it all to be over. Writing and mothering, unlike so much else in those endless days, were "pitched towards futurity" in ways that many other of our activities were not: even as we inhabited a continuous present, the kids still needed new shoes, needed haircuts, and the writing was there to "endure, withstand and return to" (Micciche 84). It has only been recently that it's felt possible to imagine a future that looks different from the hundreds of days that have gone before and to thus shape our writing days differently.

Throughout most of her illness, Riggs wrote about her cancer: first on her blog, "Suspicious Country," and then through *The Bright Hour*. Her *New York Times* article, published on September 23, 2016, came out when her cancer was quite advanced; she completed the manuscript of her memoir two months later, and died in February 2017. She describes her project—not just for writing, but for her life—as one of "accepting absurdity and the beauty of the everyday when there isn't really a future you can count on" ("Nina Riggs" 2:03–2:12). Riggs had to make her writing a part of her days because, she writes, "it is clear there will not be enough days" (288). In her only interview about the book before her death, Riggs told Nora Krug that "in fact, I had a hard time *not* working on the manuscript, and occasionally had to be reminded to take breaks, pace myself a little" (Krug). Even in a memoir in which Riggs is so committed to being in each day with her family, she is compelled to write. Our exigencies are different from Riggs's, but the lack of a reliable future is similar, as is the strong drive to write even during—or perhaps even because of—crisis.

For both of us, the pandemic changed time and writing. For Heather, writing was the only thing that could take her outside the house, give her something "else" to do, something to imagine the future when the present was so uncertain. Writing was something to get up early for, to create structures for, something that connected her with her professional self. She wrote where and when she could—in the interstices of the day and in blocks of time claimed from her family via the online calendar invitations that she and her wife would send to each other—and, when she would disappear, as far as she was able. Supervising online school in spring 2020 and for ten weeks during the worst weeks of the pandemic in the winter of 2020–2021, the blocks felt luxurious but were never enough. And so, scraps of time grabbed early in the morning, or between monitoring online first and third grade, were when the writing had to happen.

In the spring and summer of 2020, Melissa could still manage to find chunks of time in which to write. She scheduled her writing times around virtual school and virtual camps and worked on different projects during different blocks of time that were available to her. She usually worked on two to three writing projects simultaneously, which kept her interested and motivated in the work and kept her from getting too stuck on one project. In the fall, however, things in New York began to open up. Teaching and administrative labor, although still online, became more demanding; her children returned to school, at first in a hybrid format and then fully in person. But everything still felt more difficult because while the state touted "back to normal," life was anything but. We could go places, but separation was still advised. Activities restarted but with extra requirements for caregivers to observe and fulfill. The blocks of time Melissa was able to schedule before became scraps. She was no longer able to work on multiple writing projects but could manage to plod through one at a time in the moments that weren't taken up by work and family responsibilities. Part of the shift from block scheduling to scrap scheduling was due to a decline in her own mental bandwidth. The struggles of maintaining a productive work schedule over the spring and summer had taken a tremendous toll and the quick push to "back to normal" put work and family schedules into chaos. Writing in sporadic scraps in the morning and at night and while waiting in the car became the best she could manage. But yet, through the scraps, the writing continued to happen, and this was in large part due to collaboration in its many forms.

STRATEGY TWO: CREATING COMMUNITY IN ISOLATION

The benefits of academics writing with others have been well-touted in many books. In *Acknowledging Writing Partners*, for example, Laura Micciche explores the ways in which writers recognize those with whom they write, whether they "simply" share space with them or work in active collaboration. Following Frank Martela's work, Berg and Seeber suggest that collaborative work creates a "holding environment," which functions as a kind of "supportive net" for those who participate in it, offering "gestures of care and protection . . . it offers the promise that ideas will be preserved and nurtured rather than dismissed" (86). And Helen Sword, in *Air and Light and Time and Space*, interviews several academic writers about their collaborative writing practice, describing the ways in which it provides not only intellectual stimulation and broadens the scope of possibilities of their writing, but also offers emotional support. As Lisa Ede and Andrea Lunsford write, "Collaborative writing has the 'capacity . . . to open out, to open up, to explore not only the experiential present but the theoretically possible'" (141). Many of the writers in these collections talk about writing with others by sharing physical space, either on joint or separate projects; or of the freedom of the "hand-off," where each works on a piece, and then hands it off to another, working in a different place or even time zone, reassured by the fact that the work is moving forward, even if it is out of their hands.

There is, though, little discussion of collaborative writing in historical times of crisis. In her descriptions of the process of writing her memoir, it is clear that for Riggs the writing of her illness had to be a solitary effort, even as she explores her relationships with her husband, children, friends, and parents in the text. The crisis of war and pandemic, by contrast, is a collective crisis, where lines between individual experience and public need become blurry and individual choices are scrutinized for their impact on the war effort and the common good. Navigating this collectivity means that much of Virginia Woolf's and Mollie Panter-Downes's management of writing during World War II involved finding places to be alone and making sure there was someone else to take care of the day-to-day household duties so that they could write.

However, finding isolation amid parenting and housekeeping, teaching and writing, all in the same shared space, is an entirely different proposition. For us, during the COVID-19 pandemic, one of collaboration's main values has been the way it reasserts connection with a world outside the particular versions of the pandemic that we are enduring. This experience seems to be a common one: collaboration—writing groups, accountability partners, and co-writing—has been a popular coping mechanism specifically during the COVID-19 pandemic, and this popularity in crisis seems new. The prodigious amount of writing on the pandemic's impact on academic work practices (for example, Mar Pereira and citations therein) speaks to its singularity: there is no experience, in the last hundred years, to which we can compare it.

Scholars of the 1918–19 influenza pandemic have remarked upon the ways in which we are still coming to understand the impact of that pandemic on the day-to-day life of its "guilt-stricken survivors" (Outka 940). Most of the few near-contemporary narratives that are extant concern the individual experience of illness, even though, as Thomas Ewing writes, "it is also important . . . to recognize that survival was also part of the experience of the epidemic" (Nichols et al. 651). Just like during the COVID-19 pandemic, participating in the public health strategies developed in the 1918–19 pandemic—closures of schools, strict limits on movements and gatherings—created a scene of survival that requires isolation. However, in 1918–19, isolation was not mitigated by virtual connection: collaboration without sharing physical documents would have been expensive (phone bills and postage) or impossible. The point is that there is no precedent of this collaborative response to crisis for women writers. Panter-Downes and Woolf both sought solitude and built spaces where they could write alone. Riggs found that she couldn't write alone even when she had the opportunity to do so: she needed to be with her family as she wrote about her experiences with cancer. Riggs's narrative gets somewhat closer to our experiences, although we had no choice as we had nowhere else to go. And so, the pandemic has, for us, reinforced how important creating structures for writing that reach outside our domestic spaces are, not only for productivity, but for the sustainability both of our writing projects and our identities as writers.

Early in the COVID-19 pandemic, Tulley suggested collaborative work as a way through, exhorting her readers to "reach out" to colleagues and see if they can create faculty writing groups, suggesting that these "moves help connect us, even if we are not on our campuses and at conferences to discuss research" ("Resetting"). Joint projects, online co-writing (shared, regularly scheduled in an online space in which to write), and working with accountability partners became more important for us and for many other women academics writing during the pandemic. These joint or group writing spaces and projects created structures in the endless days that held us accountable to someone who saw us as more than a domestic partner, parent, or teacher. Distributing the energy and labor needed for writing made writing more possible.

But this distribution too required adaptation: older models of two writers sitting with two pads of paper and two pens, or even two computers in the same room banging out text, simply could not happen.

Seeking feedback from fellow writers and editors has always been part of an author's process. But the extreme isolation and mental toll of living through a pandemic with families always at home led us to seek new opportunities and ways to collaborate with others. Melissa, for example, formed an accountability/writing partnership with a research colleague on the other side of the country. The two spoke weekly to discuss writing goals, share drafts, and offer feedback. Some weeks these calls would serve as support check-ins, with conversations turning to pandemic fears, family stresses, and general wellness. This partnership became as important to Melissa's writing productivity as it was to her mental well-being. Heather maintained a weekly, two-hour virtual co-writing session with two work colleagues; this became not only a predictable, protected time for writing, but also provided connection with the world of our college from which she had been severed. These co-writing sessions provided a different kind of accountability than the one Melissa describes, but the effects were similar: being expected to appear on a screen once a week and needing to be in the midst of a writing project on which she could work for two hours reoriented Heather to the future amid the continuous present of pandemic time. For both of us, the accountability and collaborations kept us connected to our professional lives as writers and scholars.

A sister-alternative to the accountability partner is the writing group, which many of Melissa's and Heather's friends and scholarly colleagues formed during the pandemic. The goal of the writing group is in part accountability, but it may not always include the discussion of goals and personal support as can be offered in a partnership (although it certainly can). Writing groups often require participants to produce a certain number of pages on a specific schedule. During the pandemic, this kept people writing and reading. But more importantly, as with accountability partners, it helped us feel less alone in our work and personal lives and hang on to our identities as writers.

The last form of collaboration that we wish to touch on, and one that this essay illustrates, is joint publication. While not new to the scientific disciplines, collaborative publishing is somewhat uncommon in the humanities, and specifically within English literature, in which Melissa works. Heather, by contrast, working in applied linguistics and writing studies, has collaborated with several co-authors throughout her career using different strategies for collaboration with her various writing partners. Shortly before the pandemic, we decided to form a writing partnership, which was strengthened during the crisis. Not only did this enable us to continue to supplement our individual scholarship but it also allowed each of us to venture into other areas of research that were new to us, thus broadening our research area expertise. And, frankly, it was a deeply enjoyable and satisfying experience in a time when many things were not very enjoyable or satisfying. The unique scheduling demands of writing together allowed for each of us to take turns writing and editing, which meant that even when one of us was taking a break from the essay, it was still moving forward in the other's hands. This form of collaboration is not new: Cindy Selfe, interviewed in Tulley's "How Writing Faculty Write," describes the pleasure of the hand-off to her regular collaborative writing partner, Gail Hawisher: "I totally give it over. I don't care if they change every single one of my blessed words as long as they're doing something and moving the piece forward. . . . I just assume [Gail] is constantly making the piece better when it's out of my hands" (37). The possibility of surrendering a piece into another pair of trusted hands during a time when there was only one other adult to hand off domestic and childcare responsibilities provided deep relief during the pandemic days.

Like Selfe's and Hawisher's partnership, collaboration for us was not contemporaneous. Instead, we handed off shared documents from late at night to early in the morning; we popped in for short intervals of time during our days and texted or called each other about what we had done. Most of our conversation about writing happened in the writing itself, in comments and text messages. We rarely tracked our changes, neither monitoring nor approving each other's contributions to the piece; since neither of us has much time, we must trust what each other has done rather than combing through each other's changes. Our pandemic collaborations have been such that we have merged our voices in the pieces that we write, and we have taken responsibility for individual sections while being each other's editors, critics, and accountability partners for the texts that we are writing together. The endless days have facilitated this kind of daily back and forth. Our collaborations have created structures for writing that have threaded our time scraps together.

EMERGING FROM CRISIS

As we write this essay, the United States is emerging, haltingly, from the crisis of the COVID-19 pandemic. Case counts are well down from their January 2021 peaks; a majority of adults are vaccinated with highly effective vaccines, and our workplaces are opening up. Now, our questions and concerns revolve around what our future writing practice will look like as we reintegrate working on-site with our domestic lives. Thus, as a conclusion to this essay, we articulate some of our questions for ourselves about how the relationship between writing and time might change for us in the future. As mothers of growing children, we know that the ways in which we write will continue to evolve as our children's needs change and as we progress in our careers. Melissa goes up for tenure in 2022; her tenure decision may well, again, shift her relationship to writing and time. Heather, promoted to full professor in August 2020, is establishing a new rhythm and reason for writing that is disconnected from institutional metrics.

So what are the changes to our writing practices, brought on by the pandemic, that we hope to sustain as we go "back to normal"? (We note that we always write this in quotation marks, because we really don't know what this is or, indeed, if we even want it.) We had initiated our first collaborative writing project in October 2019, but at that time we didn't really know what style of collaboration would suit us or, indeed, if it would even work. As we found during the pandemic, our working rhythms and paces are very compatible, so we will continue writing with each other in the ways that we describe above and also talk to each other about other writing projects, filling out for each other the picture of who we are as writers as well as affirming each other's writerly identities. We will also continue to foster accountability partnerships and groups, which allow us to imagine our writing futures even when the present moment isn't conducive to writing.

Pandemics have a way of fracturing narrative. Writing of the impact of the trauma of the 1918–19 influenza pandemic, Catherine Belling observes that "the silence that surrounds the 1918 pandemic may not only have been due to selective memory's normal erasure. There may also have been a refusal or inability to describe a trauma that might still have haunted its survivors. Perhaps the flu overwhelmed language in ways that war did not" (57). As we wrote this piece, we noted that the stories of our individual lives and our struggles to shape pandemic time so we could write seemed banal in the face of the massive trauma the world has experienced. So perhaps that is the conclusion of this piece: we have tried to offer descriptions of the shape of our days even as we are still trying to shape them in such a way that we get through these late pandemic months. It has felt, at times, that language is overwhelmed by this pandemic, and that the only stories we can even try to make sense of are the smallest ones. Thus, we offer a fractured account of our pandemic writing lives: we woke up early in the morning, stayed up late at night, and tried to find time that is ours in the midst of the relentless claims upon it within a space—our homes—where too many parts of our lives have happened.

WORKS CITED

Ahmed, Sara. "Orientation Matters." *New Materialisms: Ontology, Agency, and Politics*, edited by Diana Coole and Samantha Frost, Duke, 2010, pp. 234–57. https://doi.org/10.1515/9780822392996-013.

Belling, Catherine. "Overwhelming the Medium: Fiction and the Trauma of Pandemic Influenza in 1918." *Literature and Medicine*, vol. 28, no. 1, 2009, pp. 55–81.

Berg, Maggie, and Barbara Seeber. *The Slow Professor: Challenging the Culture of Speed in the Academy*. U of Toronto P, 2016.

Boice, Robert. *Professors as Writers: A Self-Help Guide to Productive Writing*. New Forums Press, 1990.

Charney, Noah. "Barbara Kingsolver: How I Write." *The Daily Beast*, 5 Dec. 2012, https://www.thedailybeast.com/barbara-kingsolver-how-i-write.

Connelly, Rachel, and Kristen Ghodsee. *Professor Mommy: Finding Work-Family Balance in Academia*. Rowman & Littlefield, 2011.

Deryugina, Tatyana, et al. "COVID-19 Disruptions Disproportionately Affect Female Academics." *AEA Papers and Proceedings*, vol. 111, 2021. http://www.nber.org/papers/w28360.

Ede, Lisa S., and Andrea A. Lunsford. *Singular Texts/Plural Authors: Perspectives on Collaborative Writing*. Southern Illinois UP, 1992.

Ellinas, Elizabeth H., et al. "Winners and Losers in Academic Productivity During the COVID-19 Pandemic: Is the Gender Gap Widening for Faculty?." *Journal of Women's Health* vol. 31, no. 4, 2022, pp. 487–94.

Fulwiler, Robinson W., et al. "Rebuild the Academy: Supporting Academic Mothers During COVID-19 and Beyond." Supplemental Information. *PLOS Biology*, vol 19, no. 3, 2021. https://doi.org/10.1371/journal.pbio.3001100.s001.

Guy, Batsheva, and Brittany Arthur. "Academic Motherhood during COVID-19: Navigating our Dual Roles as Educators and Mothers." *Gender, Work and Organization*, vol. 27, no. 5, 2020, pp. 887–99.

Krug, Nora. "Before I Go: A Mother's Hopeful Words about Life in its Waning Moments." *Washington Post*, 1 June 2017. wapo.st/2qEfETZ?tid=ss_mail.

Mar Pereira, Maria do. "Researching Gender Inequalities in Academic Labor during the COVID-19 Pandemic: Avoiding Common Problems and Asking Different Questions." *Gender, Work and Organization*, 2021, pp. 498–509.

Micciche, Laura R. *Acknowledging Writing Partners*. WAC Clearinghouse, 2017.

Nichols, Christopher McKnight, et al. "Reconsidering the 1918–19 Influenza Pandemic in the Age of COVID-19." *The Journal of the Gilded Age and Progressive Era*, vol. 19, no. 4, 2020, pp. 642–72.

"Nina Riggs on the Essay that Changed her Life." *YouTube*, uploaded by Off the Shelf, 22 May 2017, youtu.be/_SP_BGpfY78.

Outka, Elizabeth. "'Wood for the Coffins Ran Out': Modernism and the Shadowed Afterlife of the Influenza Pandemic." *Modernism/modernity*, vol. 21, no. 4, 2014, pp. 937–60.

Panter-Downes, Mollie. Letter to William Shawn, 19 Sept. 1942, Box 381, Folder 2, *New Yorker* records, *NYPL Archives*.

Riggs, Nina. *The Bright Hour: A Memoir of Living and Dying*. Simon and Schuster, 2017.

Tulley, Christine. *How Writing Faculty Write*. Utah State UP, 2018.

208 MELISSA DINSMAN AND HEATHER ROBINSON

Tulley, Christine. "Resetting Your Research Agenda." *Inside Higher Ed*, 2 Apr. 2020. www
.insidehighered.com/advice/2020/04/02/how-continue-push-your-research-forward
-while-staying-home-during-pandemic-opinion.

Tulley, Christine. "Rhet Comp Moms Project." Christine Tulley, 2021. christinetulley
.wordpress.com/rhet-comp-moms-project/.

Silvia, Paul. *How to Write a Lot: A Practical Guide to Productive Academic Writing.* American
Psychological Association, 2007.

Smith, Zadie. *Intimations: Six Essays.* Penguin, 2020.

Squazzoni, Flaminio, et al. "Gender Gap in Journal Submissions and Peer Review During
the First Wave of the COVID-19 Pandemic: A Study on 2329 Elsevier Journals." *PLOS
One*, vol. 16 no. 10, 2021.

Sword, Helen. *Air and Light and Time and Space: How Successful Academics Write.* Cambridge
UP, 2017.

Woolf, Virginia. *Between the Acts.* Harcourt, 1941.

Woolf, Virginia. "Thoughts on Peace in an Air Raid." *The Essays of Virginia Woolf vol. 6: 1933
to 1941*, edited by Stuart N. Clarke. Hogarth Press, 2011, pp. 242–48.

13
(INTRA-)ACTIVE NOTEBOOKING AS BECOMING

Kevin Roozen and Steve Lamos

Tags: collaboration, identity

In the careful and profound analysis of her great-great-great aunt Annie's diary that emerges from the pages of *The Extraordinary Work of Ordinary Writing*, Jennifer Sinor argues that we can better understand the remarkable work that writing does in the world by paying attention to the seemingly mundane and ordinary texts and textual practices that animate people's everyday lives. For Sinor, attending to "what we first might take as simple, unsophisticated, and plain becomes one of the few opportunities to access the ways in which subject and text are made every day by ordinary people" (187). Sinor further asserts that central to the extraordinary work of the kind of "ordinary" writing that gets done in diaries and notebooks is its ability to access "the in-between, unmarked moments of our daily lives" (184). Throughout this chapter, we attend to the powerful life-making affects that emerge from the in-between—i.e., the virtual space of possibility and becoming (e.g., Massumi)—that is harnessed by a particular kind of notebooking activity in which the both of us have been engaged for many years.

We are Kevin and Steve: two mid-career, middle-aged, white academics who have found increasingly profound value in analyzing our long-term work with, through, and beyond notebooking as a kind of self-sponsored writing.[1] By "notebooking," we mean the activities (e.g., the practices and processes of recording experiences, jotting notes, making lists, musing on events), the materialities (e.g., the tools and technologies including bound notebooks, laptop computers, pens, pencils, and word processors), and the conditions of composing involved in producing records of and reflections on life events. While both of us have been engaged in notebooking for many years across multiple periods of life (nearly thirty years for Kevin and nearly ten years for Steve), we have found such activity to be especially rich during our mid-career,

https://doi.org/10.7330/9781646424870.c013

post-tenure periods, including during the COVID-19 era. We have also found notebooking to be enriching as a point of recent and increasingly regular discussion in this phase of our more than twenty-year friendship.

While we have long conversed about life, family, and work at least monthly (and often more) since our time together in graduate school back in the early 2000s, we have lately found ourselves discussing and even theorizing notebooking from a more academic and autoethnographic perspective in ways that both of us have found increasingly fascinating. For instance, when Steve asked Kevin to characterize his notebooking in a September 2019 email, Kevin wrote the following:

> In a box at work (and scattered in some of my dresser drawers and other odd places around my house) are more than twenty years (maybe more like 25 years) of these little monthly notebooks that I have carried around in my wallet. . . . I have kept almost every single one of these that I have ever used, save the 24 from the first two years of using them while I was working at an outdoor power equipment store, which must have gotten lost in one of my many moves over the past two or more decades. Why I kept them, I do not know. Why I have lugged them across the country is a mystery. But, for some reason, I have become fascinated with them. . . . What an exciting thing, I think, to examine my use of these notebooks, and to get a sense of the story they tell about myself and my textual practices. That, I think, would be pretty cool.

In the first section of this article, Kevin will examine the various in-betweens of two seemingly mundane pages of his notebook entries, exploring their rich connections both to various sorts of becoming processes and to the strong affects that he associates with them. In the second section, Steve will reflect on how intra-active discussion with Kevin about this notebooking—what amounts to an "intra-view" methodology as will be outlined shortly—has generated still other forms of collective becoming rooted in other strong affects that entangle the both of us as co-researchers and co-authors. Lastly, we will comment together on the significance of this work for understanding how seemingly mundane writing accesses the in-between in order to play a profound role in literate life-making.

NOTEBOOKING AS INTRA-ACTIVE HABIT(S)

We view notebooking as an "intra-active" phenomenon in Karen Barad's sense of this term—i.e., a phenomenon evincing the "mutual constitution of entangled agencies" (33). Notebooking involves, this is to say, a sort of bringing-forth-into-newness across a range of heterogeneous activities and materialities. Such intra-action is initiated by writers as they

(Intra-)Active Notebooking as Becoming   211

sit down to notebook on a given occasion; however, it ultimately operates in excess of these writers, well beyond any specific intentions, aims, or goals that they might ostensibly harbor. Intra-action among and through elements of notebooking—materials, discourses, practices, processes, and so on—ultimately enables a kind of newness to emerge from the in-between that operates *with* but ultimately *beyond* those entangled in it.

We have further come to understand our work as co-researchers in this project as indicative of a kind of "intra-view" approach to co-research activity—that is, a version of qualitative interview activity in which traditional roles of interviewer and interviewee are themselves set into intra-active relationship. Aaron Kuntz and Marni Presnall characterize intra-view as an open-ended interview and discussion process aimed at "making accessible the multiple intersections of material contexts that collude in productive formations of meaning" (733). These authors further stress that intra-view sees meaning itself "as a becoming" (731): While it certainly involves asking questions and recording answers, it is ultimately less concerned with traditional epistemological questions (e.g., concepts such as validity or reliability) than it is with ontological issues reflecting "the primacy of more processual ways of encountering the world in which we live" (736).

Here, we employ a kind of intra-view methodology enabling both of us to ask questions, engage in reflection, and otherwise analyze the in-between of notebooking. In particular, we have

> prompted Kevin to choose representative examples of his notebooking work for discussion;
> prompted Kevin to reflect explicitly on the examples he selected;
> facilitated recursive cycles of talk between the two of us, both on the phone and via email, about these choices and reflections (including explicit talk about bodily states, feelings, and affects/sensations); and
> reflected together, as an intra-active co-authoring unit, on this larger analytical process.

Intra-view has thereby set us into intra-active assemblage with, through, and beyond Kevin's initial notebooking into a kind of co-researcher and co-author relationship.

We further regard our intra-active notebooking and intra-view work to be rooted squarely in three "habits" related to writerly entanglement described by Marilyn Cooper; namely, the habits of "observation" (94), "connection" (94), and "wonder" (95). Cooper describes this first habit of observation as that of "being attentive to the materials, to the subject matter of writing" (94). This habit involves, that is, careful attention to the activities, materialities, and conditions under investigation. Cooper describes the habit of connection, meanwhile, as "mixing one's sentient awareness with the flows of everyday life" (94)—that is, as attempting to bring seemingly distinct observations above into a kind of intra-action. Finally, she characterizes the habit of wonder as especially fundamental to the sort of thinking engaged in by scientists and other knowledge-creators, a habit "essential" in terms of trying to "answer the world" (95). Wonder thus serves for Cooper as a kind of "felt recognition that something matters in a particular way" (95)—that is, as an energy that can both *activate* the in-between of notebooking and *fuel* its extended becoming.

Cooper further illustrates the importance of these habits through analysis of the published notebooks of Nicholas Harberd, a working plant biologist who has kept extensive scientific and personal notebooks as part of his professional work. She notes first that Harberd spends a great deal of time

> being attentive to the materials, to the subject matter of writing. Harberd is explicit about the importance of observation for a field naturalist . . . detailed observation is important in writing about almost any subject. It is a standard methodology in studies of cultures, central in news reporting and travel writing, a means of supporting project and policy proposals and arrangements, and essential in offering testimony. (94)

Cooper suggests here that Harberd deploys the habit of observation carefully, noting dimensions of material conditions in ways that both enable and propel his scientific investigation.

Cooper further notes that Harberd spends a great deal of time making habitual connections among, across, and beyond observations; for example, "Harberd continually sees patterns and makes connections among observations, experiences, memories, and feelings. Thinking of things as structured as levels connects a range of experiences and memories" (94). These sorts of connections enable Harberd to "mak[e] a new thing from the old" (96) as well as to begin "connecting past and present with the subject material through memories and experiences of daily life" (96). The habit of connection thus plays a crucial role for Harberd in begetting a kind of newness by bringing seemingly distinct concepts into intra-action.

Finally, Cooper spends an extended amount of time highlighting Harberd's focus on wonder. She writes that

> Harberd asks questions and speculates about every detail of plants he observes, and he wonders about many other things, such as why science seems so cut off from everyday life. Wonder might be thought of

(Intra-)Active Notebooking as Becoming   213

as the habit of critical thinking so popular in education, but as Harberd describes this feeling it aligns better with the felt recognition that something matters in a particular way. (95)

As elaboration on this "felt recognition that something matters in a particular way," Cooper stresses that wonder drives and powers the kinds of connections that Harberd is ultimately able to make as a scientist: "Insights and ideas emerge from Harberd's juxtaposition and connection of observations of plants and the landscape and his emotions and memories with scientific explanations of plant growth, a process he experiences with 'real excitement' [and a self-described] 'widening of vision'" (97–98). She further highlights passages in Harberd's notebooks where he mentions wonder explicitly: "Wonder is what really drives us, and wonder is what we feel" (qtd. in 97). Cooper concludes from such passages that "Wonder . . . is clearly identified in the notebook as the motive of science" (97). Cooper thereby establishes that the habit of wonder provides energetic impetus for additional intra-active observation, connection-making, and becoming in ways that help us to understand more fully both Kevin's notebooking and Kevin and Steve's intra-view activity.

KEVIN'S NOTEBOOKING: HABITUATING TO OBSERVATION, CONNECTION, AND (ESPECIALLY) WONDER

I, Kevin, began notebooking in 1993 through a job I held working the sales and repair counter at an outdoor power equipment store. Much of my work involved selling equipment or taking in equipment to be repaired, which necessitated having a readily available textual space for writing down the model and serial numbers of pieces of equipment that I needed to keep track of; repairs that customers requested; parts that needed to be ordered; and the dates, times, and locations of deliveries I needed to make. I had noticed that my boss and my co-workers all had small notebooks that were kept in their wallets and that they used them constantly throughout the workday. When I asked my boss about his notebook, he helped me order one of my own from Day-Timer, a company that sells planners and organizers. It proved quite useful for making notes to myself while on the job. I was also taking undergraduate classes at the time; woven into the notebooking entries during that period are due dates for course assignments I was working on, titles of readings that I needed to complete, reminders about study sessions with classmates, and notes about tuition payments. Scattered throughout those entries were also notes regarding tasks associated with renting an apartment and taking care of my car, such as dates for mailing payments

214 KEVIN ROOZEN AND STEVE LAMOS

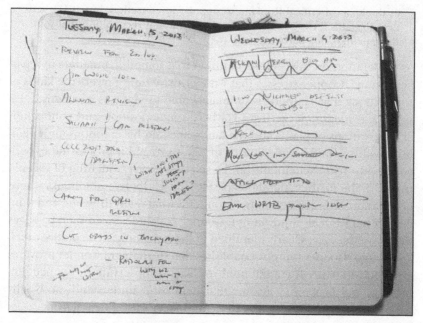

Figure 13.1. Photo of Kevin's notebook.

on time, notes to contact my landlord, and reminders to make appointments for auto service and renew my registration and insurance.

Although the context for my writing has changed significantly over the years through different jobs, marriage, having a family, graduate school, obtaining an academic position, and the like, many of the basic forms and functions of my notebooking activities have remained consistent. Those general forms and functions are visible in the two pages I offer in figure 13.1, both from the 3½-inch by 5-inch notebook I kept in my wallet from March and April of 2013. The entries on each page tend to be organized in roughly chronological order, with events and tasks occurring earlier in the day listed toward the top of each page and events and tasks occurring later in the day listed more toward the bottom. Entries related to tasks that are not associated with a particular time tend to be jotted wherever space is available. Each entry is typically separated by a line I draw beneath each one to help ensure that I can see each individual entry clearly and distinctly. Throughout the day, I tend to mark through items I have accomplished so that I can readily see what I have completed and what still needs my attention.

The series of entries I jotted on these pages for Tuesday, March 5 and Wednesday, March 6 of 2013, for example, specify the major events and tasks for each of those days. Many of the entries for this particular Tuesday and Wednesday relate to my teaching, such as the ones indicating a meeting with two first-year composition students, a graduate student's thesis defense, and my teaching and office hours. Other entries on these pages relate to my research, including the one about my upcoming CCCC conference talk and a reminder to send some of my colleagues some ideas for another conference proposal. Still other entries on these pages relate to additional facets of my work, such as those on Tuesday's page regarding a manuscript review that was coming due and obtaining some candy for the upcoming Qualitative Research Network (QRN) meeting. Finally, my notebooking for these two days addresses a number of family-related matters, such as those regarding yard care and finances.

As I have examined the many hundreds of pages like these that I've generated over many years (including these two as they have served as the focus of intra-views that Steve and I have conducted), I have glimpsed all three of the habits Cooper describes. As the subject matter of my writing is my daily activities, my notebooking is clearly animated by each of Cooper's habits.

Notebooking Habits of Observation

I readily see how my notebooking has consistently habituated me toward observation—that is, toward a close and careful attention to my life's activities, what I needed to do, and when I needed to do it. Jotting short entries across the small space of each page was a means of not just paying very conscious attention to things I needed and wanted to do each day but also of prioritizing and arranging those things into the space of my life. To borrow Cooper's language, my notebooking has oriented me toward developing a "clear description" of what I regarded as the important things and tasks facing me as well as toward developing a sense of how they could come in the temporal and spatial flow of my days.

Examining the pages of my notebooking offered in figure 13.1 renders visible a number of things about the subject matter of writing, which in this case involves observing and managing my schedule. It strikes me that the items written somewhat neatly (in terms of my handwriting, at any rate) and horizontally within the printed lines are items that were likely written in my notebook early in the week, perhaps on Sunday afternoon when I typically devoted time to planning what needed to get done between Monday and Friday. In these instances, I would have placed my notebook on a flat, stable surface like my kitchen table at home, and my wife would have had her planner open on the surface as well. The neatly written items would have been events and activities that I knew about in advance and that I could plan ahead for and work into my schedule. On the other hand, the items that are written less neatly at odd angles on the page comprise things that I likely wrote down "on the fly" as they came up during the flow of the day's activity. I would have written these down in my notebook as I had it opened against my leg while, for instance, I had stopped on the way to my classroom or to a meeting; or maybe I would have scribbled these notes as I was holding my notebook open against the console of my car as I was driving to or from campus that day.

Even as I notebooked daily for nearly twenty-five years, I doubt that I ever paid much thought to these sorts of textual practices and processes; because observing and managing my schedule was at the fore of keeping my notebook, the material practices and processes of my notebooking itself remained generally invisible to me. This invisibility is something that Cooper mentions in her analysis of Harberd's writing, noting that "when one uses tools, one is not aware of them" (102). Plus, the particular kind of writing that drives my notebooking—brief lists consisting of short phrases separated by a series of lines—seems so fragmented, so ordinary, so mundane, that it evidently failed to capture my attention as a writing researcher and scholar for many years.

Ordinary writing, Sinor asserts, "resists simple, comfortable ways of reading and knowing" (87). But by looking closely at and talking through these pages, including during intra-views with Steve, I've come to realize how much textual work I've invested in attending to and marking these in-between moments of my daily life. Sinor asserts that it is this kind of noticing and writing that enables her aunt Annie to "make order and keep the unstable at bay" (19) in ways that "create necessary stability" (20) for day-to-day living. In much the same manner, my notebooking has created a textual space where I could proceed with making and living a life.

Notebooking Habits of Connection

My notebooking further evinces what Cooper describes as the habit of connection. I have grown increasingly curious about, and frankly quite amazed at, the far-flung network of other texts at play in my notebooking. The pages by themselves are quite remarkable in the sense that imagining their actual use makes visible the wealth of other texts they intra-act with as well as the vast network of texts that animate the scheduling and ordering of my life's activities. Generating and using the entries for March 5 and March 6, for example, involved a series of different print and digital calendars that I kept in connection to similar print and digital calendars used by members of my family and my co-workers. This network also includes a wide array of other kinds of texts. I notice reminders to finish crafting a manuscript review that was due the next week and to begin drafting my annual reviews of my teaching, research, and service, which were due at the end of April. I see a reminder to finish my upcoming CCCC conference talk, which I would deliver the next week in Las Vegas. There is also a note jotted at an odd angle beneath "CCCC 2013 Talk," which reads, "What does this case study suggest about transfer?" that offers a version of the opening sentence I could use to open the concluding portion of my talk. At the bottom of the March 6 page, the note "Email WRAB proposal ideas" references an email that I had been delayed in sending to some colleagues regarding a panel we were proposing for the 2014 Writing Research Across Borders (WRAB) conference. Finally, the note about Nichole's thesis defense reminded me to bring copies of the defense paperwork that other committee members would need to sign.

Looking at those March 5 and March 6 pages of my notebooking also prompted me to think beyond written texts to consider other semiotic modalities that those pages would have been connected to as I would have actually used them throughout those days, including spoken interactions and visual images. My notes regarding cutting the backyard or shifting money into my savings account, for example, might have been written in response to spoken conversations with my wife as we planned out our weekly activities or talked about our family finances. My note about how to begin the concluding section of my upcoming conference talk might well have been the actual words I uttered during my presentation.

I notice, too, how my use of this particular kind of notebook functions as what Jamie White-Farnham refers to as a "rhetorical heirloom" (208), a textual practice or artifact that connects multiple generations of people. In this sense, my notebook links me to the people I worked with in that outdoor power equipment shop back in 1993 who introduced me to the wallet-sized Day-Timer notebooks. It also connects me to my son: when at age nine he first asked me about getting his own wallet, he did not ask for a new one; instead, he asked me if I had "one of my old wallets with a notebook" that he could use for his own. In short, many habits of connection, short-term and long-term, are included here.

Reflecting on these connections brings to mind Sinor's careful tracing of the interactions among the pages of her aunt Annie's diary and a

218 KEVIN ROOZEN AND STEVE LAMOS

host of other texts, activities, and relations; for example, reading books for pleasure, keeping track of family and business expenditures, recording the weather and the crops, commenting on her relationships with her husband and friends, and observing her physical health (103–13). For Sinor, mapping the network of interactions that texture each page "allows us to move away from what Annie says of a day (the sparse content of her diary and the value we might place on that content) and toward how she replicates, through writing, the experience of being in the days" (113). In a similar fashion (and much like Harberd as well), the connections I am making on these pages allow me to put these seemingly disparate texts and experiences in conversation with one another as I engaged in similar daily being and becoming.

Notebooking Habits of Wonder

While the long history of my notebooking has been dominated by a habituation toward observation and connection, my recent life has been marked by a profound shift toward what Cooper refers to as a "habit of wonder" (95). My attention is still focused on organizing and accomplishing my life's activities, but the many years of my notebooking have cultivated my growing attentiveness and curiosity toward the material practices and processes it has entailed. After almost three decades of notebooking, I've become increasingly attuned toward Cooper's aforementioned "felt recognition that something matters in a particular way" (95) in regard to the various elements of my notebooking activities. This, in turn, has increasingly ushered me toward seeing the intra-acting entities "as the extraordinary things that they are" (95).

As I look back at these pages from my present vantage point, one particularly rich source of wonder for me involves the materiality of my notebooking; that is, the embodied practices and processes of acting with the small notebooks in my wallet. My notebooking began in 1993 with my use of the aforementioned Day-Timer notebooks, but increasingly I found them a bit too pricey at fifty dollars for a set of twelve. Accordingly, in 2013, I started fashioning my own notebooks to keep in my wallet. Doing so prompted me to pay close attention to not only the cost but also the importance of the physical dimensions of my notebooks, as their height, width, and thickness all need to fall within a fairly narrow range if they are to fit effectively in my wallet so they can remain close at hand when I need them. If the notebook is too tall or too wide, it won't fit inside the wallet and thus won't be handily within reach. But if it is too short or too narrow, it can't offer enough space for a day's worth of entries in my handwriting and thus won't allow me to readily see on a single page everything that needs to be done and when. The same is kind of true of the notebook's thickness. If it is too thick, it makes my wallet quite difficult to remove easily from my back pocket, and it shifts my posture uncomfortably when I'm seated. But if the notebook is too thin, it doesn't have enough pages to use for multiple months. The notebooks that I finally settled on as I began fashioning my own were ones that I happened upon quite by accident; I caught a quick glimpse of them on a small display at my university's bookstore, and after looking them over I found that they had suitable physical dimensions and price tag.

Marveling at the materiality of my notebooking has also illuminated the affective intensities that it has long held for me. While I had long regarded my notebooking as too bare, utilitarian, and functional to entail any consideration of emotion and affect, this project helped me to see how such work might be opened up for both examination and reflection. I don't recall ever explicitly attending to the affective dimensions of my notebooking before beginning this project—a lack of attention especially striking given that I had encountered a wealth of scholarship addressing affect and emotion in relation to literate activity (Prior; Prior and Shipka; Leander and Boldt; Sinor) and that I myself had written up a number of detailed case studies addressing the affective dimensions of other people's writing (Roozen "Acting"; Roozen "Mapping"; Roozen and Erickson).

What eventually prompted me to start thinking about the affective valences of my notebooking was a question that Steve posed in September 2019 via email about crossing things out as he was examining these March 5 and March 6 notebook pages. Steve's seemingly simple question—"Why is everything crossed out?"—proved a crucial source of wonder that drew me toward considering issues of affect and my notebooking. Although I don't recall immediately being able to come up with much to say as I thought about Steve's question, it did prompt me to browse back through some of my many notebooks over the next few days, just to see if anything regarding affect jumped out at me, such as how long I had been crossing out items, when and why I might have started that practice, whether it was a fleeting or more sustained practice, and so on.

I first noticed that I started to consistently cross items off my list beginning in the latter months of 2012. Then, during a phone conversation with Steve in October 2019, I started both to make connections between the traces of my notebooking practices visible on those pages and what I was experiencing in my life at the time and to wonder about the incredibly powerful affects that were animating those seemingly simple inscriptions. I began to realize that the crossing out of items held some fairly negative affective entanglements for me.

Specifically, I started to recall that I had been immersed during this time in some labor-intensive and time-consuming WPA work, which I found incredibly stressful and which often prevented me from accomplishing much of what I needed to do. I slowly recognized that crossing out items on the pages of my notebook was a means of dealing with the stresses I was feeling at this particular time of my life. It provided a way for me to visually acknowledge to myself that I had accomplished something despite all of the challenges that the world had thrown at me—that in some small way I had prevailed.

At the same time, this particular phone conversation with Steve helped me to realize that the crossing off of items held some positive affective entanglements as well. Crossing off items was functioning for me as a visible, tangible sign of being someone who can accomplish things for my research, teaching, and service for my job; for taking care of my home and my family's finances; and for all of the other things involved in the continual making of a life. These constitute the seemingly insignificant in-between things that would likely go unnoticed and unheralded but that are nonetheless vitally important.

What this all illustrates, I think, is how I both cultivated a habit of wonder through reflection and intra-view as well as how this wonder seemed to gain its own momentum as observation and connection morphed into something new and exciting. These habits, first as I saw them in my original notebooking and then as Steve and I have intra-acted with, through, and beyond them over the years, make clear to me that this work has both had profound affective impacts on me and has contributed to new forms of my own becoming via the in-between. This sense of wonder is enhanced for me still further by the fact that I had not previously taken the time to wonder about my own literate activities in this way at any point before engaging in this work.

It now feels deeply satisfying to examine my own notebooking practices in these ways: they reveal a powerful and life-affirming affect operating in the in-between of seemingly mundane textual practices. Ordinary writing, Sinor notes, is often perceived as "writing that is typically unseen or ignored [and] . . . primarily defined by its status as discardable" (5). Importantly, however, making it a source of wonder and curiosity can reveal "how the unmarked moments of our days equally and fully participate in the continual making of identity and the making of texts" (202). My own thrill at seeing this important, affectively rich survival activity emerging from the in-between feels quite significant: I marvel at just how much meaning has emerged—and continues to emerge—from this notebooking.

STEVE: NOTEBOOKING INTRA-ACTION THROUGH INTRA-VIEW

I, Steve, am struck by the ways in which habits of observation, connection, and especially wonder operate within Kevin's account above. Kevin's revelations suggest a profound power to examine and understand the role of the in-between as it relates to notebooking. But I am equally struck about revelations that Kevin and I have shared via the enjoyable, energetic, and often messy intra-view activity that we have regularly performed together, work that itself reveals interesting goings-on in the in-between of our literate work together as co-notebookers and co-researchers.

These revelations began a little over two years ago when Kevin and I started talking about his notebooks as a specific site of interesting textual activity. At first, our discussion was quite informal: we'd be talking on the phone about something else and the subject of notebooking would come up naturally in conversation, often as a pleasant diversion from departmental politics or WPA headaches or other drains on time, energy, and spirit. A few months into such informal discussion, we decided that we would each send each other a couple of snippets of specific pages of our notebooks, read them over, and then ask each other questions about them.

One example of what has evolved into our collective intra-view method is included below. In figure 13.2, readers can see my versions of the same two of Kevin's notebook pages referenced earlier in figure 13.1. They feature several lines of text along with crossings-out included in black and white. Readers can also see two types of my questions and comments: the typed comments in "Track Changes" are those that I sent along before an October 2019 phone call; the handwritten comments are those that I jotted while talking with Kevin during that call.

Examining these comments in retrospect, I see myself engaging in habits of observation and connection directly related to the materiality of Kevin's notebooks. The typed questions that I first included via Microsoft "Comments" seem aimed very much at trying to make sense of what I am seeing in Kevin's work: I ask about times and places, and I ask about why the notebook is arranged the way that it is. Furthermore,

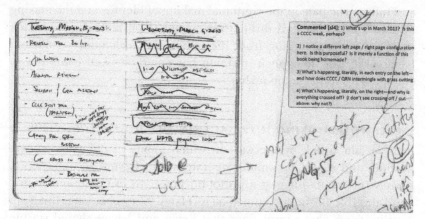

Figure 13.2. Steve's annotations on Kevin's notebook.

I ask what I see as fairly innocuous questions about why certain things on these pages are crossed out: "Why is everything crossed off?"; "I don't see crossing out / off above, why not?" Each of these questions asks that Kevin elaborate on what I'm seeing.

What I see myself doing in green, in a bit of a contrast, is trying to jot down key words and phrases that Kevin uses as he answered these questions during our October 11, 2019, phone conversation: The word "ANGST" sits at the center of this page along with the phrases "Job @ UCF," "make it," and "constant in my life." These phrasal answers constitute a kind of habit of connection: Kevin was verbally answering my questions about these specific notebooking elements by connecting them back to the time and the place in which they were written. He revealed to me that this particular set of pages took him back to a difficult period at one institution that featured much juggling of research, teaching, administration, and parenting. Each crossing out, as it turned out, constituted a kind of small victory over the challenge of a particular day.

As I assess my own two habits as an intra-viewer in this situation, I see myself in a role similar to Sinor's as she engages at length with her aunt Annie's diary. Through her detailed observation and the detailed connections that she draws, Sinor begins to understand that notebooking ultimately serves to "document the transparent process of thinking, by naming all that would typically pass unnoticed and unmarked" (181). I found myself here trying to make sense of the ways in which Kevin had documented his own day-to-day thinking here through scribblings, crossings out, and other seemingly everyday inscription tactics. These markings and un-markings ultimately "document[ed] the transparent process of thinking" in ways that I would otherwise have missed as key sites of becoming.

Immediately after we got off the phone on October 11, 2019, I jotted down the following summary of our conversation, which I think illustrates these habits of connection more explicitly:

> We talked next about the scratching out. I assumed that this was just a way of indicating that something had been done, and I said so. Kevin agreed to a point, but then said something interesting: at this time in his life, he equated crossing out with what he called "angst": each thing he crossed out, he said, was a kind of graphical "I made it" statement—a statement about having survived another day. I certainly remember talking to Kevin often around this time of the transition from [University X] to [University Y], and I remember just how upset and depressed he was: I think that this was probably also around the time that he came out to ski and lost his toenails with [our mutual friend]. And so I'm not surprised to hear this particular narrative about "scratching out" things.

Here, readers can see me making this connection between scratching out entries and angst more explicit: I write that the "angst" that Kevin was feeling at the time was reflected in part in the very lists of things that he was notebooking about. I also write explicitly that each crossing out was a miniature kind of "I made it" declaration—a miniature pronouncement of small triumph and having "survived another day." I even make a connection to a vacation trip that Kevin and I took around the time when he wrote the entries on March 5 and March 6. We had gone snow skiing on some difficult terrain with a third friend, and Kevin actually lost one toenail in the aftermath on account of ill-fitting ski boots.

In the immediate wake of these connections, I began to wonder regularly about the larger goings-on within and beyond the in-between of these two pages. This wonder became especially obvious to me once Kevin wrote me back on email about these specific pages nearly one year later. He began to make additional sense of our conversation through notes that he typed up on August 10, 2020, and then sent to me soon thereafter:

> I always felt like I was just barely making it through the day, and so, as a way to kind of celebrate the little victories of getting things accomplished, I had started to cross through items on my list each day. It was a practical move, as it made it easy for me to glance at the page of my notebook and see what still needed to be done. But it was also something else—it was a way for me to visually see for myself that I was getting things done each day, that despite how overwhelmed I felt, that feeling that shit could all go wildly off the rails at any moment, I was still able

224 KEVIN ROOZEN AND STEVE LAMOS

> to get something accomplished each day, I was still able to make some progress, to carry on with my life and all that needed to get done. I can still remember how good it felt, and still feels, to cross things off of my lists. When I get to cross something off my list, it feels really good. I get this feeling of being competent. And sometimes, I get this feeling like "hey world, I got it done."

I still feel clearly here a sense of wonder at Kevin's words—wonder at his retrospective reflection some ten months later on his part about "how good it felt" to "get this feeling of being competent." The reference to "hey world, I got it done" stands as a final emphasis on the energy he needed to keep moving forward such that other things might likewise get done in the present and future.

Even as illustrated in this short snippet of exchange, our intra-view activities index a powerfully emergent habit of wonder rooted in the in-between of notebooking. How fascinating that something as simple as crossing off one element of a list could simultaneously generate and be propelled by so much powerful affect over such an extended period of time! As I thought about this revelation as a newly minted intra-viewer, I found myself once again in a position akin to Sinor: "Thrilled because years ago I would not have known what I had nor had the tools to read it. A few years ago, these notebooks surely would have been tossed" (182). I was quite thrilled at the emergence of profound revelation in the midst of something so seemingly everyday.

CONCLUSIONS: THE POWER AND SURPRISE OF INTRA-ACTIVE NOTEBOOKING

Based on her analysis of the ordinary textual activities that link the professional and domestic lifeworlds of a civil engineering professor, Sarah Durst asserts that "the practices that appear 'everyday' need our attention, for it is in the 'everydayness' of practice that a life is built" (493). Viewed through intra-active habits of observation, connection, and (especially) wonder that have infused our work together on this project, our own notebooking processes and practices illuminate how the in-between of seemingly mundane and everyday writing both indexes powerful instances of life sustenance and animates our continual becoming. I, Kevin, have been struck by the fact that I've been notebooking for nearly thirty years before developing a curiosity about its dense materialities, expansive intertextual reach, and deeply affective dimensions. I have also been moved by the fascinating connections that I now see between my efforts to assemble a life and Sinor's aunt Annie's daily survival in the late nineteenth century. Meanwhile, I, Steve, have been quite surprised at how posing ordinary questions about snippets of Kevin's notebooking can reveal the life-affirming power of habits so otherwise seemingly simple and plain.

Both of us have been surprised further by the ways in which our regularly routine (and slightly chaotic) intra-view talk about these note-booking activities has revealed new sources of becoming, both from the in-between of the palimpsest that comprises these original notebook pages and from the in-between of our relationship together as friends, co-researchers, and co-authors. Intra-viewing around notebooking has come to organize our days; it has come to reinvigorate our research and scholarly agendas; it has also come to entangle us further as long-time friends and colleagues. Intra-viewing has thus helped us to realize that attending to everyday textualities greatly increases our chances of glimpsing the richness of our literate life-making activities even in the most seemingly mundane spaces.

No less importantly, we are both now imagining ways to use assign-ment sequences in our writing courses that are rooted explicitly in intra-view-based notebooking practices, particularly as framed by both Sinor's perspective and Cooper's three-part framework. We imagine, that is, inviting regularized, rhythmic, and routinized writing about life events (both remarkable and quotidian) as central to our students' activities. We also imagine both stressing habits of observation, connec-tion, and wonder explicitly as we ask students to engage in this work and assigning intra-view activity among groups of students such that they can collaboratively co-explore the in-between of their own notebooking activities. Finally, we imagine referencing our own experiences here as we engage with our students. On the one hand, we will need to remind them that habit-based notebooking and intra-viewing can function for weeks, months, or even years without fully knowing or predicting what might become. On the other hand, we will need to nonetheless assure them that regularly engaging in these practices can yield powerful access to the richness of the in-between as a fundamentally important source of their life-making activities.

NOTE

1. This chapter is drawn from a larger project that examines both of our individual notebooking activities. Here, however, we will be foregrounding Kevin's notebook-ing activities as the explicit focus of analysis.

WORKS CITED

Barad, Karen. *Meeting the Universe Halfway: Quantum Physics and the Entanglement of Matter and Meaning*. Duke University Press, 2007.

Cooper, Marilyn. *The Animal Who Writes: A Posthumanist Composition*. U of Pittsburgh P, 2019.

Durst, Sarah. "Disciplinarity and Literate Activity in Civil and Environmental Engineering: A Lifeworld Perspective." *Written Communication*, vol. 36, no. 4, 2019, pp. 471–502.

Kuntz, Aaron, and Marni Presnall. "Wandering the Tactical: From Interview to Intra-view." *Qualitative Inquiry*, vol. 18, no. 9, 2012, pp. 732–44.

Leander, Kevin, and Gail Boldt. "Rereading 'A Pedagogy of Multiliteracies': Bodies, Texts, and Emergence." *Journal of Literacy Research*, vol. 45, no. 1, 2013, pp. 22–46.

Massumi, Brian. *Parables for the Virtual*. Duke UP, 2002.

Prior, Paul. "How Do Moments Add up to Lives: Trajectories of Semiotic Becoming vs. Tales of School Learning in Four Modes." *Making Future Matters*, edited by Rick Wysocki and Mary P. Sheridan, Computers and Composition Digital Press/Utah State UP, 2018. http://ccdigitalpress.org/makingfuturematters.

Prior, Paul, and Jody Shipka. "Chronotopic Lamination: Tracing the Contours of Literate Activity." *Writing Selves/Writing Societies: Research from Activity Perspectives*, edited by Charles Bazerman and David R. Russell, The WAC Clearinghouse, 2003, pp. 180–238.

Roozen, Kevin. "Acting with Inscriptions: Expanding Perspectives of Writing, Learning, and Becoming." *Journal for the Association of Expanded Perspectives on Learning*, vol. 26, 2021, pp. 23–48.

Roozen, Kevin. "Mapping Translingual Literacies: Encouraging and Enacting Transnational Perspectives of Literate Life." *Translingual Affordances: Globalized Approaches to the Teaching of Writing*, edited by Alanna Frost et al., The WAC Clearinghouse, 2020, pp. 133–59.

Roozen, Kevin, and Joe Erickson. *Expanding Literate Landscapes: Persons, Practices, and Sociohistoric Perspectives of Disciplinary Development*. Computers and Composition Digital Press/Utah State UP, 2017. Web. https://ccdigitalpress.org/expanding.

Sinor, Jennifer. *The Extraordinary Work of Ordinary Writing: Annie Ray's Diary*. U of Iowa P, 2000.

White-Farnham, Jamie. " 'Revising the Menu to Fit the Budget': Grocery Lists and Other Rhetorical Heirlooms." *College English*, vol. 76, no. 3, 2014, pp. 208–26.

14
EXTERNALIZED PROCESS AND WRITING TOOLS

Laura R. Micciche

Tags: productivity, adaptability, technology, embodiment

In this chapter I describe how writers externalize their processes through online tools and software programs, including time-tracking software, ambient sound programs, research- and project-management tools, writing accountability groups, distraction-free writing tools, and shared task boards. By "externalize," I refer to writers' deliberate and serendipitous use of physical and digital tools to address defined or extemporaneous writing needs. The deliberate, intentional part of this framing is similar to Paul Prior and Jody Shipka's description of ESSPs (environment-selecting and -structuring practices), described as the "intentional deployment of external aids and actors to shape, stabilize, and direct consciousness in service of the task at hand" (44; see also Lotier). Prior and Shipka are especially interested in writers' use of ESSPs to curate their physical environments, whereas I focus on external resources that advanced writers choose or happen upon to match the complexity of the tasks they undertake and the changing conditions of their professional and personal lives.

Derek Van Ittersum and Kory Lawson Ching have likewise studied "how invested writers can become in actively shaping their writing processes through the selection and structuring of their tools." Their study of software programs reveals "writers who tinker extensively with the tools they use to write." Also focused on writers and their tools, Tim Lockridge and Van Ittersum, in *Writing Workflows: Beyond Word Processing*, explore the writing processes of Markdown bloggers, illustrating how software and hardware programs mediate writing (57). They describe writers' "modular" writing approaches, which enable them to "rotate tools in and out" of their workflows (18). Workflows, they write, "aren't about tools used in isolation or in perfect test conditions. Rather, a workflow is a habituated, mediated, and personal means of accomplishing

https://doi.org/10.7330/9781646424870.c014

something" (82). This chapter builds on such insights, and similar ones advanced by scholars of the sociomaterial aspects of writing processes (C. Haas; Miller; Hensley Owens; Rule), by illuminating how intentional and serendipitous tool selection and usage plays out in the writing lives of advanced writers.

I've led faculty and graduate writing workshops since 2013 that have afforded me a view of writers' efforts to adapt and change their relationships with tools, and the subsequent ways in which they've been changed by them. I've worked with over three hundred student and faculty writers in fields ranging from aerospace engineering to botany to architecture and design. During summer 2020 and again in spring and summer 2021, I taught a dissertation workshop remotely, with an enrollment of thirty students in each section (see Micciche on converting this class from f2f to remote). Simultaneously, I led three weeklong faculty workshops remotely, each enrolling approximately twenty-five participants at varying ranks from multiple colleges. Because of COVID-19 restrictions, participants were cut off from their research communities and forced to adapt their personal lives to the limits imposed by social distancing. Writing was newly defined by the smallness of the worlds they were inhabiting, calling for creative innovations and flexibility at a moment when we all craved normalcy, consistency, and stability. In the absence of these security markers, participants formed communities of practice that cohered around writing and sharing strategies, tools, and resources to support writing. In these sessions, I began thinking like an ethnographer studying a vigorous culture of writing practitioners. Participants showed me how expert writers in diverse fields approach writing when stakes are high, adaptation is crucial, and time is premium.

Our workshops included an optional resource-share session during which I invited participants to share a writing program or application, research management tool, organizational method, database, sensory assist, or other resource they found valuable to their writing and research activities. Participants frequently shared their screens during these sessions, showing how they use and adapt various resources for often idiosyncratic purposes. That is, writers do not always use resources "out of the box"; instead, they create workarounds for mismatched features, apply usage strategies learned from peers, and generally exert agency driven by their professional and personal positionalities and pressing writing situations. The resource-share sessions created opportunities for writers to learn from one another how to work differently, exposing participants to resources they didn't know they needed or may have never thought to try.

Externalized Process and Writing Tools   229

In this way, tools were positioned as more than instruments for getting things done and solving problems; they became inventive and self-reflective. Tools came to represent new ways to imagine one's relationship to writing, as Evelyn,[1] an educational studies student, demonstrates in her reflection about dissertation writing:

> I bought a subscription to Scrivener which has made a world of difference
> to my writing organization. The binder feature shows my chapter sections
> in totality—I can see every part within the whole. . . . Using Scrivener
> helped me to visualize and actualize a writing process of this magnitude.
> I found the Word document folders/files so cumbersome and unruly for
> a project of this length. What had worked for writing course papers or
> manuscripts was not working for me in this dissertation process.

In her pre-workshop goals statement, focused largely on content concerns (weaving narrative into her dissertation), Evelyn did not express concerns about visualizing, organizing, and taming the sprawl of her project. Once introduced to Scrivener, though, recognition of her needs shifted, came into relief, or became defined anew. Seeing "every part within the whole" became important during the dissertation stage, whereas it wasn't such an issue before. This writer's positionality—ABD (all-but-dissertation) and ready to graduate and begin a tenure-track job—affected her needs as well as her relationship to writing. Drawing on other examples from graduate student and faculty workshop participants' discussion board postings, end-of-workshop reflections, and discussion comments, I'll describe the inventive ways that writers externalize their writing processes in efforts to make manageable the projects they undertake at specific stages in their careers and personal lives. We'll also see how external tools emerge within communities of writers and end up shaping participants' relationships with writing.

EXTERNALIZED TOOLS

A successful tenured associate professor in sociology writes her book during twenty-five-minute chunks using the Pomodoro technique; a graduate student in literary studies enters her writing and research hours in Clockify, an online program frequently used by freelancers, lawyers, and consultants to track billable hours; an international student in romance languages uses Coffitivity, an ambient sound program, to create a sense of community while writing alone in her apartment during a global pandemic.

Writers have described to me the crucial role that these and other tools play in their work routines and identities as researchers and

230   LAURA R. MICCICHE

writers. Comp scholars have studied technologies of writing, especially in materialist-focused research over the past two decades or so, investigating how writers use tools, objects, and their own bodies to create a writing environment (Prior and Shipka; Rule; Wyche), compose digitally (C. Haas; Pigg; Selfe; Takayoshi; Yancey) and with software (Ching; Van Ittersum and Ching; Lockridge and Van Ittersum; Hensley Owens), accommodate bodily needs (Gibson; Miller), communicate in and with culturally diverse contexts and materials (Canagarajah; A. Haas), and form a writerly identity (Alexis). I add to this research a focus on community crowd-sharing that leads writers to view (or not view) external tools as viable forms of writing support. As I'll describe below, participants most often mentioned tools that coalesce around goal-setting, research management and community, and sensory enhancement. Worth noting is that writers identified tools that addressed problems and needs in the moment, and not always successfully. While writers sought new tools to solve problems, those same tools sometimes created new problems, sending writers on a cyclical search for something better.

Writers regarded tools with what I would call pragmatic instrumentalism, based on the idea that writing problems can be mediated by external resources to solve practical problems (with the recognition that what constitutes a problem is always changing, so resources must also). This problem-solving approach to high stakes writing situations, which was visible in peer-to-peer resource-share sessions, offered a salve to writers intent on progressing toward completion, even when those same writers acknowledged the artificiality or psychological tricks afforded by external tools. Take, for instance, the ambivalence about the benefits and contrived quality of external writing tools expressed by fourth-year educational studies student, Sammy: "I believe that using some of the research and project management and other writing tools and resources we discussed in the workshop such as Write or Die, Written Kitten, Pomodoro and others work well for keeping me motivated (albeit sometimes a little gimmicky)." The tools left a mark on writers' practices, changed routines, and created new ones; at the same time, writers made tools do things they weren't explicitly made to do. One writer's willingness to share practices—how they take notes, organize research, structure writing time—became another's serendipitous find. In effect, writers sharing their contextual experiences made permissible instrumental and "gimmicky" strategies or tools that might have otherwise seemed too gauche to try or believe in.

Goal-Setting Tools

A junior anthropology colleague eagerly introduced her KanbanFlow board to us over Zoom. An online bulletin board, KanbanFlow enables users to visualize workflow, track time spent on a given task, share with collaborators, and much else. Of note is that it's not marketed to an academic audience. Sample boards on the website feature tasks like "produce financial report for Q2" and "load database with customer data," making clear that, first and foremost, KanbanFlow is a tool for managing business or corporate workflows. Academics hack the program, creating boards that fit their purposes. While this is to be expected with most any application, the individualized work that writers put into their boards makes especially apparent the inventive workarounds generated by writerly needs. We gushed at the elaborate color-coded, multi-column system our colleague had created to track her goals and accomplishments, both academic ("do first pass of data" and "send edits to team members") and personal ("dentist appointment," "yoga on Tuesday"). We admired the organization and commitment to life management that was so evident in her board. We recognized, simultaneously, that she wasn't fully in charge. KanbanFlow imposes a system for tracking flow through its very features and default presentation. Agency is located in both the board creator—who tailors the program to specific tasks, selects color schemes, and decides what to include—and in the program itself, whose design establishes parameters for how to visualize and categorize one's work, evident in the default columns (to-do, do today, in progress, and done).

Whereas KanbanFlow visualizes workflow, Clockify visualizes time spent on tasks. The program markets itself as a means to boost productivity by enabling users to see how they spend their time, track billable hours, organize collaborative teams, and assess the efficiency of a business. Introduced by Rebecca, an English graduate student who had tried several different programs before discovering this one met her needs, Clockify was soon after adopted by a handful of workshop participants. A student in communication sciences and disorders who had to study a new population after the pandemic made it impossible to study preschool-age children, the original focus of her research, Sisan noted in her pre-workshop goals statement that she needed to "stick to a strict timeline." Because she's always multitasking, she worries that her dissertation won't take precedence. Clockify helps her understand "in a visual way how much time I put in daily." Rebecca, a former high school teacher, explained why the program worked well for her: "I'm more in need of a trick to get me started, not a trick to keep me going. Once

I start writing, I don't need to set a time to be sure I work a minimum amount of time—I get into the flow and work plenty. What I need is to be able to see how many hours I've worked each day/the entire week, since I'm so conditioned to have this tracked and dictated for me by an employer."

Others expressed concerns about how to account for labor and time as well. Fourth-year chemistry student Sheeniza seeks a balance between writing and lab work as well as a process for writing her dissertation without a hard deadline to motivate her. Given the pressure she was under, she tried to binge write, finding that "it is unrealistic to dedicate 6 hours to writing because I have other tasks to get done for the day." Julia, a fourth-year student in Romance languages, struggles with self-criticism, stress, and guilt about her difficulty achieving work-life balance. She confides that "I am worried about the amount of writing I should be doing each day. I need to write more." Nola, a fourth-year sociology student, prioritized "set writing hours" in her goals statement so that she could make headway on her dissertation before returning to her home country, Oman, with her family. Nola's reflections were dotted with concerns about finding time to write, establishing accountability partners, and staying focused while in the midst of a transcontinental move. Writing a dissertation under these conditions is extremely challenging, made more so by the fact that academic work is largely independent and characterized by deadlines that are frequently extended or revised. As a result, some writers invent structure and accountability through external tools, which present ways to manage and record writing time, satisfying the need to legitimize labor.

Notably, writers are not identified as the target audience of Clockify, which, on its website, is praised by entrepreneurs, sales managers, software engineers, and marketing managers. Yet, writers are undeterred. In the case of Clockify, they create for themselves constructs of productivity based on "normal" working conditions within capitalist culture. Writers earn capital in exchange for labor that has beginning and end points; writing and time are trackable, visible through the online interface, rather than spectral, happening out of sight or visible only through words on the page, which may not seem commensurate with time spent. Normalcy provides a sense of accomplishment that Clockify records and makes real for writers, something often missing from independent writing sessions. Sisan put this succinctly when she writes that Clockify "helps me to look back at the end of the week and give myself credit for what was accomplished and was left undone." Invented or adopted tools offer writers external ways to structure what is often an unstructured, nonlinear, recursive process that can stretch into years (e.g., 63% of students enrolled in the spring 2021 section of the workshop were in their fifth year or beyond).

Other tools that offer an enabling structure for writers include Microsoft Outlook's calendar, where writers schedule writing time as a way to preserve space each week for their own work—no meetings, no doctor appointments, and no grocery shopping during writing blocks. A simple enough strategy, but writers nonetheless noted that it only became necessary for them to schedule writing time—to declare it part of their job—once they were ABD. Others began using screen limit programs on their phones and computers to remove the temptation to scroll social media when they wanted to focus on writing. A biomedical engineering student and three-time attendee of the dissertation workshop, now on the cusp of graduation, noted in his final reflection that he was grateful for a classmate's recommendation to try the app and website Freedom, a website blocker. For months he had been searching for a way to block YouTube on his Windows OS (prior to that, he used SelfControl on a Mac). Telling himself not to visit the site wasn't enough; he needed external discipline while writing in an environment where everything imaginable is literally at his fingertips. The internet is important to his work, but it also presents problems that need to be solved—namely, creating boundaries and limits in order to achieve focus. Thought of this way, user and tool vie for control, both exerting agency on the writing scene.

One of the most widely discussed and adopted tools by faculty and students is Pomodoro, a simple timer that defaults to a twenty-five-minute activity session followed by a five-minute break (time increments can be customized). Pomodoro promises transformation of issues that often plague advanced writers—productivity, focus, and intellectual ability: "Over 2 million people have already used the Pomodoro technique to transform their lives, making them more productive, more focused and even smarter" (Cirillo). And yet, while many writers try Pomodoro because they need external motivation to find writing time in their busy lives, the path toward productivity is not always a straight one. Writers define productivity in their own terms, revealing that they do more than use a tool; they also craft what productivity means for themselves. To this point, Claire, a creative nonfiction student, describes how Pomodoro transformed her writing while at home during the pandemic:

> Suddenly, there was a low-pressure, low-commitment way to experience a mini version of that 'permission-granted,' 'sacred time'—by setting that timer for 25 minutes, and using that time, there was a mental shift. It

234   LAURA R. MICCICHE

tricked my brain: instead of that pit of dread, that I was starting some huge
project, worrying about writing 'forward' or making sure it was 'on topic'
or 'useful' enough, I was simply writing, for 25 minutes.

Claire prioritizes "simply writing" over specific outcomes or productivity
benchmarks, in line with her initial goal for the workshop: "I've been
particularly interested in challenging the ways we've forced a more nov-
elistic form on memoir and am hoping to do something a little more
free-flowing, playful."

"Tricking my brain" comes up a lot in conversations with advanced
writers. The world is noisy and full of distractions. Writers often need
strategies to claim time and focus. It's not that they don't have intrinsic
motivation; they do, in abundance. But stress, personal and professional
responsibilities, mental and physical challenges, and the stakes of writing a dissertation, book, or other high-stakes project threaten to overwhelm on the regular. Externalized tools offer ways to mediate stress and
create agency during a process that often feels unwieldy and chaotic.

Research Management and Community

An assistant professor in anthropology shared with me her Summer of
Pain Writing/Reading Challenge that she participates in with geograph-
ically separated colleagues. Conducted through Google Drive, group
members record their daily reading and writing accomplishments on a
color-coded spreadsheet. The group creates rules for how to determine
a unit of work each week, assigns points based on agreed-upon rules,
and establishes a structure for rewarding units completed. While writers
can work ahead, they can't work backward, meaning they can't make up
points for missed work.

This complex system, which the group has maintained for over five
years, helps members hold one another accountable during the coveted
summer research period, especially important to pre-tenure researchers
who crave structure to keep pace with the "clock." Hyper-individualized
and game-like, complete with punishments, rewards, and multiple
players, this approach to research management reveals the deep social
needs of writers. The "pain" in this challenge is real, but it's also shared
and tinged with dark humor, removing some of the sting. The group
uses Google Drive as a meeting place where they can offload their collective anxieties about tenure into a spreadsheet. The clean lines of rows
and columns, highlighted in pastel colors as each participant completes
a block of writing, are meant to document productivity—or its lack—not
to track feelings, doubts, or other negative emotions (cf. Tarabochia).

As group members get closer to tenure, it's no surprise that pragmatic instrumentalism drives their productivity. We might be tempted to critique the drive toward progress assumed by this model (during a pandemic, no less), but doing so misses the reality that advanced writers sometimes need a reprieve from airing the emotional weight of writing, so well-chronicled in academic publications like *The Chronicle* and *Inside Higher Ed*, and instead need social mechanisms—instrumental, contrived, or gimmicky—to stay on track.

Another social motivator, Focusmate, is a virtual coworking program that pairs creators who work in tandem during a fifty-minute session with cameras off and sound on. Alejandro introduced Focusmate to workshop participants. A student in Romance languages whose dissertation analyzes creative writing handbooks and includes a series of writing prompts, Alejandro was eager to try new writing resources and share them with the group (unsurprising, given his research topic). Focusmate is aimed at achieving a "flow state," defined as "long stretches of intense focus," by pairing "accountability partners" who are working on any variety of projects. Alejandro noted that he especially appreciates that not everyone is an academic. Working alongside people who are writing a business proposal, composing a piece of music, or just doing their bills untangles his work from the stressors and isolation of academic work. Alejandro is another doer among many; writing a dissertation becomes less rarified, more achievable, by virtue of proximity to people doing "normal" things.

Focusmate, anchored in psychological research, integrates "behavioral triggers to achieve a flow state: pre-commitment, implementation of intentions, social pressure, accountability, and specificity in task definition." Reading through the application's description, I'm struck by similarities to cognitive writing theory, particularly the emphasis on goal-directed behavior to effect change. Cognitive theory understands writing as a goal-directed process. For instance, Linda Flower and John Hayes note that "writers create a hierarchical network of goals and these in turn guide the writing process" (377).

What's different about Focusmate, and other digital and virtual tools, is that they emphasize the goal-directedness of *doing* a task rather than the choices one makes *while doing it*. In other words, users turn to Focusmate to help them get work done. They begin by signing up for a session with a partner, effectively linking behavior (accountability) and sociality as key to achieving a flow state. Step one, as noted above, is pre-commitment, the purpose and effect of which is "a specific and concrete commitment *to another person*—when you book a Monday 9am session

236   LAURA R. MICCICHE

you're essentially saying, 'I commit to work with my partner on Monday at 9am for 50 minutes.'" Committing to a partner is another difference from cognitive approaches, which are mostly built for individual writers, not for the sociality of writing. Focusmate establishes the parameters of working alongside another person—fifty-minute one-on-one sessions, showing but muting oneself on camera, and booking in advance—and creators use those constraints however they choose. Program and user are interdependent; they co-construct what "focus" looks like and how it's achieved.

Sensory Enhancement

In weekly discussion board postings about their writing practices, students regularly mentioned sensory assists that served their mental and physical health while also helping them to persist in their projects. For example, A Soft Murmur, a site that allows users to select from a range of "ambient sounds to wash away distraction," came up with some frequency. Fourth-year educational studies student Sammy entered the workshop with clear goals to write a dissertation proposal, create good writing habits, and learn more about scholarly writing. Sammy found value in less goal-driven aspects of writing as well, attaching affective values to the writing process. They had this to say about listening to a thunderstorm on A Soft Murmur: "It was great for blocking out the rest of the world while I was writing and it made me think of summer, which made me happy." Aurality surfaced in other ways too. Rebecca wrote that after completing a draft, she draws a bubble bath, soaks, and reads the paper aloud to herself so that she can edit for a conversational tone. Claire referred to the multisensory satisfaction that results when the "sound of the sentence and the rhythm . . . all come together to make something pleasing, to the eye, the ear, the mind."

The need for change while writing is another important sensory motivator, as Sammy notes: "When the weather is warm, I like to take my computer or pad of paper outside. I think it is important to switch things up a bit and try out some different ideas and scenarios to keep myself motivated to write." Echoing the idea that newness links to motivation, Julia has incorporated new elements into her writing environment as a way to feel more connected to her work and to offset some of the stress she feels: "I tried to have something that connects me with the four elements, plus 'my own element': a plant (earth), a window (air-landscape), a candle (fire), a drink (water, a cup of coffee/tea), and my notebook and fountain pen (paper and ink)."

These writers' symbiotic relationships with their writing environments illustrate the importance of feeling connected to something beyond themselves and their tasks.

In the last section, I noted writers' need to sometimes sidestep emotional talk about writing, but in the realm of sensory influences, writers are awash in feeling. Whether deliberate (choosing elements to enhance one's environment) or spontaneous (head outside when weather permits), sensory enhancements are entangled with writers' felt experience of being in the world while doing the internal, individual work of writing. To experience writing with and through external tools or resources is to challenge individuated cognition, the lonesomeness of one writer writing alone. Doing so has seemed especially important to those who have disclosed mental and physical health challenges; in many cases, their uptake of tools is also an uptake of self-care.

Many sensory elements emerged in response to the following discussion board prompt: What brings you joy while writing? Hot tea or coffee and relaxing music, candles, plants, notebooks, bookmarks, and animal companions. Some emphasized the lift they get from achieving a "flow state," when words and ideas come together and writing feels easy, even effortless. Abby, a paleoecology doctoral candidate who studies the ecology of big mammals, addresses writing flow: "I love that 'flow state' where the connections between ideas come easily and the writing is fluid. When I am in that groove, writing feels like discovery." An enthusiastic blog writer, Abby has a passion for writing about science creatively but struggled during the pandemic to focus on her dissertation, to feel again excitement for her topic. Her description of the "flow state" seems directly related to her ability to "regai[n] enthusiasm," as she wrote in her reflection, during the writing workshop. The connection between affect and flow is not limited to internal states, of course. Sarah, a seventh-year PhD candidate in classical archaeology, writes about the tactile quality of typing as a source of pleasure that helps with flow: "I genuinely enjoy typing. I bought a nice mechanical keyboard in the fall and I just love the way it feels to press the keys." Such pleasures, along with a need for a "strict schedule," are important to Sarah, who identifies her main problem as self-motivation, "a problem that has just been exacerbated by this pandemic and the fact that I am working from home."

Ambient sound and the effects of voice, aromatherapy, candles, plants, keyboards—these tools affect the sensory experience of writing. We are in the neighborhood of Sondra Perl's "felt sense." Her description aligns with student depictions of the elusive flow state:

238 LAURA R. MICCICHE

> You are drafting a paper. After an initial struggle, trying this, trying that, jotting down a few sentences and then rereading them, you hit your stride. The words are coming quickly. Everything about the composition starts to feel right. Maybe your body tingles. . . . You love what is happening and wish there were some way to hold on to this experience, to enter this free-flowing realm whenever you want. (3)

Like Perl's felt sense, achieved (or at least encouraged) by following writing guidelines, writers describe achieving a flow state *with assistance*. However, distinct from Perl's guidelines, which are largely focused on a writer's singular mind and body, advanced writers seek assistance from both internal and external resources. They try new routines and tools, learn from others, connect physically and virtually. They enact an expansive construct of writing that doesn't hinge exclusively on internal cognition, good ideas, organization, the right research, or any number of common resources associated with productive writers. Writers are hungry for motivation, companionship, accountability, and sensory inspiration. External tools might be adopted out of a need for pragmatic instrumentalism, affective or sensory intervention, as well as physical and mental needs, which I'll turn to in the final section.

EXTERNAL TOOLS AND BODILY CHANGE

Reflecting on my writing life, I can pinpoint key transitions entangled with tools. While working on a master's in poetry, I upgraded from an electronic typewriter to a Brother word processor with a pop-up screen that showed seven or eight lines of text before they were printed on a piece of paper. Seeing writing in this still-forming state revolutionized my writing both practically and conceptually. Editing on-screen made lines seem fluid, imbued with movement in ways that I hadn't experienced before.

A new mother in 2004, I wrote using the Pomodoro method: twenty-five minutes of writing, five minutes of break. Without the luxury of time or energy, I found myself incapable of focusing for more than twenty-five minutes at a time. I felt like I could do anything for twenty-five minutes, including getting some words down between feeding and naps.

Since then, changes linked to embodiment have defined my writing practice. I've shifted from a traditional desk chair to a yoga ball (for achy back), added a stationary bike with attached desktop to my routine (for improved circulation), switched out prescription eyeglasses for blue light–filtering non-prescription glasses (for eye strain and presbyopia), and replaced Microsoft Word with Scrivener, a word processing program and management system for integrating files, data, research, and most anything else into one window (for mental focus challenged by multitasking). Tracing my writing tools is tracing my embodied and professional evolution. Sometimes I feel like my body is in charge of my writing practices; other times, my tools, which expand and limit how writing evolves for me.

The reality is that both are in charge at different moments. As I type this while sitting on a yoga ball, I'm keenly aware of moving while writing. My trunk wobbles, but I plant my feet firmly on the floor in front of me and actively use my core to keep a straight back. Leaning slightly forward causes the ball to move behind me, shifting my center of gravity and making typing difficult. I have to right myself in order to continue. The ball is writing material; my body, a technology of writing. Kory Lawson Ching, writing about distraction-free writing tools, addresses the interdependence of tool and user in a way that resonates with my experience: "Technological mediation . . . is transformative; it leaves its mark upon the user. In the case of writing, we should expect technologies like word processing software to shape not only texts but also the habits and durable practices of writers who compose with them" (348). Physical writing tools, like the ball, also function as mediators that help us compose and, in turn, compose us and leave a mark (in my case, a tired core).

While my system of networked tools solves problems and better aligns with my physical and intellectual needs, it also reveals the worn-ness of old writing tools, ones that have trained my body for writing practices that are no longer sustainable. In other words, I have integrated new tools into my repertoire to deal with those (stationary desk, chair with backrest, single-vision glasses without blue light filter, etc.) that no longer match my bodily experience of writing. That writing should happen at a desk suggests a stable activity at a fixed location. Writing on a yoga ball introduces physical movement and bodily balance into writing sessions. Both stability and movement reflect values attached to writing—the former places importance on writing as discrete, rooted in place, and the latter emphasizes writing as bodily, connected to place. Value systems, as sociocultural writing researchers have shown, are embedded in tools, marking them as non-neutral partners in composing and synecdoches for motivation, productivity, collaboration, and much else (e.g., C. Haas; Van Ittersum and Ching; Prior; Shipka; Spinuzzi).

As projects and stakes change, as writers change, writing needs change too, making once reliable processes insufficient, obsolete, unsustainable. For example, Evelyn's comment about the infrastructural differences between writing a seminar paper and a dissertation, which she came to after discovering Scrivener, illustrates conscious awareness of process and routine limitations when scale, complexity, and scope shift. Sisan uses a running metaphor to describe the difference: "Dissertation writing is not like working on other projects. This is a marathon and small persistent goals take me farther than the sprint." Faculty, too, have noted during our large group discussions that they can't rely on their success with short-form writing as they develop book projects while juggling numerous other professional and personal responsibilities. While "a workflow is a habituated, mediated, and personal means of accomplishing something" (Lockridge and Van Ittersum 82), it is subject to change as professional and personal conditions require that we habituate differently to writing over time.

Bodily changes over a lifespan, like those that have altered my writing routines, affect how and which tools get taken up to accomplish something. Tools are never as visible as when they stand in for actions or behaviors that our bodies can no longer accomplish, operating as prosthetics for writing. In her study of asphasic writers, Elisabeth L. Miller uses the phrase "literate misfitting" to describe "conflicts readers and writers encounter when their bodies and minds do not fit with the materials and expectations of 'normal' literate practice" (36). These conflicts, she notes, "she[d] light on how the relationship between the embodied, material, and social aspects of literacy operates on all writers, disabled and normatively abled" (34). Miller's analysis shows that able-bodied ideologies permeate composing tools and technologies, giving rise to writers' creative strategies to "critique and revise normative practices" (40).

Michelle Gibson, in "Revising a (Writer's Life)," vividly illustrates this point as she details changes to her writing process in response to her diagnosis of progressive multiple sclerosis (MS). Her disease keeps changing, and so does her writing practice, prompting continual revision—what she calls the "Revision Hag." Gibson writes:

> Just when I revise my ways of moving from place to place, of navigating my computer, of reading (because I can no longer turn the pages in a book, all of my reading is done on a computer or tablet), and of writing, my symptoms progress and I hear that cackling voice commanding, "Revise, revise, revise." I have been forced to revise long-held beliefs and habitual ways of functioning as a writer. I have had to revise my physical practice of writing, the value I place on certain types of writing, and my ideas about the very purpose of writing. (13)

Gibson ends her piece by sympathizing with students she's worked with, those who "responded with horror" when she suggested revisions of their writing. "I understand like never before that the Revision Hag's command to revise, revise, revise sometimes represents not only the reconsideration of a piece of writing, but also of ways of seeing and living in the world" (14). One revision Gibson describes as a positive change involves her use of voice-recognition software, which she began using after losing strength and coordination in her hands. About the software program Dragon, Gibson writes: "All my life I have found it difficult to transfer my thinking from my mind, through my body, and onto the page. . . . [W]riting with my voice helps me forget my disabled body" (13). Like Gibson, Kim Hensley Owens describes her use of voice-recognition software when typing became impossible due to acute tendonitis in her wrists and hands. Hensley Owens describes the interactive relationship between software and user: "Voice-recognition software . . . has some agency in that it 'learns.' It becomes better able to recognize my voice and my terms with practice; I, too, with practice become better able to tailor my speech to its needs." Writers form relationships with tools rather than simply *use* them or *get used* by them.

Those relationships are often defined by writers' tendency to offload physical and mental tasks, memory, structure, organization, social needs, affective and ambient pleasures onto external tools. Those tools, in turn, shape writing practices and relationships with writing, regulating behavior and feeling, and likely much else. In addition, the writing tools and usage practices described in this chapter underscore the role community plays in technologies of writing—a factor that hasn't gotten much attention in sociomaterial studies of writing tools. Beyond the workshop context, for example, Gibson notes that blogs became her "primary intellectual and creative outlet" after she retired from university life because of her progressive MS (14). Her online MS support group provides a strong social network, and her awareness of the benefits and disadvantages of Dragon, "definitely the most popular among people I know with MS" (13), emerges from a variety of online sites and forums. Communities of writers influence and model, question and affirm, what tools can do for us and what we can do with them.

Acknowledgments. I'm grateful to faculty and graduate student participants who attended writing workshops with me in 2020 and 2021 and gave me permission to include their words in here. Their eagerness to share ideas about their writing processes gave me the idea for this chapter. Thanks to Hannah Rule for offering crucial feedback on an earlier draft.

NOTE

1. First names of participants are used throughout this chapter. Two are pseudonyms: Evelyn and Sammy.

WORKS CITED

Alexis, Cydney. "The Symbolic Life of the Moleskine Notebook: Material Goods as a Tableau for Writing Identity." *Composition Studies*, vol. 45, no. 2, 2017, pp. 32–54.

Canagarajah, A. Suresh. *A Geopolitics of Academic Writing*. Pittsburgh UP, 2002.

Ching, Kory Lawson. "Tools Matter: Mediated Writing Activity in Alternative Digital Environments." *Written Communication*, vol. 35, no. 3, 2018, pp. 344–75.

Cirillo, Francesco. "Cirillo Consulting GmbH: Services, Products, Software to Enhance Your Productivity." *Cirillo Company*, https://francescocirillo.com/.

Flower, Linda, and John R. Hayes. "A Cognitive Process Theory of Writing." *CCC*, vol. 32, no. 4, 1981, pp. 365–87.

Gibson, Michelle. "Revising a (Writer's) Life: Writing with Disability." *Composition Studies*, vol. 41, no. 2, 2013, pp. 12–14.

Haas, Angela M. "Wampum as Hypertext: An American Indian Intellectual Tradition of Multimedia Theory and Practice." *Studies in American Indian Literature*, vol. 19, no. 4, 2007, pp. 77–100.

Haas, Christina. *Writing Technology: Studies on the Materiality of Literacy*. Routledge, 1996.

Hensley Owens, Kim. " 'Look Ma, No Hands!': Voice-Recognition Software, Writing, and Ancient Rhetoric." *Enculturation*, no. 7, 2010. http://enculturation.net/look-ma-no-hands.

Lockridge, Tim, and Derek Van Ittersum. *Writing Workflows: Beyond Word Processing*. U of Michigan P, 2020. https://doi.org/10.3998/mpub.11657120.

Lotier, Kristopher M. *Postprocess Postmortem*. WAC Clearinghouse & UP of Colorado, 2021.

Micciche, Laura R. "Dissertation Assistance During COVID-19." *Inside Higher Ed*, 4 Aug. 2020, https://www.insidehighered.com/advice/2020/08/04/phd-students-need-more-support-their-dissertation-writing-opinion.

Miller, Elisabeth L. "Literate Misfitting: Disability Theory and a Sociomaterial Approach to Literacy." *College English*, vol. 79, no. 1, 2016, pp. 34–56.

Perl, Sondra. *Felt Sense: Writing with the Body*. Heinemann, 2004.

Pigg, Stacey. *Transient Literacies in Action: Composing with the Mobile Surround*. WAC Clearinghouse & UP of Colorado, 2020.

Prior, Paul. *Writing/Disciplinarity: A Sociohistoric Account of Literate Activity in the Academy*. Lawrence Erlbaum Associates, 1998.

Prior, Paul, and Jody Shipka. "Chronotopic Lamination: Tracing the Contours of Literate Activity." *Writing Selves/Writing Societies: Research from Activity Perspectives*, edited by Charles Bazerman and David R. Russell, WAC Clearinghouse, 2003, pp. 180–238.

Rule, Hannah J. *Situating Writing Processes*. WAC Clearinghouse & UP of Colorado, 2019.

Selfe, Cythnia L. "The Movement of Air, the Breath of Meaning: Aurality and Multimodal Composing." *CCC*, vol. 60, no. 4, 2009, pp. 616–63.

Shipka, Jody. *Toward a Composition Made Whole*. U of Pittsburgh P, 2011.

Spinuzzi, Clay. "Compound Mediation in Software Development: Using Genre Ecologies to Study Textual Artifacts." *Writing Selves/Writing Societies*, edited by Charles Bazerman and David Russell, The WAC Clearinghouse, 2003, pp. 97–124.

Takayoshi, Pamela. "Writing in Social Worlds: An Argument for Researching Composing Processes." *CCC*, vol. 69, no. 4, 2018, pp. 550–80.

Tarabochia, Sandra L. "From Resilience to Resistance: Repurposing Faculty Writers' Survival Strategies." *Peitho*, vol. 23, no. 3, 2021. https://cfshrc.org/article/from-resilience-to-resistance-repurposing-faculty-writers-survival-strategies/.

Van Ittersum, Derek, and Kory Lawson Ching. "Composing Text/Shaping Process: How Digital Environments Mediate Writing Activity." *Computers and Composition Online*, 2013, http://cconlinejournal.org/composing_text/webtext/index.html.

Wyche, Susan. "Times, Tools, and Talismans." *Essays on Writing*, edited by Lizbeth A. Bryant and Heather M. Clark, Pearson, 2009, pp. 52–64.

Yancey, Kathleen Blake. "Writing in the Twenty-First Century." *A Report from the National Council of Teachers of English*, 2009.

INDEX

adapt, 6, 18, 19, 21, 46, 68, 92, 102, 112, 228; adaptability, 6, 18, 54; adaptation, 3, 43–44, 204, 228; adapting, 18, 19, 45
Advice for New Faculty: Nihil Nimus (Boice), 91, 100
Ahmed, Sara, 94–95, 196
Andriamanalina, Noro, 13, 15–16
Anson, Chris, 32, 65
Anttila, Eeva, 29
anxiety, 15, 16, 18, 20, 56, 69, 76, 80, 82, 107, 143, 146–148, 150, 151, 153, 155, 156, 162, 168, 194
Anzaldúa, Gloria, 126, 129

Bailey, Moya, 54, 160
balance, 15, 19, 49, 74, 90, 91, 92, 99, 109, 112, 168, 173, 195, 232, 239
Banks, William, 28, 90, 93
Barnard, Ian, 119, 121
Becker, George, 74
Berg, Maggie, 33, 52, 62, 64, 182, 193, 195, 202
Bjork, Collin, 52
Black, Indigenous, and People of Color (BIPOC), 15, 16, 159, 165, 166, 169
Black woman, 93, 158–162, 164, 165, 167, 168, 170–172; Black women, 20, 158, 160, 164, 166–169, 172
block, writer's, 16, 53, 59–60, 78, 110, 117
block, of time, 32, 135, 163, 166, 173, 195, 197, 199, 201, 233, 234
Boice, Robert, 4, 65–66, 91, 100, 110, 117, 124, 135, 195
Borderlands: La Frontera (Anzaldúa), 126
Braiding Sweetgrass (Kimmerer), 8
Brand, Alice G., 14
"Bring Back the Nervous Breakdown" (Useem), 68
Brown, Nicole, 161
Buhre, Frida, 52
Burqueño, 19, 124, 126, 127, 134

children, 3, 4, 7, 8, 38, 57, 76, 77, 91–93, 97, 144, 145, 193, 194, 196–199, 201, 206, 231
chronic illness, 20, 41–43, 48, 49, 159–164, 172, 173

collaborate, 204; collaborating, 169; collaboration, 6, 18, 21, 52, 57, 62, 115, 169, 174, 175, 189, 190, 201–206, 239
Coronavirus, 3, 5, 194
crip time, 14, 18, 22, 42–45, 47, 49, 51–53; crip, 42, 50, 105, 116; cripping, 62
crisis, 21, 43, 48, 85, 193, 194, 197, 198, 200–203, 205
Crow, Jim, 99
Cyprus, 89, 90, 94, 96, 97, 103

DeSalvo, Louise, 105, 106, 113, 116–121
disability, 18, 19, 41–44, 46–54, 62, 73, 74, 106, 111–115, 118, 119, 121, 145, 148, 160–162, 164, 166
Downs, Doug, 36
Draft No. 4, On the Writing Process (McPhee), 80
Dreads and Open Mouths: Living/Teaching/ Writing Queerly (Rallin), 119, 145, 149
Driscoll, Dana Lynn, 15, 73, 82

Elbow, Peter, 3, 65
Elfenbein, Madeleine, 91
embodiment, 11, 18, 21, 26, 51, 52, 72, 74, 91, 93, 101–103, 107, 111, 112, 115, 120, 143, 238, 251
Enoch, Jessica, 65, 66
equity, 42, 51, 53, 99, 143, 162
"Exploring Options in Composing" (Selzer), 69
Extraordinary Work of Ordinary Writing, The (Sinor), 209, 216–218, 219, 220, 222, 224, 225
expressivism, 3, 28

Family Medical Leave Act (FMLA), 97
Faris, Michael, 7
Fleckenstein, Kristie S., 29
Floyd, George, 56
freewriting, 3, 110
"From Resilience to Resistance: Repurposing Faculty Writers' Survival Strategies" (Tarabochia), 146, 154
Furtak, Erin Marie, 32

246 INDEX

Garrett, Bre, 105, 106, 113–116, 121
gender, 51, 55, 71, 76, 92, 104, 160, 173, 207, 208
Gladman, Renee, 36
Gladwell, Malcolm, 109
Goffman, Irving, 48
Greek, 19, 89, 91, 93, 94, 96, 98, 101
grind culture, 20, 164, 166, 170–172
guilt, 7, 15–17, 43, 66, 76, 203, 232
Guttom, Hanna, 29

healing, 72, 82, 100, 105, 113, 116–120, 155
Healthy Writer, The (Penn), 80
Hensley Owens, Kim, 72, 73, 90, 92, 228, 230, 241
Hjortshoj, Keith, 59
How Writing Faculty Write (Tulley), 65, 125
Howard, Rebecca Moore, 74

identity, 6, 18–21, 24, 28, 31, 35, 60, 61, 70, 74, 75, 89, 91, 94–99, 101–103, 124, 126, 127, 133, 134, 142–144, 146, 147, 152, 158, 160, 166, 193, 195, 209, 221, 230
"Increasing the Productivity of 'Blocked' Academics" (Boice), 110, 122
Intern Nation: How to Earn Nothing and Learn Little in the Brave New Economy (Perlin), 184
Interrogating Privilege: Reflections of a Second Language Educator (Vandrick), 27
intersectional, 13, 18, 162
intersectionality, 160
Introduction, Methods, Results, and Discussion (IMRAD), 34, 38
invention, 16, 115, 116, 125
isolation, 25, 59, 82, 134, 194, 202–204, 227, 235

Jensen, Joli, 35

Karpen, Ruth Ray, 33
kids, 4, 8, 101, 181, 194, 199, 200
Knoblauch, A. Abby, 28

labor, 15, 20, 21, 23, 33, 42, 46, 48, 53, 61, 63, 100, 106, 110, 124, 125, 128, 131, 144, 160, 164, 167, 172, 175, 176, 180, 182, 183, 184, 185, 187, 191, 194, 196, 201, 203, 207, 220, 232
Lawson, Euan, 80, 88
Leigh, S. Rebecca, 15
Lesbian, Gay, Bisexual and Transgender (LGBTQ), 146, 147
Life-Changing Magic of Tidying Up, The (Kondo), 8
Living a Feminist Life (Ahmed), 94

lockdown, 62, 70, 71, 175, 179
Lockridge, Tim, 11, 36, 112, 116, 125, 227, 230, 240
Löytönen, Teija, 29

Martinez, Aja, 99
McPhee, John, 80
mental health, 20, 57, 69, 71, 73–75, 82, 142, 147, 150–153, 156, 166
Micciche, Laura, 5, 13, 14, 16, 63, 64, 83, 124, 127, 129, 130, 140, 181, 195, 196, 199, 200, 201, 228
Miller, Carolyn, 43
Mountz, Alison, 33

National Council of Teachers of English, 175
neoliberal, 5, 21 39, 47, 49, 52, 54, 83, 87, 90, 106, 111, 112, 118, 175, 180, 182, 183, 188; Neoliberalism, 19, 86, 182, 183
North, Anna, 62
notebooking, 21, 209–225

pandemic, 3–7, 9, 13, 18, 21, 24–27, 30, 31, 35, 54, 56–59, 67, 68, 71, 74, 76, 79, 85, 91, 92, 100, 103, 104, 111, 134, 136, 145, 159, 162, 165, 166, 167, 172, 175, 179, 186, 193–208, 229, 231, 233, 235, 237
Pantelides, Kate L., 91
Patterson, Chakita, 100
Penn, Joanna, 80
Perl, Sondra, 26, 237
Price, Margaret, 47, 50, 148
Prior, Paul, 4, 227

queer, 19, 20, 22, 42, 47, 55, 106, 111, 113, 116, 119, 121–123, 144, 145, 147–151, 153; queerly, 20, 119, 122, 142–145, 147, 149–153, 155

Rhetoric and Writing Studies (RWS), 124, 126–130, 133, 135, 137
race, 50, 51, 154, 160, 167
Rallin, Aneil, 119, 145, 149, 150, 154, 155
remote, 4, 7, 24, 25, 111, 162, 228
Restaino, Jessica, 5, 105, 106, 111–113, 117–119, 121
revise, 3, 4, 28, 36, 70, 148, 187, 240, 241
revision, 6, 36, 44, 52, 69, 97, 110, 240, 241
Room of One's Own, A (Woolf), 92, 198
Roozen, Kevin, 219
Rose, Mike, 16
Royster, Jacqueline Jones, 32, 51, 61, 65, 137
Rule, Hannah, 8, 12, 13, 14, 67, 180, 228, 230, 241

Seeber, Barbara, 33, 52, 62, 64, 182, 193, 195, 202
"Self-Authorship and Faculty Writers' Trajectories of Becoming" (Tarabochia), 146, 151, 152, 154
Selfe, Cindy, 32, 65, 135, 205, 230
Sharer, Wendy, 60
Shipka, Jody, 4, 6, 10, 12–13, 83–84, 115, 124, 130, 131, 219, 227, 230, 239
Silences (Olsen), 60
Sinor, Jennifer, 21, 209, 216–218, 219, 220, 222, 224, 225
Surrender: Feminist Rhetoric and Ethics in Love and Illness (Restaino), 5, 105, 106, 111–113, 117–119, 121
Sword, Helen, 66, 124, 195, 202

Tarabochia, Sandra L., 146, 151–152, 154, 234
technology, 6, 18, 38, 43, 44, 112, 125, 179, 180, 239
Tinberg, Howard, 65
tinderbox, 10, 11
transformation, 3, 7, 233
Tulley, Christine, 3, 4, 7, 12, 15, 32, 33, 36, 63, 65, 66, 67, 91, 92, 124, 125, 130–131, 134, 135, 136, 137, 195, 197, 199, 203, 205

Understanding Writing Blocks (Hjortshoj), 59
Unlocking the Power of Sleep and Dreams (Walker), 74
Upsetting Composition Commonplaces (Barnard), 121

Valkeemäki, Anita, 29
Van Ittersum, Derek, 11, 72, 73, 78, 90, 105, 112, 116, 125, 227, 230, 239, 240

Vandrick, Stephanie, 27
Villanueva, Victor, 28, 29, 124, 129
vulnerability, 105, 124, 139; vulnerable, 133

WPA, 63, 64, 142, 143, 144, 147, 220, 221
walk, 25, 30, 31, 76, 87, 88, 92, 96, 163, 174, 185, 187, 197; walking, 30, 31, 34, 78, 116, 161
Walker, Alice, 92–93
Walker, Matthew, 74
Wendell, Susan, 47, 48
Wenger, Christy, 26
Wetherbee Phelps, Louise, 33
Wheatley, Phyllis, 92
Wilkerson, Isabel, 95
Wintering (May) 8
Women's Ways of Making It in Composition (Bailiff, Davis, and Mountford), 92
Woolf, Virginia, 92, 105, 194, 198, 199, 202, 203
work ethic, 19, 89, 90, 93, 99, 100, 101, 103
writing advice, 16, 53, 65, 124, 125, 129, 140, 146
"Writing Out on a Limb" (Yoo), 37
writing routine, 113, 117, 145
writing process, 6–9, 11, 17, 19, 20, 22, 26, 36, 66, 67, 80, 105, 109–111, 114–116, 118, 124, 125, 130, 134, 137, 139, 142, 143, 145, 148, 150, 153, 155, 159, 162, 167, 169, 171, 229, 235, 236, 240
writing tools, 9, 21, 42–45, 53, 227, 229, 230, 231, 233, 235, 237, 239, 241, 243

yoga, 79, 106, 113–116, 120, 121, 231, 238, 239

Zamin, Nadia, 15, 73
Zoom, 7, 8, 114, 134, 168, 179, 180, 183, 190, 231

ABOUT THE AUTHORS

Ann N. Amicucci is associate professor of English at the University of Colorado Colorado Springs, where she teaches writing pedagogy, social media rhetorics, and first-year research writing. Her recent work has appeared in *Computers and Composition, Preserving Emotion in Student Writing*, edited by Craig Wynne, and *Writing Spaces: Readings on Writing, Volume 4*, edited by Dana Lynn Driscoll, Megan Heise, Mary K. Stewart, and Matthew Vetter. She blogs with Tracy Lassiter at twoprofsfromohio.wordpress.com/.

Tatiana Benjamin (she/her/hers) is an assistant professor in the Department of Justice Studies at James Madison University (JMU), serves as co-coordinator of the African, African American, diaspora studies minor. She is a scholar-practitioner with a long-standing commitment to centering the identities and experiences of the African diaspora. Her teaching includes courses on global migrations, social justice, and popular culture. Her research includes Black feminist political economy; African diasporic history; immigration policy and advocacy; Caribbean American identity formation; transnationalism; intersectionality; and anti-Black racism.

Beth Buyserie is the director of composition and assistant professor of English at Utah State University. Her work focuses on writing program administration, the teaching of composition, critical pedagogies, professional learning, and the intersections of language, knowledge, and power through the lenses of queer theory and critical race theory.

Melissa Dinsman is assistant professor of English at York College, CUNY and author of *Modernism at the Microphone: Radio, Propaganda, and Literary Aesthetics During World War II* (2015). Her research focuses on WWII women writers, the politics of the domestic, and information networks. Dinsman is currently at work on her next book project, which explores the ways British women writers sold the war to the American public.

Andrew Harnish is an assistant professor in the Department of Writing at the University of Alaska Anchorage. His research investigates how pragmatic rhetorics intersect with rhetorics of queerness and disability in first-year writing classes. He teaches courses in introductory composition and technical communication and serves as departmental liaison to the Writing Center. His work has appeared in *Disability and Society* and *Literacy in Composition Studies*.

Kim Hensley Owens (she/her) is director of the University Writing Program (until 2023) and professor of English at Northern Arizona University. With Cathryn Molloy, she serves as co-editor of *Rhetoric of Health and Medicine*. Publications include *Writing Childbirth: Women's Rhetorical Agency in Labor and Online* (2015); recent articles in *College English, Present Tense*, and *Rhetoric of Health and Medicine*; and chapters in various edited collections. Her current project is an auto/ethnographic exploration of Threshold Choir.

Kellie Keeling is an undergraduate English major with a writing and publication concentration at the University of North Georgia.

ABOUT THE AUTHORS

Melanie Kill is an assistant professor of English at the University of Maryland. She studies digital rhetorics and rhetorical genre studies with attention to disability, feminism, and social justice. Previous work has appeared in *CCC, JAC,* and *Digital Humanities Pedagogy* (2012). She is founding chair of the CCCC Wikipedia Initiative.

Steve Lamos is an associate professor in the Program for Writing and Rhetoric and the English Department at the University of Colorado Boulder. His work includes the 2011 book *Interests and Opportunities: Race, Racism, and University Writing Instruction in the Post–Civil Rights Era* (Pitt UP), articles in *CCC, College English, Composition Studies, JBW,* and *WPA,* and chapters in several edited collections.

Tim Laquintano is associate professor of English and the director of the writing program at Lafayette College.

Laura R. Micciche is professor of English and director of the rhetoric and composition graduate program at University of Cincinnati. Her research focuses on composing processes, feminist pedagogies, and affect. Recent books include *Failure Pedagogies: Learning and Unlearning What It Means to Fail* (Peter Lang 2020), co-edited with Allison D. Carr, and *Acknowledging Writing Partners* (Parlor 2017). For six years, she served as editor of *Composition Studies,* an independent journal in rhetoric and composition.

Zakery R. Muñoz is a Burqueño—born and raised in Albuquerque, New Mexico. He is a doctoral student of composition and cultural rhetoric at Syracuse University. He studies graduate student writing pedagogy, Indigenous methodology, settler colonialism, and digital writing methods.

Kate L. Pantelides is an associate professor and director of general education English at Middle Tennessee State University. She teaches rhetoric, composition, and technical communication courses at the undergraduate and graduate levels. Her research addresses rhetorical genre studies, research methods, and feminist rhetorics. Her most recent works include *Try This: Research Methods for Writers,* with Dr. Jennifer Clary-Lemon and Derek Mueller, and *A Theory of Public Higher Education,* co-authored with the TPHE Collective.

Emily Pridgen completed her bachelor's degree in English with a concentration in writing and publication at the University of North Georgia. Currently, she is studying to become a teacher by earning a Master of Arts in Teaching, English Education (Secondary) through Western Governors University while living in Italy.

J. Michael Rifenburg, professor of English at the University of North Georgia, USA, serves as senior faculty fellow for scholarly writing with UNG's Center for Teaching, Learning, and Leadership. He authored *The Embodied Playbook: Writing Practices of Student-Athletes* and *Drilled to Write: Becoming a Cadet Writer at a Senior Military College.* He is a recipient of the University System of Georgia Regents' Scholarship of Teaching & Learning Award.

Heather Robinson is a professor of English at York College, CUNY. Her research spans applied linguistics, feminist academic administration and literary criticism of twentieth- and twenty-first-century women's writing. She is the co-author of *Translingual Identities and Transnational Realities in the U.S. College Classroom* (Routledge, 2020), and author of *Language, Diaspora, Home: Mother Tongues,* forthcoming from Routledge, alongside various articles and book chapters. This is her second co-authored publication with Melissa Dinsman.

About the Authors

Kevin Roozen is professor of writing and rhetoric at the University of Central Florida. His research examines the complex pathways that people's literate becoming traces throughout their lifespans and across their lifeworlds. Kevin's research has appeared in a number of journals and edited collections and in his co-authored book *Expanding Literate Landscapes: Persons, Practices, and Sociohistoric Perspectives of Disciplinary Development*. His current research explores people's histories with ordinary inscriptions in their everyday lives.

Hannah J. Rule is associate professor of English in composition and rhetoric at the University of South Carolina, where she teaches graduate and undergraduate courses in writing and the teaching of writing. Her scholarship—found in venues including *CCC, Composition Forum*, and *Composition Studies*—focuses on composition theory and pedagogy, embodiment and materiality, and histories of the writing process paradigm. She is the author of the monograph *Situating Writing Processes* (2019) and co-editor, with Cydney Alexis, of the recent collection *The Material Culture of Writing* (2022).

Derek Van Ittersum is professor of English at Kent State University, where he teaches in the Literacy, Rhetoric, and Social Practice graduate program. With Tim Lockridge, he is the author of *Writing Workflows: Beyond Word Processing* (2020), winner of the 2018 Sweetland/UM Press Book Prize.